GETTING STARTED IN

ADVANCED OPTIONS

OPTIONS

ILLUSTRATED EDITION

NOTES OF A
SCANDAL

HDCP
UNAUTHORIZED.
CONTENTS DISABLE

BOOKS IN THE *GETTING STARTED IN* SERIES

Getting Started in Currency Trading, Third Edition by Michael D. Archer

Getting Started in Forex Trading Strategies by Michael D. Archer

Getting Started in Asset Allocation by Bill Bresnan and Eric P. Gelb

Getting Started in Chart Patterns by Thomas N. Bulkowski

Getting Started in Internet Auctions by Alan Elliott

Getting Started in Mutual Funds, Second Edition by Alvin D. Hall

Getting Started in Stocks by Alvin D. Hall

Getting Started in Estate Planning by Kerry Hannon

Getting Started in a Financially Secure Retirement by Henry Hebeler

Getting Started in Online Personal Finance by Brad Hill

Getting Started in REITs by Richard Imperiale

Getting Started in Rebuilding Your 401(k), Second Edition by Paul Katzeff

Getting Started in Security Analysis by Peter J. Klein

Getting Started in Global Investing by Robert P. Kreitler

Getting Started in ETFs by Todd K. Lofton

Getting Started in Futures, Fifth Edition by Todd Lofton

Getting Started in Candlestick Charting by Tina Logan

Getting Started in Project Management by Paula Martin and Karen Tate

Getting Started in Value Investing by Charles Mizrahi

Getting Started in Financial Information by Daniel Moreau and Tracey Longo

Getting Started in Emerging Markets by Christopher Poillon

Getting Started in Technical Analysis by Jack D. Schwager

Getting Started in Hedge Funds, Third Edition by Daniel A. Strachman

Getting Started in Fundamental Analysis by Michael C. Thomsett

Getting Started in Options, Eighth Edition by Michael C. Thomsett

Getting Started in Options, Illustrated Edition by Michael C. Thomsett

Getting Started in Real Estate Investing, Third Edition by Michael C. Thomsett

Getting Started in Rental Income by Michael C. Thomsett

Getting Started in Six Sigma by Michael C. Thomsett

Getting Started in Stock Investing and Trading by Michael C. Thomsett

Getting Started in Stock Investing and Trading, Illustrated Edition by Michael C. Thomsett

Getting Started in Swing Trading by Michael C. Thomsett

Getting Started in Annuities by Gordon M. Williamson

Getting Started in Bonds, Second Edition by Sharon Saltzgiver Wright

Getting Started in Retirement Planning by Ronald M. Yolles and Murray Yolles

GETTING STARTED IN
ADVANCED OPTIONS

ILLUSTRATED EDITION

MICHAEL C. THOMSETT

WILEY

Published by John Wiley & Sons Singapore Pte. Ltd.
1 Fusionopolis Walk, #07-01, Solaris South Tower, Singapore 138628

Other Wiley Editorial Offices
John Wiley & Sons, 111 River Street, Hoboken, NJ 07030, USA
John Wiley & Sons, The Atrium, Southern Gate, Chichester, West Sussex, P019 8SQ, United Kingdom
John Wiley& Sons (Canada) Ltd., 5353 Dundas Street West, Suite 400, Toronto, Ontario, M9B 6HB,
    Canada
John Wiley& Sons Australia Ltd., 42 McDougall Street, Milton, Queensland 4064, Australia
Wiley-VCH, Boschstrasse 12, D-69469 Weinheim, Germany

Library of Congress Cataloging-in-Publication Data:
ISBN 978-1-118-34363-0 (Paperback)
ISBN 978-1-118-34369-2 (ePDF)
ISBN 978-1-118-34368-5 (ePub)

Typeset in 11/15 pt. Adobe Garamond Pro Regular by Aptara, India

10 9 8 7 6 5 4 3 2 1

CONTENTS

Acknowledgments   vii
Element Key   ix
Introduction   xi

CHAPTER 1:   STRATEGIES IN VOLATILE MARKETS:
              UNCERTAINTY AS AN ADVANTAGE   1
Avoiding 10 Common Mistakes   3
Modifying Your Risk Tolerance   10
The Nature of Market Volatility   13
Market Volatility Risk   14
Options in the Volatile Environment   19

CHAPTER 2:   COMBINATIONS AND SPREADS:
              CREATIVE RISK MANAGEMENT   31
Overview of Advanced Strategies   34
Vertical Spread Strategies   41
Horizontal and Diagonal Spread Strategies   52
Altering Spread Patterns   57

CHAPTER 3:   HEDGES AND STRADDLES: MORE CREATIVITY   73
The Two Types of Hedges   73
Hedging Option Positions   77
Straddle Strategies   83
Theory and Practice of Combined Techniques   89

CHAPTER 4:   OPTIONS FOR SPECIALIZED TRADING:
              LEVERAGING THE TECHNICAL APPROACH   95
Swing-Trading Basics   97
The Setup Signal   100
Testing the Theory   103
A Strategic View of Options for Swing Trading   107
Options Used for Other Trading Strategies   110
Swing- and Day-Trading Advanced Strategies   111

CHAPTER 5: **OPTIONS ON FUTURES: LEVERAGING YOUR LEVERAGE** **117**
Important Distinctions 118
Regulatory Differences 124

CHAPTER 6: **TRADING INDEX OPTIONS: PLAYING THE BROADER MARKET** **131**
Advantages to Trading Index Options 133
Exercise and Expiration Rules 135
Index Option Strategies 137
Structured Index Options 140

CHAPTER 7: **SYNTHETIC POSITIONS: TRACKING THE STOCK** **147**
Synthetic Put (Protected Short Sale) 149
Synthetic Long Call (Insurance Put or Married Put) 151
Synthetic Long Stock 152
Synthetic Short Stock 155
Split Strike Strategy (Bullish) 157
Split Strike Strategy (Bearish) 159
Collars 162
Synthetic Straddles 169

CHAPTER 8: **RISK: RULES OF THE GAME** **177**
Identifying the Range of Risk 178
Evaluating Your Risk Tolerance 188

CHAPTER 9: **TAXES: THE WILD CARD OF OPTIONS TRADING** **195**
Qualified Covered Calls—Special Rules 200
Looking to the Future 206

CHAPTER 10: **CHOOSING STOCKS: FINDING THE RIGHT INGREDIENTS** **213**
Developing an Action Plan 217
Selecting Stocks for Call Writing 220
Averaging Your Cost 225
Analyzing Stocks 230
Applying Analysis to Calls—the "Greeks" 250
Acting on Good Information 258

Glossary **267**
Recommended Reading **285**
About the Author **287**
Index **289**

ACKNOWLEDGMENTS

Thanks to those many readers who wrote to offer their suggestions for and insights into previous editions of *Getting Started in Options*, including constructive criticism and clarifying questions. Their letters have helped to improve the ever-changing set of explanations and examples, definitions, and other materials used in this book.

Very special thanks go to Debra Englander, my editor for many years at John Wiley & Sons, whose encouragement through many editions of this and other books has been greatly appreciated.

Also, many thanks to Nick Wallwork and Gemma Rosey, my editors in Singapore, for their excellent help and guidance through the production process.

ELEMENT KEY

Definitions
This symbol is found in boxed notations providing specific definitions of options terms. These are placed within the book to accompany and augment discussions relevant to each definition.

Key Points
These highlighted sections emphasize key points or offer observations, rules of thumb, and added points that options traders can use.

Valuable Resources
These sections provide links to websites where you will find added value for particular options discussions, to further help in expanding your options knowledge base.

Examples
Numerous examples illustrate points raised in context and provide a view of how the issues might apply using actual options trades. They are intended to demonstrate practical application of the principles being presented.

INTRODUCTION

Every investor and trader wants to combine several attributes in the stock portfolio: diversification, leverage, safety, and profitability.

This is a big order. How can you create all of these elements in the same portfolio? Tradition advises that if you want profits, you have to give up safety, and that if you want to use leverage, you have to take on greater risk.

In this book, these traditional problems are challenged by demonstrating how to combine the desirable attributes while managing and even eliminating the undesirable ones.

Options, once reserved for speculators and those able to tolerate high risk, have become mainstream devices for portfolio management. Many advanced option strategies can be applied so that risks are held down or even hedged entirely, while even conservative investors may create profits by combining options with stock positions.

Can options be used in a conservative manner? Yes; in fact, one of the best aspects to this market is that it can be designed to fit a range of risk tolerance profiles. The highly conservative investor may use options to reduce risk in long stock positions. On the far end of the spectrum, the speculator can continue to use options to swing trade, leverage, and seek fast profits. The range of strategies covers the entire risk spectrum.

This book presents a range of advanced strategies. It demonstrates how market volatility works as an advantage when options are properly used to profit from uncertainty. Spreads and straddles provide the means for designing an options portfolio to accomplish many goals. These include creation of a small but consistent profit potential in exchange for equally limited risk exposure.

The later chapters in the book examine some very interesting option strategies for even greater profits than those available from option trading on equities. Options on futures are very exciting; since futures are leveraged instruments already, options on futures are "leverage on leverage." Trading options is much safer than trading directly in futures, however. Just as trading options on stocks is cheaper and often safer than trading shares directly, you can trade options on futures directly or through commodities-based exchange-traded funds (ETFs) or index funds. This market opens up many possibilities for large profits, while limiting risks to the relatively low cost of the option.

Index options are equally exciting. An index provides built-in diversification and broad exposure, in comparison to the very limited diversification available when you trade shares.

The flexibility of options opens many additional possibilities, including trading not in the underlying security, but in synthetic stock positions. The use of offsetting options is low-cost or no-cost (because the cost of long options is covered by income from short options); and the synthetic position moves exactly like the underlying security. Using synthetics allows traders to benefit from changes in the security price, but without needing to place a large amount of capital at risk.

The discussion of risk itself is often left out of investment and trading books, and this is a mistake. Clearly, risks have to exist in all markets, especially in options, or there would be no opportunity for profit. In options, traders need to understand the range of risks before placing capital into strategies. Too many option traders take on greater risks than they can afford, not so much because they don't understand risk but because they are attracted to the trade itself. You are far better off settling for smaller and more consistent profits than going for broke . . . and going broke. The risk discussion is always one of the most important and essential elements in any investment strategy.

A later chapter explains how taxes work on option trading. As odd as the tax code is, rules for options are among the most complicated. This chapter by no means provides a comprehensive explanation of the technical rules applied to option profits and losses; but it does highlight the major considerations every trader needs to be aware of and should discuss with a tax adviser before entering into advanced strategies.

This book is designed to provide you with all of the tools you need to master the strategic and management aspects of advanced option trading. These attributes include:

- *Definitions in context.* Every term is defined in the space next to the text as it is introduced. All definitions are also summarized in the Glossary at the end of the book.
- *Illustrations.* The book includes dozens of illustrations designed to visually summarize key points and to show how strategies play out and are applied.

- *Key Points.* These highlighted, brief statements provide you with the brief major points to be taken away from each section as it is presented.
- *Valuable Resources.* These link you to the world of options resources and provide the benefits of access to topics and features that will improve your trading capabilities.
- *Examples.* The text includes many examples that emphasize the points being offered, and show how strategies apply when put into trading modes.
- *End-of-chapter comic summaries.* Each chapter concludes with a summary of highlights in the form of a comic strip. This is meant to highlight the key points, but in an entertaining and amusing manner seldom found in books on such technical subjects. This makes the book enjoyable on a new and different level.

The purpose to this series is to help investors and traders master advanced strategies—not only to understand the techniques and steps of each, but also to develop a context for them. This means being aware of risks as well as opportunities.

Advanced options as a strategic approach to portfolio management are exciting because you can design your own level of risk as a basic step in folding options into the risk-reduction strategies. Portfolio health should always be a primary goal and purpose for every investor. In spite of the long-standing reputation of options as having high risk and not being appropriate for most people, this book shows you how these amazing intangibles can be used to *reduce* risks while increasing profits.

CHAPTER 1

STRATEGIES IN VOLATILE MARKETS: UNCERTAINTY AS AN ADVANTAGE

The business of life is to go forward.
—Samuel Johnson, *The Idler*, 1759

Options traders have to be concerned with many different aspects of how and why they make decisions. The selection of stock, degree of risk, exposure, use of capital, which option to trade, whether to go long or short, and whether to use *calls* or *puts*—all of these decisions determine how successful you are in your options trades.

This book presents a range of advanced options strategies and is based on an understanding that there are many different kinds of traders. Some are speculators and enjoy the high risk with its amazing profit potential (and of course, the equally high potential of loss). Other traders are quite conservative and want to use options to manage their portfolios, reducing risk while increasing income.

calls

options providing their owners the right, but not the obligation, to purchase stock of an identified underlying security, at a fixed strike price, and on or before a fixed expiration date.

puts

options providing their owners the right, but not the obligation, to sell stock of an identified underlying security, at a fixed strike price, and on or before a fixed expiration date. Every put provides these rights over 100 shares.

With all of this in mind, a good starting point is to examine how a strategic approach to options trading is best designed in volatile markets. It seems that in the modern market, holding periods have been reduced from years to months, and in many cases to weeks. This fast turnaround is one change in the market that adds to volatility, which also drastically affects how stock ownership has changed—and where options trades fit in this new environment.

Volatility—the feature that stockholders are most concerned with—may serve as a big advantage to options traders. Stockholders like steadily rising markets because that makes profits. If you are like so many first-time investors, you probably began your investment program during bull markets; unfortunately, markets are cyclical and those uptrends can and do turn suddenly.

Valuable Resource
The Chicago Board Options Exchange (CBOE) provides a "volatility finder" among its services. This is of great interest to you as an options trader: **www.cboe.com/tradtool/ TBVolatilityFinder.aspx**.

If you are a more experienced investor, you understand that success has to be defined in terms other than the absolute of either winning or losing. You know that being right more often than wrong defines investing success. You also know how to diversify and limit risk even in a rising market, and you understand the old wisdom that stocks climb a wall of worry.

Key Point
Success in the market may be defined as being right more often than being wrong. Expecting loss is realistic; if a loss takes you by surprise, then you need to take a second look at your expectations.

Hindsight always clarifies observations of upward and downward trends. When you look back, the signals appear obvious, as though they could have been anticipated easily. However, it is far more difficult to identify the type of market you are experiencing at this moment, and to anticipate correctly what is going to happen next. At any given time, some observers think the market is rising, others think it is falling, and a third group adopts a wait-and-see approach. Each of these groups can cite plenty of market data to support their points of view, but they cannot all be right. Your dilemma in this environment of uncertainty is finding a way to build your portfolio of stocks while also minimizing your risk of catastrophic losses. You want to take advantage of emerging increases in the prices of stocks and, at the same time, limit your risk exposure. You may be tempted to flee the market in times of uncertainty, and this is understandable. But fleeing is not the only prudent decision. You can also employ options in volatile markets to take advantage of that volatility, and to improve profits while protecting yourself against unexpected losses.

AVOIDING 10 COMMON MISTAKES

As a starting point in defining your market strategy, examine the basic assumptions that go into how and why you have made past decisions. How do you pick a company? Do you study its fundamentals, follow price chart patterns, or buy stocks on the basis of name recognition?

Key Point

Your methods for picking stocks should be carefully and completely defined. Otherwise, it is easy to fall into the trap of picking stocks on the wrong assumptions: by past profits, name recognition, or rumors.

Some common errors characterize the way that some investment decisions are made. These include the following 10 mistakes:

1. *Failing to follow your own rules.* Many people define themselves as believers in the fundamentals, and then

insider information

any information about a company not known to the general public, but known only to people working in the company or having nonpublic knowledge about matters that will affect a stock's price.

contradict their own standards. Instead of monitoring trends in the important areas of companies' financial statements, they find themselves tracking stock charts or making decisions based on index movements.

The market is full of temptations, promises of easy money, and artificial excitement. But it is also a dangerous place. With the benefit of history, it is easy for you to recognize the real situation at any given time. However, in the heat of the moment, many investors give way to an emotional response to information. If you hear that a stock is about to take off, the human tendency is to want to buy some shares before that happens. A logical, rational approach would tell you otherwise. If the person giving you this tip does actually have *insider information*, it is illegal to pass that information on to others—and it is illegal for others to act on the information. If the person does not have insider information, then it could be only a rumor, in which case you should not act on the information. It could also be a *pump and dump* move. This occurs when people who own a stock whose price has fallen want to get the price up so they can sell their shares at a profit, so they promote (pump) the company to get others to buy; this causes the price to rise, and then they sell (dump) inflated shares.

pump and dump

action by an individual holding shares of a company who spreads false rumors in order to get people to buy shares and increase the price of the stock, and then sells shares at a profit.

2. *Forgetting your risk tolerance limits.* More than anything else, continually examine and reexamine your limitations. *Risk*

tolerance means just that: the amount of risk you can afford to take and are willing to take. If you cannot afford to lose, then you should not expose yourself to a high risk of loss.

Identifying risk tolerance levels should be thought of as the first step in beginning an investment program. When people buy their first house, they identify how expensive a home they can afford, the level of down payment required, market trends, and other important factors. This is all part of risk tolerance. However, the same people may enter the market with little or no thought to the level of risk. Unfortunately, this approach has consequences. If you cannot afford to lose money, you need to question whether a particular strategy is appropriate. This applies not only to trading in options, but to every market and strategy. Knowing your risk tolerance is essential.

risk tolerance

the amount of risk that an investor is able and willing to take.

Valuable Resource
To better define and understand your personal risk tolerance, take a free test offered by Rutgers University, at **http://njaes.rutgers.edu/money/riskquiz/**.

3. *Trying to make up for past losses with aggressive market decisions.* Losses can happen very suddenly, or they can accumulate over time, eroding your portfolio value. In either case, losses represent ill-timed decisions. Avoid the tendency to try to make up for big losses by taking unacceptable risks.

The reason it is so important to identify your risk tolerance is to avoid making big mistakes when your decisions don't go the way you planned. Many investors try to offset unexpected losses by taking ever-higher risks in the hope of getting their losses back. When those investors begin this practice, they cease being investors and become gamblers. And most gamblers lose. It makes more sense to accept losses as part of the outcome within your portfolio, learn from those losses, and take steps to decrease losses in the future. Those steps can include better stock selection, protective measures (including the use of options, for example), and diversification.

4. *Investing on the basis of rumor or questionable advice.* The Internet chat room is not a good place to get

market information. Unsolicited phone calls, pop-up advertisements, or mail solicitations for investment solutions, promising fast and easy profits, are not going to make anyone rich. Advice from friends, relatives, coworkers, or people you talk to on the bus or train should be discarded.

If you are intent on getting advice from someone else, think carefully before you pay for that advice. The record of analytical services offered by the big brokerage firms has been quite poor. Not only have these firms given historically poor advice, but it would often have been more profitable to do the exact opposite. The big firms have also been fined millions of dollars for knowingly giving poor advice to clients. With today's Internet-based market, a lot of free advice is available from many different places. You may also receive advice from friends, relatives, or coworkers. But the truth is that no one is going to give you free *good* advice. Making smart investment decisions invariably requires that you perform your own research, apply your own clearly identified risk standards, and do your homework directly.

5. *Trusting the wrong people with your money.* As a group, analysts' advice has led to net losses for their clients. The problem is not limited to analysts' conflicts of interest. As a group, analysts tend to pick earnings and price targets rather than try to find solid fundamental strength in

companies. This makes analysts a poor source for market information; you are better off on your own.

If you do intend to hire someone to advise you, make sure they base their investment advice on sound fundamentals. If you check, you will discover that the majority of financial advisers and analysts know little or nothing about accounting standards and rules and do not base decisions on tried-and-true fundamental principles. It is more likely that a financial adviser will try to steer you into *mutual funds* rather than stocks because funds pay more than 8 percent commission to salespeople; and, of course, investors pay this through a *sales load.* For example, if the commission is 8.25 percent, that means that out of every $100 you invest, only $91.75 goes into the investment; the rest goes to the salesperson (financial adviser). You do not need to pay commissions to find sound investments; and by definition, anyone buying stocks and trading options should be making his or her own decisions and not relying on expensive advice.

Valuable Resource
The Securities and Exchange Commission (SEC) provides a free calculator to help compare fees and expenses of mutual funds: **www.sec.gov/investor/tools/mfcc/mfcc-int.htm**.

mutual funds

investment programs in which money from a large pool of investors is placed under professional management. For a fee, management invests in stocks and bonds. Mutual funds may be set up to pay a sales load to salespeople, often called *financial advisers;* or they may be no-load, meaning investors can buy shares directly and not pay commissions.

sales load

a commission charged when a financial adviser places a client's capital into a load mutual fund.

6. *Adopting beliefs about the markets that simply are not true.* The market thrives on beliefs that, although strongly held, are simply not true. Widespread beliefs are difficult to overcome, but it is wise to question convention, especially when you see time and time again that those beliefs are invariably misleading.

For example, many investors insist on believing that there are secret, magic formulas that guarantee success in the stock market. Even though the facts clearly dispute this belief, thousands of people send away money every year to learn these so-called insider secrets to market wealth. You will never meet anyone who has become rich in the market by following any formula that they paid to find out about.

7. *Becoming inflexible even when conditions have changed.* You may find a method that works for you, so you stick with it even when conditions have changed and the strategy is no longer working. However, you need to maintain your flexibility, because markets are in a continual state of change.

The market is constantly evolving. Very little remains true for long, so even today's favorite stock or market sector could easily be out of favor next month. You only need to look back over history to realize how easily an industry can become obsolete. Before 1900, auto and airline stocks did not exist, and before 2000, digital cameras were not widely known so companies such as Polaroid and Kodak dominated the film markets. A review of the fundamentals for any company out of favor today reveals falling stock prices, lower profits, and a relentless decline in all of the fundamental indicators. There are good lessons to be learned from history, and the market reflects change as a constant element.

8. *Taking profits at the wrong time.* The temptation to take profits as soon as they are available is a strong one. However, the timing of profit taking should depend more on your overall strategy than on a momentary opportunity. If you always take profits when available, you will end up with a portfolio full of stocks whose current market value is lower than their original cost.

Using options as a secondary strategy in your stock portfolio enables you to take profits without needing to sell stock. This can be accomplished in several ways. For example, when stock values climb high, you can sell covered calls or buy puts. If and when market values fall back to previous levels, the short call or long put positions can be closed at a profit—but you continue to hold your long-term stock. When stock values fall, you can also take advantage of the temporary panic by buying calls (you can also sell puts in this situation). When the stock prices rise back to previous levels, the option positions can be closed at a profit.

9. *Selling low and buying high.* The advice to buy low and sell high is easily given but harder to follow. It is all too easy to make investment decisions on the basis of panic (at the bottom) or greed (at the top). A worthwhile piece of market wisdom states that bulls and bears are often overruled by pigs and chickens.

It is not easy to resist the emotions of greed and panic; but you need to think long-term when you invest in stock. If you select companies based on sound criteria, you do not need to be concerned about short-term price movement, not to mention rumor and speculation about what will happen tomorrow. Options can also be useful in overcoming the paradoxical temptation of long-term investors, which is to act like short-term speculators and against their own best interests. Options are excellent instruments for hedging other positions, riding short-term price movements, and taking profits, all without having to sell your stock before you really want to (on the upside) or because prices fall temporarily (on the downside).

10. *Following the trend instead of thinking independently.* Crowd mentality is most likely to be wrong. Crowds don't think; they react. So mistakes are likely to occur when you follow the crowd instead of thinking for yourself.

Successful investors learn to think for themselves and to avoid crowd thinking. This means not only resisting the temptation to follow the majority, but also to recognize that the majority is usually wrong. This *contrarian* approach to investing has proven to be successful historically because crowd mentality is a misguided way to think.

contrarian

an investor who invests opposite popular opinion in recognition of the tendency for the majority to be wrong more often than right.

MODIFYING YOUR RISK TOLERANCE

Recognizing common mistakes in approaches to investing is a good starting point in determining how *not* to approach stock and options investing. All of the mistakes involve perceptions or misperceptions about the markets, but they share a common element: a perception about risk. If you can identify risk levels to a particular strategy and quickly decide whether they are good matches for your own risk tolerance, you will be far ahead of most other investors and traders. Risk exposure is the central determining test for every investing strategy you will consider.

Your ability and willingness to be exposed to risk is a matter of degree. Risk tolerance is defined by capital resources and income, investing experience, family status, condition of the market, and your personal attitude. It is ever changing because as your own circumstances evolve all of these areas evolve as well.

> **Key Point**
>
> Risk tolerance is an ever-changing matter, reflecting your attitude, experience, knowledge, and resources at the moment. It will be different next year and the year after, so you need to review risk tolerance constantly.

- *Capital resources and income* define your ability to undertake certain risks. If you have a large amount of capital to invest, you will be able to consider a wider array of possible investments than if your assets are more limited. Of course, that also means that you will likely be unaware of the risks associated with some decisions. Having a large amount of capital available might contain risk of its own in that regard; so if you inherit a large sum of money, sell your house, or take other actions that bring you a large nest egg to invest, you need to still pay attention to risk. The same arguments apply to income levels. An individual with a comfortable level of income will be more inclined to diversify in terms of investment products *and* risks. As a strategy, it makes sense to vary the risk levels of your portfolio as long as it is part of a plan. The danger arises when risks come about unexpectedly.

- *Investing experience* has a lot to do with the risks you take on and how you evolve as an investor. As you become familiar with options, for example, you will be willing to try advanced strategies, use options in different ways within your portfolio, and diversify risks with option positions. Experience has another side: those who have lost money in the market have learned about risk the expensive way. Many people walk away from the market permanently, which is a risk decision. They conclude that the market is simply not a safe investing environment. In fact, it can be, if you learn how to mitigate specific risks.

- *Family status* has a lot to do with the types of investments you choose. If you are a young single person making good money, you will be inclined to take greater risks; if you are married, buying a home, and raising young children, you will by necessity think about security, college education expenses, and retirement savings. Major events, like marriage, birth of a child, divorce, losing a job or starting a new career, relocating, health problems, or the death of a loved one, will understandably have a major impact on how you invest, because such events change your risk tolerance profile.

- *Condition of the market* will also change your risk tolerance. When the market is going through a broad-based bull period, it is easy to feel confident about investing. As a result, there is a tendency to lower your attentiveness. In these conditions, it makes sense to buy and hold securities as long as the good times last; but at the same time, be aware of risks. Markets can turn around quickly.

Key Point

Even recognizing the fact that markets change continually, it is easy to make the mistake of fixing your definition of risk and never changing. As a consequence, your profile can become outdated.

- *Personal attitude* will have more than anything else to do with your definition of risk tolerance. If you consider yourself ultraconservative, you will prefer to leave the majority of your portfolio in low-yielding, insured money market accounts. Others can tolerate high risk and seek the best possible returns, and they will speculate in long-shot investments. Most people are somewhere in between.

THE NATURE OF MARKET VOLATILITY

Risk comes in many forms and, as a result, your definition of risk tolerance has to take the different forms of risk into account. A study of price volatility is a good place to start. Volatility can and should be applied to individual issues. This does not mean that overall volatility trends should be ignored; however, because listed options are specific to a single stock, the study of volatility can be used to measure risk, to identify market conditions, and to find option opportunities.

Market volatility follows cyclical patterns, just as prices do. When prices for specific stocks, sectors, or the overall market rise rapidly, we usually also see increases in the volume of shares traded. A short-term rally is characterized by corresponding short-term volatility, meaning prices can change in both high and low directions within a single day or week. A longer-term rally—lasting several weeks, for example—will tend to be broader based. Market volatility will slow down as the rally begins to lose its momentum, which is one way to identify the top of the market—not always, but often.

Being aware of the patterns and tendencies of market volatility does not necessarily provide you with a key to the timing of option decisions.

premium

the price of
an option,
expressed in
dollars and cents
but without
dollar signs.
For example,
if an option
has a premium
of $200, it is
expressed as 2;
if an option has
a value of $325,
it is expressed as
3.25.

time value

that portion
of an option's
premium
attributed
specifically
to the time
remaining to
expiration. Time
values decline
as expiration
approaches
and the rate
of decline
accelerates
within the final
month.

In fact, in the most volatile of markets, it is the uncertainty of the timing of events that makes the market the most interesting, and the most dangerous.

Key Point

Volatility introduces both risk and opportunity. The very uncertainty associated with big price swings provides options traders with the best environment for profits—if properly understood.

Volatility is an expression of conflicting investor interests converging at the same moment. A high demand or a high supply resulting from greater than usual volume has an immediate effect on stock share prices and on option *premium* levels. When *time value* is distorted during high-volume periods, it creates a momentary advantage for options traders. Distortions occur most often during highly volatile periods for a specific stock, but the offsetting market reaction tends to correct the condition within the same trading day. So to take advantage of time value price distortions, you will need to track the market throughout the day.

Key Point

Options traders who plan to take advantage of short-term price aberrations have to be prepared to track prices closely, and to act quickly.

MARKET VOLATILITY RISK

Understanding the nature of volatility is essential. When you use options to accompany open stock positions, you may eventually realize that volatility is going to affect your equity position and is not just a short-term profit opportunity in options. The risk feature of volatility is going to determine the safety of your portfolio.

This danger—market volatility risk—is especially important if you write covered calls. Selecting stocks for long-term growth as the primary means for finding investment candidates is a fundamental strategy.

However, picking stocks primarily based on the richness of option premium levels is a shortsighted strategy that may lead to losses. There is no sense in exchanging short-term option profits for losses in stock value. Richer option premiums are associated with more volatile stocks. The higher premium levels exist because the stock itself has higher risk.

This is a trap for options traders. When you think about buying stock without considering the related options, you look at financial information, long-term competitive stance, the sector, management, dividend yield, and price history, among other indicators. However, when you are looking for covered call writing opportunities, it is tempting to buy 100 shares and sell an option at the same time, using the discounting effect (return from the option) as your primary consideration. If you ignore other risk elements of the stock, you invite greater risk. The more volatile stock is, the more likely it will be to lose market value in a market decline.

Key Point

Beware the tempting rates of return available from buying stock and selling covered calls at the same time. Don't overlook the importance of analyzing the stock as a starting point, not as a subordinate point to the option's value.

The question should be: does the option discount the share price adequately to justify the higher risk? If the option profit serves only to equalize the market risk of the stock, are there more sensible alternatives? It makes more sense to purchase the stocks of less volatile companies and wait out price movement, and then sell covered calls with *striking prices* (also called *strikes*) well above your purchase price, ensuring higher profits even in the event of *exercise*. While this strategy is more conservative and requires time to build profits, it also avoids

striking prices

the dollar value of shares equivalent to the prices at which options are exercised.

strikes

price points at which an option can be exercised.

exercise

the act of buying stock under the terms of the call option or selling stock under the terms of the put option, at the price per share specified in the option contract.

the problems of market volatility. Because the federal tax rules affecting capital gains also affect after-tax profits, it makes more sense to sell out-of-the-money calls than in-the-money calls, or to accept short-term gains in exchange for higher premium income.

The comparative analysis of market volatility emphasizes a stock's share price and trading range, which are technical indicators. An equally important form of volatility involves a study of trends in the financial results of the company. An analysis of *fundamental volatility* is a valuable method for picking stocks wisely.

Investors like predictability. You may take comfort when a company's sales increase gradually and predictably from one year to the next, and when profits remain within an expected and predictable range. This preference has led to pressure on companies to equalize earnings through accounting decisions. You will also take comfort in the low volatility of financial reports, even when this results from creative accounting treatment of a less certain reality. You may feel safe with predictable outcomes when fundamental volatility is low.

For example, Table 1.1 compares fiscal years 2007 through 2011 for three retail corporations: Wal-Mart, Target, and JCPenney.

Note how different these revenue, net profit, and net return outcomes are. Wal-Mart's numbers are very consistent, growing by approximately the same degree every year. This makes estimates of future growth highly predictable and reliable.

However, Target's revenues also rose but net profits were inconsistent. As a result, the net yield was also unpredictable. Future projections of the same numbers will be much more difficult.

JCPenney reported the most inconsistent returns. Revenues declined through the five-year period, and so did profits and net yield. The results for the three companies demonstrate how the differences in fundamental volatility appear.

Table 1.1 Fundamental Volatility Comparisons

Wal-Mart (WMT)

Fiscal Year	Revenues ($ millions)	Net Profits ($ millions)	Net Yield
2011	$421,849	$15,355	3.6%
2010	408,214	14,414	3.5
2009	405,607	13,254	3.3
2008	378,799	12,884	3.4
2007	348,650	12,178	3.5

Target (TGT)

Fiscal Year	Revenues ($ millions)	Net Profits ($ millions)	Net Yield
2011	$67,390	$2,920	4.3%
2010	65,357	2,488	3.8
2009	64,948	2,214	3.4
2008	63,367	2,849	4.5
2007	59,490	2,787	4.7

JCPenney (JCP)

Fiscal Year	Revenues ($ millions)	Net Profits ($ millions)	Net Yield
2011	$17,759	$ 378	2.1%
2010	17,556	249	1.4
2009	18,486	567	3.1
2008	19,860	1,105	5.6
2007	19,903	1,134	5.7

Source: S&P Stock Reports.

fundamental volatility

the tendency for a company's sales and profits to change from one period to the next, with more erratic change representing higher volatility.

Sales and profits do not materialize consistently and steadily. Actual outcome is far more chaotic. How do companies even out their results, and isn't that fraud? The generally accepted accounting principles (*GAAP*) rules give corporations a lot of flexibility to interpret and report their numbers.

The GAAP guidelines exist in no one place, but consist of a series of published opinions, guidelines, and regulations developed by many groups, with the American Institute of Certified Public Accountants (AICPA) serving as central authority for GAAP standards. The Financial Accounting Standards Board (FASB) develops new guidelines and also serves as a clearinghouse for rules within the auditing profession.

GAAP

acronym for generally accepted accounting principles, the rules by which auditing firms analyze operations, and by which corporations report their financial results.

Valuable Resource
Check the AICPA and FASB websites to learn more about these organizations and the role they play in developing GAAP standards: **www.aicpa.org** and **www.fasb.org**.

GAAP has been the sole standard for U.S.-based companies for many years. However, the Securities and Exchange Commission (SEC) has set a deadline of 2015 for all publicly traded companies to begin reporting under a uniform system in which GAAP rules will be replaced by rules of the International Accounting Standards Board (IASB), whose

International Financial Reporting Standards (IFRS) will be the new guiding force for preparing financial statements. This change, whether put into effect in 2015 or moved to a later date, will be difficult for investors because any long-term trends they have been following may be altered under the new system.

The two systems—GAAP and IFRS—are quite different in how certain expenses are treated. For options investors and traders relying on fundamental trends and ratios, the change could distort the tracking unless older fiscal year results are restated. Although having one international standard is highly desirable in today's global market, this change is sure to create short-term chaos and, potentially, distortions in fundamental tracking systems.

An investor or a trader who is less informed than a more sophisticated one may be the most vulnerable, since reliance on a short list of fundamentals may change quite suddenly as the new standards go into effect. Because IFRS profits are generally higher than GAAP-based calculations, an uninformed trader may mistake a change for a bargain-priced stock and view this—as well as related options trades—as an opportunity, when in fact it may be a reflection of the change in accounting systems between fiscal years. Potentially, the change in systems may also affect volatility in stocks and valuations of options, at least in the short term. At the very least, the potential inaccuracies should be kept in mind when the change does occur. In the meantime, U.S.-based companies continue to rely on GAAP rules for preparation of financial statements.

Inflating current results to improve an otherwise dismal operating result requires a different type of manipulation. For example, current-year expenses may be capitalized and then amortized over several years, increasing the current year's profits. Depreciation can be spread out over a longer period than normal by making an election under Internal Revenue Code rules. Or reserves set up during acquisitions can be reversed to inflate current profits.

All of these types of entries *might* be allowed under GAAP; but regardless of whether accountants can justify questionable interpretations, the fact remains that these practices are deceptive. They give you a distorted and inaccurate picture of operations. If you make investment decisions based on inaccurate or unreliable information, you are being deceived. And to the extent that stock prices are distorted by misleading accounting decisions, option values are distorted as well.

Full disclosure and application of a universal reporting standard would be desirable. Full disclosure might also mean higher fundamental volatility. While this might be unsettling, it is always better to see an accurate result than to settle for the short-term comfort you gain from low fundamental volatility. Remember, higher volatility could have a positive effect on premium levels.

Key Point

More accurate, consistent reporting probably would also mean greater fundamental volatility. Ironically, the more honest financial statements could reflect higher than average year-to-year volatility; this could require the market to change widely held opinions about the nature of volatility and risk.

OPTIONS IN THE VOLATILE ENVIRONMENT

The more uncertain a trading environment, the greater your concern for the safety of your capital. When prices are very low, you may be fearful about placing capital at risk, especially if you have already lost money in the market. At the same time, such moments are buying opportunities.

If you have cash to invest but you are concerned about market volatility, limited speculation could be a wise strategy. Although buying calls is highly speculative due to the unavoidable *expiration* factor, the decision can work as an alternative strategy. Instead of putting all of your capital at risk in purchasing shares, you can buy calls as a method for controlling stock. If and when those shares climb in value, the calls can be exercised and you can purchase shares at the fixed striking price. But if the stock price declines, you are not obligated to exercise and you will lose only the money invested in call premium.

Considering that time works against the buyer, is it wise to buy calls as an alternative to simply buying stock? It can be. Using long-term equity anticipation *security* (LEAPS) calls with long-term life spans can make a lot of sense in volatile markets. Because LEAPS options last up to 30 months, they are more interesting than shorter-term listed

expiration

the end of an option; after expiration, every option becomes worthless. This date is the third Saturday of expiration month, and the preceding third Friday is the last trading day.

options. In the market, 30 months is a very long time. If you select stocks that you believe have a better than average chance to appreciate in value, going long on LEAPS calls could be a profitable form of speculation.

When you buy long-term LEAPS calls, you will have to expect to pay extra premium for more time value. So LEAPS calls are going to be far more expensive than shorter-term calls; but with the time element in mind, the longer-term speculation can work to your advantage. There are ways to reduce the cost of long-term LEAPS positions as well. For example, you can purchase a call and then sell earlier-expiring calls with higher striking prices. This strategy reduces the cost of the long call. It is a relatively safe strategy, because the long position covers the short. Because you will have up to 30 months before the long LEAPS call expires, you can sell a series of short calls and allow them to expire during the holding period.

Another possible strategy for those who already own shares and want to acquire more is to sell a covered call and an uncovered put at the same time. Using LEAPS options, this can create a substantial rate of return. So there are numerous LEAPS strategies, both long and short, that provide you with alternatives to the popular stock-specific strategies: dollar cost averaging, hold-and-wait strategies, profit taking, or simply getting out of the market. The use of options, especially longer-term LEAPS options, allows you to remain in the market and to create new opportunities with minimum risk.

Key Point

LEAPS-based strategies can be tailored to match your risk tolerance. The big advantage with LEAPS is the extended time until expiration.

The problem of investing more capital in a down market is well known. Typically, when prices are down, there are numerous buying opportunities available; but it is also common for people to hesitate, fearing further declines. In this condition, it requires a cool head and calm nerves to go against the crowd mentality of the market and to recognize the opportunity. Using LEAPS options, you can take advantage of depressed prices without risking capital in long positions.

Example

Solving the Capital Problem: You have approximately $10,000 to invest. You have been following five stocks that you believe will increase in value over the next two to three years; but you cannot buy 100 shares of all of these with your limited capital. And because the market has been very volatile lately, you are not even sure that the timing is right for committing money right now. You don't want to miss an opportunity, and you remain uncertain about short-term volatility.

In the circumstances just described, there are three problems: (1) limited capital, (2) uncertainty about short-term price volatility, and (3) the desire to profit from longer-term change. Everyone faces these conditions from time to time, and many investors face them continually. LEAPS options address all three concerns. With a $10,000 capital base as described, it is possible to buy calls for all five of the stocks. As long as out-of-the-money options are chosen, the premium cost will be lower than it would be for an in-the-money option on the same 100 shares. This diversifies the $10,000 capital into five different 100-share lots; but because these are options and not shares, the risk of loss is limited. The entire $10,000 could be lost if none of the stocks rises in value. But if they are selected well, that is a remote possibility. Three years is a very long time, and in the cyclical market, today's depressed conditions are likely to reverse and prices will advance.

Key Point

The LEAPS option removes the most inhibiting factor of the options market, the short-term nature of contracts and ever-looming expiration. A three-year life span is an eternity in the stock market.

Is it prudent to buy LEAPS calls, given the risks of long positions as a general rule? It could make more sense than buying shorter-expiring standardized calls, which will expire in a few months. Remembers, a LEAPS contract has a life up to three years, and a lot can happen in that time. If you believe that stocks will rise in value during those months, then buying long-term options represents a smart strategic choice.

If the market value does not rise, you lose the option premium. However, since you will be spreading a limited amount of capital among options on several different stocks, you stand a good chance of profiting overall as long as the general market direction is upward during the lifetime of the LEAPS.

There are three possible outcomes in this strategy:

1. The LEAPS expires worthless. If the stock fails to rise above the LEAPS striking price, the strategy produces a loss (the premium paid).
2. The LEAPS increases in value and you close it at a profit. You decide that you would rather take the option profit when available, and give up the opportunity to buy shares later.
3. The stock value rises and you exercise the LEAPS option, purchasing shares at the fixed (lower) striking price. This is the outcome to aim for; LEAPS are used to own the right to buy 100 shares at a fixed price, with the idea that you will want to make the purchase as long as the stock value rises and fundamental conditions do not change.

LEAPS can be used in all of the ways that short-term options can be used. LEAPS calls can be bought to insure against losses in short stock positions, and LEAPS puts can be used to insure against losses in long stock positions. You can also sell LEAPS, either naked or covered. The covered call strategy will produce far higher premium income because of higher time value. In exchange, you will also be required to keep your stock tied up to cover the short option for a longer period of time. The typical time value pattern for a LEAPS covered call is that it remains fairly stable at first and then rapidly falls off during the final four to six months. Thus, covered call writing on very long-term periods should be analyzed and compared with shorter-term alternatives. When comparing likely rates of return, remember to annualize the outcomes to make them comparable; a 10 percent return on a one-year covered call is twice as profitable as a 15 percent return on a three-year covered call.

Key Point

The risk/reward question for LEAPS covered call writers has to be analyzed carefully. The question of time is one aspect only, and the other aspect—exposure to exercise—is much longer-term than for standard short-term options.

The potential uses of LEAPS beyond expected purchase (or sale) of shares in the future can become quite interesting. When you combine the longer expiration of LEAPS options with the features of shorter-term expirations, some of the typical trading techniques become more advantageous, especially on the short side. Remember, time works for the seller and against the buyer. As a seller of a LEAPS option, you are going to have more time value to work with and a longer time until expiration. As a buyer of a LEAPS option, you still work against time; but because expiration is so far away, the potential for profit—or at least the uncertainty of what will happen—makes buying options far more feasible.

The advantage of an extended time until expiration is partially offset by the LEAPS tendencies with *extrinsic value*, seen in variation in the LEAPS delta. When options are close to expiration, they tend to be very responsive to changes in the stock's price. However, the farther out the LEAPS, the less responsive it is likely to be.

This reality often means the LEAPS premium changes very little even when the stock price moves many points. For example, if you own a LEAPS call and the underlying stock moves up three points, you might see only one point (or no points) of movement in a 24-month LEAPS

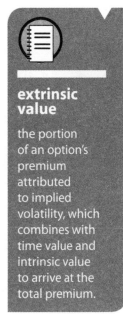

extrinsic value

the portion of an option's premium attributed to implied volatility, which combines with time value and intrinsic value to arrive at the total premium.

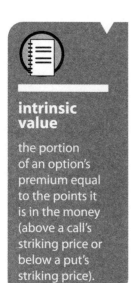

intrinsic value

the portion of an option's premium equal to the points it is in the money (above a call's striking price or below a put's striking price).

call. What actually occurs in this situation is that extrinsic value falls as an offset against *intrinsic value* (assuming the call is in the money), or, if out of the money, the extrinsic value fails to react to price movement solely because of the long time period until expiration.

As frustrating as it is to see an unresponsive trend in a LEAPS position, it is an odd reality. In spite of the usual rules for interaction among intrinsic, extrinsic, and time value, longer-term options are subject to these kinds of adjustments. So extrinsic value can act as an offset to changes in intrinsic value, or simply may hold down values of options due to the time itself. This does not mean that time value actually changes, but it does mean that the LEAPS will not act in the same, more predictable way that short-term options will act.

This can be an advantage, because the offset tendency works in both upward and downward movements. So if you are long on a LEAPS call contract and the stock declines, you are less likely to see a corresponding decline in the LEAPS call. Or if you own a LEAPS put and the underlying stock value rises, the offset can reduce the effect on the put value. Even with the offset experienced in extrinsic value, however, using LEAPS calls and puts in long positions can continue to make sense over the long term.

The same arguments favoring buying calls in anticipation of an upward-moving market apply just as well when you expect market values to fall. You can buy LEAPS puts when you have seen a big run-up in value and you anticipate a reversal. This strategy makes sense regardless of whether you own stock.

When you own shares and the market value has risen substantially, you face a dilemma. Do you take your profits now, while you can, and risk missing out on even more appreciation? Or do you wait, risking losses if prices fall? You may continue to think of the company as a sound long-term investment, so you don't want to sell; but you are worried about short-term corrections to market price. If you buy a LEAPS put in this situation, the downward price movement in the stock would be matched point for point by increasing value in the in-the-money LEAPS put. You also discount your basis by selling calls with rich time value premium, an alternative to profit taking that allows you to continue owning shares.

When you don't own shares and market value has run up, buying a put is a speculative move. You anticipate a correction; when prices fall, you will experience a corresponding increase in value of the LEAPS put. Without taking a short position or selling uncovered calls—both high-risk strategies—by owning the put you can profit if you are right when stock market prices fall. And because expiration is farther out, you have as much as three years to be proven right.

When you want to buy more shares and you believe the price is too high today, selling puts may work well for you. The premium you receive lowers your basis and risk, and as long as you consider the striking price a good price for shares, exercise would not be devastating. If share prices continue to rise, you keep the premium from selling the put. This strategy mitigates the dilemma for every stock investor: If you buy more shares today and prices then fall, you have a paper loss position. If you don't buy more shares and the stock's price rises, you miss the opportunity. Look at short puts as a possible solution to this dilemma.

Key Point

Using LEAPS to time market swings or insure other positions is more practical than using short-term options. The longer time until expiration provides better value, enabling you to protect paper profits more economically.

European-style option

an option that can be exercised only during a specified period of time immediately preceding expiration. Some index options are European-style.

The advantage of longer expiration overcomes the option buyer's ongoing struggle with time, at least to a degree. In long positions, you will pay more for time value but you have more time. In a volatile market, your chances of profiting with LEAPS calls and puts are greater because expiration is not immediate.

In addition to trading in LEAPS on individual stocks, you can also buy or sell index LEAPS. These are somewhat more complex because the relationship between striking price and index value is not the same as for individual stocks. In addition, index LEAPS may be set

American-style option

an option that can be exercised at any time before expiration. All equity options and some index options are American-style.

capped-style option

an option that can be exercised only during a specified period of time; if the option's value reaches the cap level prior to expiration, it is exercised automatically.

up in one of three ways. An *American-style option* can be exercised at any time prior to expiration. All short-term options and LEAPS in stocks are exercised as American-style options. However, some index options are *European-style options*, which means that exercise is allowed only during a shorter period of time immediately before expiration. A third variation is the *capped-style option*. This gives the owner the right to exercise, but only during a specific time period before expiration. If the option reaches its cap value before expiration, it is exercised automatically.

Even in the most uncertain of markets, the right strategy can be found to match the circumstances and your own risk tolerance. Options become most interesting when you move beyond the decision to buy or to sell and begin exploring the many strategies in the range of spreads and combinations. The next chapter shows how these work.

DON'T *UNDERESTIMATE* THE INDIVIDUAL TRADER. MOST OF THEM ARE *SMART* ENOUGH TO UNDERSTAND *ALL* OF THIS WITHOUT NEEDING A SUPER SECRET LABORATORY.

IN FACT, THIS WAS ALL KEPT SECRET FOR *WAY* TOO MANY YEARS.

IT'S TIME TO COME *OUT* OF THE SHADOWS AND GIVE *A NEW GENERATION* OF INVESTORS AND TRADERS A LOOK AT HOW OPTIONS WORK.

BUT...BUT... BUT IF THAT'S *TRUE*, THEN WHAT WOULD I *DO* FOR A *LIVING*?

MAYBE YOU COULD *TRADE OPTIONS*...

EXIT

TO BE CONTINUED!

2

COMBINATIONS AND SPREADS: CREATIVE RISK MANAGEMENT

To conquer without risk is to triumph without glory.
—Pierre Corneille, *Le Cid*, 1636

Options strategies are varied and flexible and run the gamut from highly speculative to extremely conservative. This explains a large part of the appeal of options, even when employed as portfolio management tools. You can insure paper profits, take advantage of short-term price swings, or create double-digit returns with covered calls.

Beyond this popular and effective strategy are many additional ways to use calls and puts: in long or short positions or combined within single strategies. This chapter demonstrates how many of these advanced strategies work and how you can create combinations of many kinds that will limit losses.

Remember, however, that most examples are based on the minimum number of *open positions*. The possibilities only expand once you begin trading in multiple numbers of option contracts. This is limited by

open position

the status of a trade when a purchase (a long position) or a sale (a short position) has been made, and before cancellation, exercise, or expiration.

your imagination and risk profile, and also will be limited by margin restrictions imposed by both the Federal Reserve Board's regulations and the policies of your brokerage firm. Because of these limitations, you are required to keep a portion of exercise values in your portfolio at all times, which also limits the number of open option contracts you can have in your account. The many combined and advanced strategies open many doors, but you are always limited by your own financial resources.

Options traders can employ only four basic strategies: buying calls, selling calls, buying puts, and selling puts. But these four basics can be combined in numerous strategies; for example, you can modify risks in long positions with offsetting short positions in options.

Your reasons for buying or selling options define the level and degree of risk that you are willing to assume. The utilization of options defines your risk profile as a stock investor. Any strategy has to be secondary to the more important phase in your investment program: the selection of stock. A lot of emphasis is placed on option risk or reward, but the stock risk is easily overlooked. Before even considering how or whether to employ options, you need to first identify a strategy that helps you select stocks with several important investing rules in mind, including the following:

- Protect your capital from catastrophic losses due to stock market volatility.
- Avoid long positions in stocks with severe liquidity or solvency problems.
- Select companies whose industry position is strong and growing.

This short list only defines the overall importance of selecting stocks as a starting point in your program, and that may or may not include options. The big mistake is to pick stocks to cover rich-premium options and, in the process, unintentionally fill your portfolio with highly volatile issues such that any downturn in the market is likely to cause a severe loss of value in the stocks. In that situation, a limited short-term option profit is accompanied by a larger loss in stock value and, potentially, problems recapturing value through a reversal in direction of price movement.

Key Point

Avoid filling your portfolio with high-risk stocks picked because option premiums are higher than average. You need to watch not only potential profits on options but potential losses on stocks as well.

You have the right to decide individually how much risk exposure is appropriate. Applied to the options market, defining risk levels also helps you to decide whether a particular strategy is right for you. Consider the difference between one investor who wants only to profit from buying and selling uncovered options and another who covers calls with shares of stock in order to maximize returns. The risks are on opposite sides of the spectrum, because uncovered positions are very high-risk and covered positions are very low-risk. The different uses of options by each person define and distinguish their perceptions of risk and opportunity, their desired outcomes, and even their basic ideas about how to operate within the market.

In moving beyond the four basic options strategies, you may discover value in a variety of combinations, which can be put into action for many different reasons. For example, long and short option positions can be engaged in at the same time, so that risks offset one another. Some combined strategies are designed to create profits in the event that the underlying stock moves in either direction; others are designed to create profits if the stock price remains within a specific range.

OVERVIEW OF ADVANCED STRATEGIES

spread

the simultaneous purchase and sale of options on the same underlying stock, with different striking prices or expiration dates, or both.

There are four major classifications of advanced strategies: spreads, hedges, straddles, and strangles.

The Spread

The first advanced strategy is called a *spread*. This is the simultaneous opening of both a long position and a short position in options on the same underlying stock. The spread increases potential profits while also reducing risks in the event that the underlying stock behaves in a particular manner, as will be illustrated shortly.

The *vertical spread* or *money spread* is created using either all calls or all puts with the same expiration date but different strike prices.

vertical spread

a spread involving different striking prices but identical expiration dates.

> **Example**
>
> **Vertical Spread, More than Margarine:** You buy a 45 call and, at the same time, sell a 40 call. Both expire in February. Because the strike prices are different while the expiration dates are identical, this is a vertical spread.

Spreads can have different expiration dates or a *combination* of different striking prices and expiration dates. They can be put together in numerous formations.

Spread strategies using short-term options—expiring in six months or less—are, of course, limited in value to that time range. However, spread strategies are far more complex when you combine short-term options with a long-term equity anticipation security (LEAPS). This longer-term option may have a life up to three years, so the offsetting possibilities can be far more complex. Knowing, for example, that time value declines the most during the final two to three months, you can "cover" a short-position option with a longer-term LEAPS option. We qualify the term *cover* in this strategy. Although it is widely referred to in that manner, it is in fact more accurately a form of spread.

money spread

alternate name for the *vertical spread*.

Example

Thinking Ahead: You purchase a LEAPS 40 call that expires in 30 months. The stock is currently selling at $36 per share. You pay 11 ($1,100). Although time value premium is high due to the long-term nature of this option, you believe that the stock will rise in price during this period and that this will justify your investment. A month later, the stock's market value has risen to $41 per share. You sell a 45 call expiring in four months and receive a premium of 3 ($300). Three months later, the stock is selling at $44 per share and the short call is valued at 1 ($100). You close the short call position and take a profit of $200 (minus trading fees). You now are free to sell another call against the LEAPS, and you can repeat the process as many times as you wish.

combination

any purchase or sale of options on one underlying stock, with terms that are not identical.

The preceding transaction should be evaluated with several points in mind. The LEAPS cost $1,100, and you have already recovered $200 of that cost. The LEAPS is now in the money, so the price movement direction is favorable. This transaction took four months, so you have 26 more months before the long LEAPS call expires. You could repeat the short-term call sale again and again during this period. It is possible that you could recover the entire premium invested in the long position through well-timed short-term call sales—and potentially still profit from the long position as well. This would be an ideal outcome, and you have two and a half years for it to materialize. In comparison to using only short-term calls, you have far greater flexibility using short-term options in combination with long-term LEAPS options.

Key Point

Combining short-term options with long-term LEAPS options expands the profit potential of many spreads.

A variation of the spread offers potential double-digit returns, especially using the high time value of LEAPS options. For example, you can combine a covered call and an uncovered put on the same stock and receive premium income on both. This strategy is appropriate if and when:

- You are willing to write a covered call, recognizing that if exercised, your stock can be called away.
- You are also willing to write an uncovered put, in full knowledge that if exercised, you will have to purchase 100 shares of stock above current market value. This is appropriate when the striking price, less put premium you receive, is a good price for the stock.
- You structure the short call and put so that exercise may be avoidable through rolling techniques if and when the stock moves close to either striking price.

Example

Double-Digit Returns: You own 100 shares of stock that you purchased at $26 per share. Today, market value is $30. You write 29-month LEAPS options on this stock, selling a 35 call and a 25 put at the same time. Your total premium on these two LEAPS options is 11 points, or $1,100. That represents a net return, based on your purchase price of $26 per share, of 42.3 percent.

In this example, you would experience one of four outcomes:

1. One or both of the LEAPS options may expire worthless. In that outcome, the premium is 100 percent profit.

2. One or both of the LEAPS options may be exercised. If the call is exercised, you will give up shares at $35 per share. Your basis was $26, so your capital gain is $900, plus the call premium. If the put is exercised, you will buy 100 shares at the striking price of 25, so your average basis would be 25.50 in this stock.

3. One or both of the LEAPS options can be rolled forward to avoid exercise. The call can be rolled forward and up, and the put can be rolled forward and down. With each change in striking price, you change the eventual exercise value, so that upon exercise you would be more points ahead. If the call is exercised, you will gain five points more with a five-point roll. If the put is exercised, you will buy stock at five points less than before.

4. One or both LEAPS options can be closed. As long as time value falls, you may be able to close these short positions at a profit. However, they can also be closed to reduce losses if the stock's adverse price movement is significant.

collar

a spread strategy combining long stock, a covered call, and a long put, with both options out of the money. The collar limits potential gains and potential losses.

One interesting variation on the spread is the *collar*. This strategy involves three positions: buying the stock, selling an out-of-the-money call, and buying an out-of-the-money put. It is designed to limit potential losses; however, potential profits are limited as well. While trading costs may be high when collars are used for single-contract transactions, they are viable in some situations. The further out of the money the call and put, the more bullish your point of view. This strategy combines the most optimistic points of view, and when the short call pays for the cost of the long put, the potential loss is limited as well. Potential outcomes include exercise of the short call, in which the stock will be called away; inadequate movement on either side, resulting in little or no net loss; or your exercise or sale of the long put in the event of a decline in the stock's price.

dividend collar

a collar designed to create income from quarterly dividends, using long stock, short calls, and long puts. The strategy eliminates market risk and requires monthly entry and exit.

One type of interesting collar is based on using stock and options as a no-risk method to generate double-digit returns from dividends. This *dividend collar* has three parts: 100 shares of stock, one short call, and one long put, all opened before the *ex-dividend date* and all closed as soon as possible afterward.

Ideally, the dividend collar should involve a call and put with the same striking price at the next increment above the current price of the stock.

ex-dividend date

the date on which a stockholder is no longer stockholder of record for the purpose of earning dividends. Only those acknowledged as stockholders of record before the ex-dividend date earn the quarterly dividend.

Example

The Cat Will Play: A trader bought 100 shares of Altria (MO) at $36 per share several weeks ago. On March 22, Altria is at $39.67 per share during the trading day. The next ex-dividend date will be April 5, only 14 days away. On that same day, the April 40 call is at 0.30 and the April 30 put is at 0.51. A dividend collar is opened by (a) buying 100 shares, (b) selling the 40 call, and (c) buying the 39 put.

> The cost of the long put is mostly covered by the income from the short call, netting a debit of $21 (0.51 minus 0.30). The dividend is $0.50 cents, representing a yield of 5.04% ($0.50 per quarter, or $2.00 per year; $2.00 ÷ $39.67 = 5.04%).

One of three outcomes is possible: First, the stock price rises above $40 and the short call is exercised before the ex-dividend date; in this case, the strategy fails but there is no net loss and the trader ends up with a no-cost long put. However, if the stock price rises above $40 after the ex-dividend date, the trader earns the dividend and the call will be exercised by the last trading day, April 21.

Second, if the stock price falls below the 39 strike, the trader exercises the put before April 19 and disposes of shares at $39 per share, a profit of $300 before trading costs (original purchase price of $36 subtracted from the strike of 39). This action may be taken on or before the last trading day, and in this case the short call expires worthless.

Third, the stock price ends up right between $39 and $40, an unlikely but possible outcome. In this case, the trader earns the dividend, both options expire, and stock can be sold at a profit above the $36 per share basis.

The purpose of the dividend collar is to eliminate all market risk while creating dividend income monthly instead of quarterly. Either the short call is exercised and shares are called away or the trader exercises the put and disposes of shares at the striking price of the put. In either case, the dividend is earned and capital is freed up to repeat the strategy in the following month.

The strategy also requires locating stocks with ex-dividend dates in different months. The requirement is for at least one stock with an ex-dividend date in each of the three cycles (January, April, July, October; February, May, August, November; and March, June, September, December). For example, if each of the three stocks yields 4 percent per year in dividends, the dividend collar earns 1 percent every month instead of every quarter. This converts the annual 4 percent dividend to a 12 percent dividend, and the strategy has also eliminated market risk.

The dividend collar and similar strategies provide opportunities for high profits with little or no risk. Spreads are especially well suited to this approach to the options market.

The Hedge

The second advanced strategy is the *hedge*, which is explored in greater detail in the next chapter. For example, you hedge a short sale in stock by purchasing a call. In the event the stock rises, the short seller's losses will be offset by a point-for-point rise in the call. A put also protects a long stock position against a decline in price. So using options for insurance is another type of hedge. Both spreads and straddles contain hedging features, since two dissimilar positions are opened at the same time; price movement reducing the value on one side of the transaction tends to be offset by price movement increasing value on the other side.

Advanced strategies often produce minimal profits for each option contract, given the need to pay trading fees upon opening and closing. Such marginal outcomes do not necessarily justify the associated risks, so advanced options traders apply these strategies with large multiples of option contracts. When you deal in multiples, the brokerage deposit requirements are increased as well.

In the advanced strategy, what appears simple and logical on paper does not always work out the way you expect. Changes in option premium are not always logical or predictable, and short-term

hedge

a strategy involving the use of one position to protect another. For example, stock is purchased in the belief it will rise in value, and a put is purchased on the same stock to protect against the risk that the stock's market value will decline.

straddle

the simultaneous purchase and sale of the same number of calls and puts with identical striking prices and expiration dates.

strangle

a strategy in which an equal number of long calls and puts are bought (long strangle) or sold (short strangle). These terms include different striking prices but the same expiration date, and the strategy will be profitable only if there is a large price movement in the underlying stock.

variations occur unexpectedly. This is what makes option investing so interesting; such experiences also test your true risk tolerance level. You may find that your risk tolerance is different than you thought once you employ advanced option strategies. Being at risk is daunting, so think of the *range* of risks and costs before embarking on any advanced strategy.

The Straddle

The third combination strategy is called a *straddle*. This is described in detail in the next chapter. A straddle is defined as the simultaneous purchase and sale of an identical number of calls and puts with the same striking price and expiration date. Whereas the spread requires a difference in one or more of the terms, the straddle is distinguished by the fact that the terms of each side are identical. The difference is that a straddle consists of combining calls on one side with puts on the other.

The lessons of the spread examples earlier in this chapter can also be applied in the straddle. Instead of spreading with the use of higher or lower striking prices, both options can be sold at or near the money. In this situation, premium income will be far greater, consisting of high time value on both sides. The chances of exercise are greater as well, and if you wish to avoid exercise, you will have to roll at least one of the straddle positions, and possibly both. If the stock's direction reverses itself, it could result in the need to roll the call forward and up *and* to roll the put forward and down.

If you enter an at-the-money straddle using short covered calls and short uncovered puts, you need to be prepared to accept exercise if it does occur. Because you keep the premium for selling these options, it can be a very profitable strategy.

The Strangle

A strategy combining features of both the spread and the straddle is the *strangle*. In this strategy, you will make a profit only if the stock has a significant move. A strangle consists of a long call and a long put with different striking prices but the same expiration date, and it is affordable primarily because both options are out of the money.

Example

Strangle, Not Choke: You have been tracking a stock that has traded in a narrow range for many months. You expect a large price movement, but you don't know which direction it will take. The stock currently trades at $43 per share. You enter a strangle consisting of a 45 call and a 40 put, both expiring in seven months. The total cost of these two options is 4 ($400). As long as the stock's price remains between $36 and $49 per share, the strangle cannot be profitable (striking prices expanded by the cost of both options). But if the price moves above or below that range, one side or the other will be profitable. In a short strangle, potential profits exist as long as options remain out of the money, and that profit range is expanded by the receipt of option premium.

The strangle is a strategy based on the belief that the stock will move substantially. Of course, because it requires the purchase of two options, the chances for success in this strategy are less than the chances when purchasing a single option. To enter a strangle, you should be confident that substantial price movement is likely to occur before expiration.

A related strategy partially solves the problem. As shown in the previous example, the cost of long options makes it difficult to reach and exceed a breakeven point. The *iron condor* is a variation on the strangle. It consists of four different options: long and short calls and long and short puts, all on the same underlying stock.

VERTICAL SPREAD STRATEGIES

You can use spreads to exploit time value premium. These changes are predictable because everyone knows what happens to time value as expiration approaches. And when options are in the money, it is reasonable to expect intrinsic value premium to react dollar for dollar with movement in the price of the underlying stock. Time value premium can change in predictable ways, which presents opportunities for short-term profits. The relationship between intrinsic value and time value is what makes the spread an interesting and challenging strategic tool.

iron condor

the combination of a long strangle and a short strangle on the same underlying stock. The cost is reduced due to offsetting premium payments and receipts; it is practical as long as short position exercise costs do not exceed long position profits.

Key Point

As with most option strategies, time value spells the difference between profit and loss in most spreads.

You have an advantage when offsetting long and short positions. The spread employing short-term options is likely to involve one side in the money and the other side out of the money. The in-the-money side will tend to change in value at a different rate from the out-of-the-money side, because it contains intrinsic value. By observing the differences on either side of the striking price, you can anticipate advantages that you can gain through the spread strategy, whether the market moves up or down.

Whenever you combine a long call with a higher-strike short call, you create an alternative form of "cover" for the short position. The risk disappears as long as both positions are open because, even with a large price run-up in the stock, the long position is always going to be worth more than the short position. This remains a covered position as long as the long position is open. However, if the long call expires and the short call remains open, it reverts to an uncovered position. So the safest covered spread of this type exists when both expire at the same time (or when the long position will be open longer than the short).

It is also possible to create a covered put using the same strategy. It involves creating a spread in which the long position has a *higher* strike than the short put position. If the stock's value falls so that the short put is in the money, the long put will also be in the money and will always be worth more. This is true as long as both puts expire at the same time, or when the long put remains open longer than the short put. This is the only situation in which a short put can be truly covered. In a put-based spread, you can overcome the limitation and create a low-risk strategy.

bull spread

a strategy involving the purchase and sale of calls or puts that will produce maximum profits when the value of the underlying stock rises.

Bull Spreads

A *bull spread* provides the greatest profit potential when the underlying stock's market value rises. With the bull spread, you buy an option with a lower striking price and sell another with a higher striking price. You can employ either puts or calls in the bull spread.

The following example describes the ideal situation, in which both sides of the spread are profitable, because the stock's price behaves perfectly to suit the spread. Of course, you have no control over price movement, so this outcome will not always occur. Even when only one side is profitable, however, the strategy works as long as you achieve an overall net profit.

Example

Bull Spread, Not a Bad Thing: You open a bull spread using calls. You sell one December 55 call and buy one December 50 call, as shown in Figure 2.1. At the time of this transaction, the underlying stock's market value is $49 per share. After you open the spread, the stock's market value rises to $54 per share. When that occurs, the 50 call increases in value point for point once it is in the money. The short 55 call does not increase in value, as it remains out of the money and, in fact, will drop in value as its time until expiration nears. Because of the advantage the spread creates at the time the stock has reached the $54 per share level, both sides of the spread will be profitable. The long 50 call rises in value and the short 55 call remains out of the money.

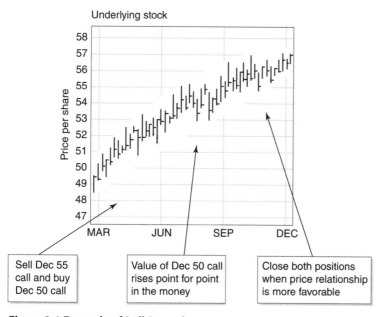

Sell Dec 55 call and buy Dec 50 call

Value of Dec 50 call rises point for point in the money

Close both positions when price relationship is more favorable

Figure 2.1 Example of Bull Spread

Key Point

The spread is most profitable when the stock's price changes in the desired direction, timing, and pattern. Both sides of the spread can work out well. This would be much easier if stock price movement could be controlled or predicted—which it cannot.

A bull vertical spread is profitable when the underlying stock's price moves in the anticipated direction. For example, a lower-priced call will be profitable if the stock rises in value, whereas the higher-priced short call will not be exercised as long as it remains out of the money, as previously illustrated.

A bull vertical spread with defined profit and loss zones is shown in Figure 2.2.

Example

Defining the Zones: You sell one September 45 call for 2, and buy one September 40 call for 5. The net cost is $300. When the stock rises between $40 and $45 per share, the September 40 call rises dollar for dollar with the stock, while the short September 45 call remains out of the money. Its premium value will decline as time value disappears. As long as the stock remains within this five-point range, both sides can be closed at a profit (as long as closing the positions would produce net income higher than your initial cost of $300). If the stock's price rises above $45 per share, the five-point spread in striking prices will be offset by the long and short positions. Both calls will be in the money. So this strategy limits both profits as well as losses.

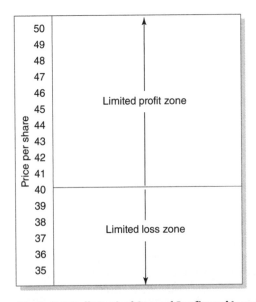

Figure 2.2 Bull Vertical Spread Profit and Loss Zones

Bear Spreads

While the bull spread seeks increases in market value, the *bear spread* will produce profits if the stock's market value falls. In this variety of the spread, the higher-value option is always bought, and the lower-value option is always sold.

bear spread

a strategy involving the purchase and sale of calls or puts that will produce maximum profits when the value of the underlying stock falls.

Example

A Bearish Idea: You open a bear spread using calls. You sell one March 35 call and buy one March 40 call. The stock's market value is $37 per share. The premium value of the lower call, which is in the money, will decline point for point as the stock's market value falls; if the stock's value does fall, the position can be closed at a profit.

Going Pessimistic with Puts: You open a bear spread using puts. As shown in the example in Figure 2.3, you sell one December 50 put and buy one December 55 put. The underlying stock's market value is $55 per share. As the price of the stock moves down, the long 55 put will increase in value point for point with the change in stock price. By the time the stock's price moves down to $51, both puts will be profitable—the long put from increased intrinsic value, and the short put from lower time value.

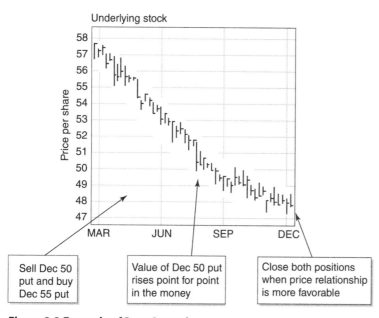

Figure 2.3 Example of Bear Spread

This scenario assumes ideal conditions in which the stock's price moves the desired number of points in the perfect time frame, which enables the bear spread writer to profit. The example illustrates the ideal outcome using a bear spread. You gain more flexibility when going long using LEAPS options in the bear spread; this enables you to write several short-term puts against the "covered" longer position. The cost for the long position will be greater due to the time factor, but the potential for profit makes the entire strategy far more flexible as well.

Key Point

Bear strategies often are overlooked, because people tend to be optimists. Look at *all* of the possibilities. You can make money when the stock goes down in value, too.

A detailed bear spread with defined profit and loss zones is illustrated in Figure 2.4.

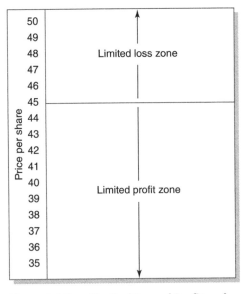

Figure 2.4 Bear Vertical Spread Profit and Loss Zones

Example

Profits on Both Sides: You sell one September 40 call for 5 and buy one September 45 call for 2; your net proceeds are $300. As the stock's market value falls below the level of $45 per share, the short 40 call will lose point value matching the stock's decline; the long call will not react in the same way, as it remains out of the money. As the $40 per share price level is approached, the spread can be closed with profits on both sides.

Consider how the preceding example would work with puts instead of calls. In that scenario, the long put would *increase* point for point with a decline in the stock's market value.

When the bear spread employs calls, profits are frozen once both sides are in the money, at least to the degree that intrinsic value changes; one side's increase will be offset by the other side's decrease. The only remaining opportunity to increase profits at that point would lie in time value premium left in the short position.

In all of these examples, the most significant risk is that the stock will move in the direction opposite that desired. Be prepared to cut losses by closing a spread in that event before the short position increases in value. You risk exercise on the short side at any time that option is in the money, and you might need to close to avoid exercise. Your maximum risk other than that of exercise is limited to the point difference between the two striking prices (minus net premium received when the position was opened, or plus net premium paid). In the preceding examples, a five-point spread was used, so the maximum point-spread risk is $500. The point-spread risk increases as the gap between striking prices changes, as shown in Table 2.1.

Example

Limiting the Risk Zone: You open a spread. The difference between striking prices on either side is five points. Your maximum risk is $500 plus trading fees, plus net premium paid when you opened the position (or minus net premium received).

Table 2.1 Spread Risk Table

Number of Option Spreads	Striking Price Interval	
	5 Points	**10 Points**
1	$ 500	$ 1,000
2	1,000	2,000
3	1,500	3,000
4	2,000	4,000
5	2,500	5,000
6	3,000	6,000
7	3,500	7,000
8	4,000	8,000
9	4,500	9,000
10	5,000	10,000

A Four-Part Position: You open a spread buying and selling four options on either side. The difference between striking prices is five points. Your maximum risk is $2,000 (modified as in the previous example), because four positions are involved, each with a five-point difference between striking prices.

box spread

the combination of a bull spread and a bear spread, opened at the same time on the same underlying stock.

Box Spreads

When you open a bull spread *and* a bear spread at the same time, using options on the same underlying stock, it is called a *box spread*. This limits risks as well as potential profits, and is designed to produce a profit on one side or the other, regardless of which direction the stock moves.

Example

Boxed in with Options: As illustrated in Figure 2.5, you create a box spread by buying and selling the following option contracts:

Bull spread: Sell one September 40 put and buy one September 35 put.

Bear spread: Buy one September 45 call and sell one September 40 call.

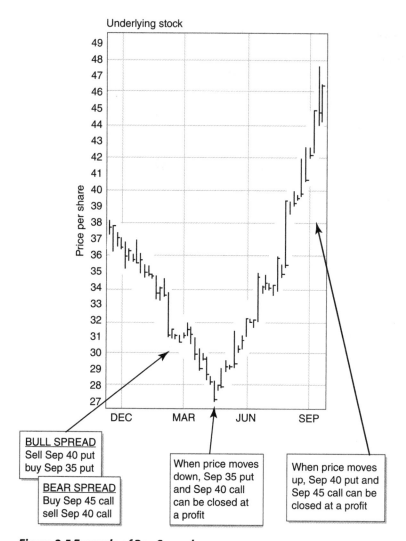

Figure 2.5 Example of Box Spread

In this example, if the underlying stock's price moves significantly in either direction, portions of the box spread can be closed at a profit. One important reminder: It makes sense to close corresponding long and short positions in the event of a profit opportunity, to avoid the risk of leaving yourself exposed with an uncovered short option. In the ideal situation, the stock's price will move first in one direction (enabling half the box spread to be closed at a profit) and then in the other (enabling the other half to be closed, also at a profit).

Key Point

When one side of the box spread expires, you might be left exposed on the other side. Keep an eye on the changing situation to avoid unacceptable risks.

The detailed profit and loss zones of a box spread are summarized in Figure 2.6. The net proceeds from this box spread result from the following outcomes:

> *Bull spread:* Sell one September 45 put for 6 (+$600) and buy one September 40 put for 2 (–$200)

> *Bear spread:* Sell one December 35 put for 1 (+$100) and buy one December 40 put for 4 (–$400)

If the stock's market price rises to between $40 and $45 per share, the bull spread can be closed at a profit. Above that level, the difference in bull spread values will move to the same degree in the money, offsetting

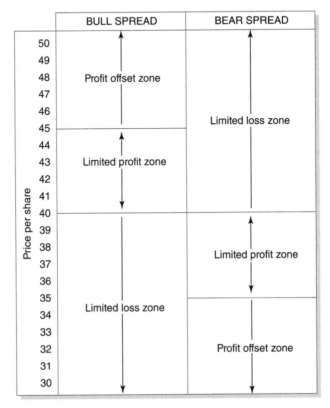

Figure 2.6 Box Spread Profit and Loss Zones

one another. At that level, you can wait out time value decline, but it could also make sense to close the position when profits are available, if only to avoid exercise.

If the stock falls to between $35 and $40 per share, the bear spread can be closed at a profit. The long December 40 will be in the money and will change point for point with change in the stock's price. Below the level of $35 per share, the long and short position will change in intrinsic value levels, offsetting one another. Closing in-the-money positions makes sense to avoid exercise, remembering that time value offsets are likely to minimize any additional profits you could earn from waiting any longer.

Key Point

When you close part of a box spread, close related long and short positions to avoid leaving open uncovered short positions.

Debit and Credit Spreads

The simultaneous opening of long and short positions involves receipt *and* payment of money. When you go short, you receive a premium, and when you go long, you are required to pay. When you receive more than you pay, that also extends your profit range in a combination strategy. While it is always desirable to receive more money than you pay out, it is not always possible. Some strategies will involve making a net payment. When you make a payment to open the position, more profit is required in changed value levels to offset the amount paid and produce a net profit.

Key Point

When a spread involves a net receipt, that broadens your profit potential; a net payment is accompanied by the requirement for greater profits in changed option premium to make up the difference.

credit spread

any spread in which receipts from short positions are higher than premiums paid for long positions, net of transaction fees.

A spread in which more cash is received than paid is called a *credit spread*. When you are required to make a payment, that is called a *debit spread*.

HORIZONTAL AND DIAGONAL SPREAD STRATEGIES

Vertical spreads involve options with identical expiration dates but different striking prices. Another variation of the spread involves simultaneous option transactions with different expiration months. This strategy is called a *calendar spread*, or *time spread*.

The calendar spread can be broken down into two specific variations:

1. *Horizontal spread:* In this strategy, options have identical striking prices but different expiration dates.
2. *Diagonal spread:* In this strategy, options have different striking prices *and* different expiration dates.

debit spread

any spread in which receipts from short positions are lower than premiums paid for long positions, net of transaction fees.

calendar spread

a spread involving the simultaneous purchase or sale of options on the same underlying stock, with different expirations; also called *time spread*.

Example

Going Horizontal: You create a horizontal calendar spread. You sell one March 40 call for 2, and you buy one June 40 call for 5. Your net cost is $300. Two different expiration months are involved. The earlier short call expires in March, while the long call does not expire until June. Your loss is limited in two ways: by amount and by time. This strategy is illustrated in Figure 2.7. If, by March expiration, the first call expires worthless, you have a profit in that position and the second phase goes into effect. The short position no longer exists. If the stock rises at least three points above striking price before expiration, the overall position is at breakeven; above that, it will be profitable.

time spread

alternate name for *calendar spread*.

Example

The Diagonal View: You create a diagonal calendar spread. You sell one March 40 call for 2, and you buy one June 45 call for 3. Your net cost is $100. This transaction has different striking prices *and* expiration months. If the earlier-expiring short position is exercised, the long call can be used to cover the short call. In other words, as owner of the long position, you can exercise the call when your short position call is exercised. If the earlier call is not exercised, the overall risk is restricted to the net cost of $100. After expiration of the short call, breakeven is equal to the long call's striking price plus the cost of the overall transaction. In this case, the net cost was $100, so the breakeven price (not allowing for trading costs) is $46 per share. This is illustrated in Figure 2.8.

horizontal spread

a calendar spread in which offsetting long and short positions have identical striking prices but different expiration dates.

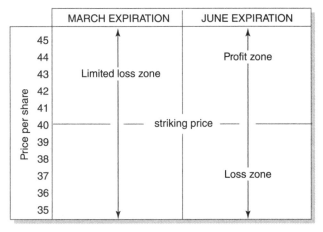

Figure 2.7 Profit and Loss Zones for an Example of Horizontal Calendar Spread

diagonal spread

a calendar spread in which offsetting long and short positions have both different striking prices and different expiration dates.

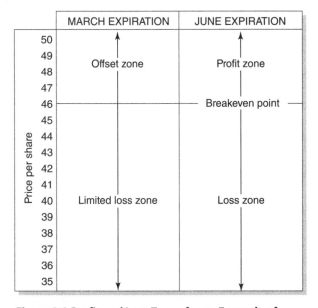

Figure 2.8 Profit and Loss Zones for an Example of Diagonal Calendar Spread

VERTICAL   HORIZONTAL   DIAGONAL

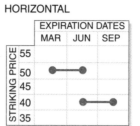
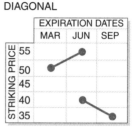

Figure 2.9 Comparison of Spread Strategies

Giving different spread strategies the names *vertical*, *horizontal*, and *diagonal* helps distinguish them from one another, and makes it easier to visualize the relationships between expiration and striking prices. These distinctions are summarized in Figure 2.9.

A horizontal spread is an attractive strategy when the premium value between two related options is temporarily distorted or when the later option's features cover the risks of the earlier-expiring short position.

Example

Unlimited Risk, Horizontally Speaking: You open a horizontal spread using calls. You sell a March 40 call for 4, and you buy a June 40 call for 6. Your net cost is $200. If the market value of the underlying stock rises, the long position covers the short position. The risk is no longer unlimited. The maximum risk in this situation is the $200 paid to open the spread. If the stock remains at or below striking price, the short call will lose value and expire worthless; or it can be bought and closed at a profit. For example, if the short call's value fell to 1, you could buy it and realize a profit of $300. Compared to the net cost of opening the spread, this puts you $100 ahead overall, but you still own the long call. If the premium value were to rise above the $600 paid for this call, it could be sold at a profit.

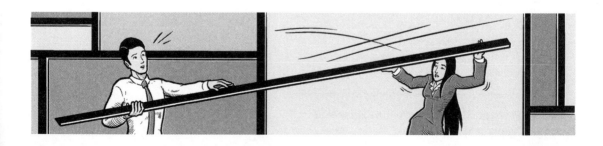

A horizontal spread is also effective in reducing risks when a position is already open. For example, if you previously sold a call and the stock begins to change in value so that you are at risk of exercise, you can reduce that risk by buying an option with a later expiration, which offsets the short position. This may be a less expensive alternative than buying the short position at a loss, because the long position has the potential to increase in value. If you own stock and do not want to go through exercise, the horizontal spread provides an alternative: you can use the long call to satisfy exercise instead of giving up stock.

Key Point

Devices like the horizontal spread sometimes come about in stages; for example, the long, later-expiring side can be opened to avoid exercise in a previously established short position.

Example

Avoiding Exercise Horizontally: You sold a covered June 45 call last month. The stock's market value is above the striking price. You do not want to close the position, because that will create a loss, and you also would like to avoid exercise. By buying a September 45 call, you create a horizontal spread. If the June 45 call is exercised, you will be able to use the September 45 call to fulfill the assignment. However, if the call is not exercised, you own a later-expiring call that has its own potential for profit within a time span of an additional three months.

A diagonal spread combines vertical and horizontal features. Long and short positions are opened with different striking prices and expiration dates.

Example

Reduced Risk with Diagonal Strategies: You create a diagonal spread. You sell a March 50 call for 4, and you buy a June 55 call for 1. You receive $300 net for these transactions. If the stock's market value falls, you will earn a profit from the decline in premium value on the short position. If the stock's market value rises, the long-position call's value rises as well, offsetting increases in the short call. Maximum risk in this situation is five points; however, because you received net premium of $300, the real exposure is limited to two points (five points between striking prices, less three points net premium). If the earlier short call expires worthless, you continue to own the long call. With its later expiration, you have potential profit for three more months.

This variety of spread becomes far more interesting when combining LEAPS options for the long side and shorter-term options for the short side. Because so much time is involved in the LEAPS option—up to three years—you have far more flexibility in designing, modifying, and developing strategies for horizontal and diagonal spreads.

For example, it is likely that by selling short-term options against the longer-term LEAPS, the strategy can be repeated many times. Enough premium income could be generated by selling calls to offset the cost of the long-position LEAPS. As the stock price changes over time, the corresponding horizontal or diagonal differences can be adjusted as well. The result could be to maximize premium income without risking exercise. Remember, the greatest decline in time value occurs in the last quarter of an option's life span. So you maximize this strategy by timing to offset long positions: You would seek short positions with higher striking prices (for calls) or lower striking prices (for puts).

The box spread adds complexity but opens the possibility for variations on this theme. A box spread employing long-position LEAPS and a series of offsetting shorter-term option short sales enables you to modify the range as the stock's price moves in either direction.

ALTERING SPREAD PATTERNS

The vertical, horizontal, and diagonal patterns of the spread can be employed to reduce risks, especially if you keep an eye on relative price patterns and you recognize a temporary price distortion. Going beyond reduction of risk, some techniques can be employed to make the spread even more interesting. Combining LEAPS options with shorter-expiring options also increases the flexibility in spread strategies. In the best possible outcome, you will be able to profit both from spreads *and* on the underlying stock.

Varying the Number of Options

The *ratio calendar spread* involves the use of a different number of options on each side of the spread, plus different expiration dates. The strategy is interesting because it creates two separate profit and loss zone ranges, broadening the opportunity for interim profits.

ratio calendar spread

a strategy involving a different number of options on the long side of a transaction from the number on the short side, when the expiration dates for each side are also different. This strategy creates two separate profit and loss zone ranges, one of which disappears upon the earlier expiration.

Example

The Geometric Approach: You enter into a ratio calendar spread by selling four May 50 calls at 5 and buying two August 50 calls at 6. You receive $800 net ($2,000 received less $1,200 paid) before transaction fees are deducted. You hope that between the time you open these positions and expiration, the underlying stock's market value will remain below the striking price; that would produce a profit on the short side. Your breakeven is $54 per share.

If the stock is at $54 at the point of expiration, you break even due to the ratio of four short calls and two long calls. Upon exercise, the two short calls will cost $800—the same amount that you received upon opening the ratio calendar spread. If the price of the stock is higher than $54 per share, the loss occurs at the ratio of 4 to 2 (since you sold four calls and bought only two). If the May expiration date were to pass without exercise, the four short positions would be profitable, and you would still own the two August 50 calls.

The profit and loss zones in this example are summarized in Figure 2.10. Note that no consideration is given to transaction costs, time value of the longer-expiration premiums, or the outcome in the event of early exercise.

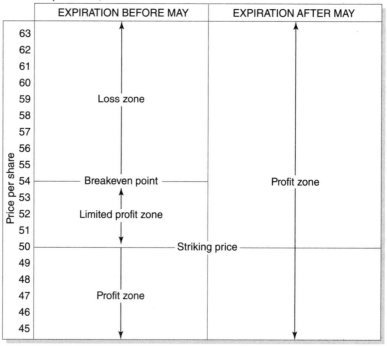

Figure 2.10 Example of Ratio Calendar Spread

Another complete ratio calendar spread strategy with defined profit and loss zones is summarized in Figure 2.11 and explained in the following example.

> **Example**
>
> **A Complexity of Zones:** You sell five June 40 calls at 5 and buy three September 40 calls at 7. Net proceeds are $400. The short position risk is limited to the first expiration period, with potential losses partially covered by the longer-expiration long calls. If the stock's market value does not rise above the striking price of 40, the short calls will expire worthless.

Once the June expiration passes, the $400 net represents pure profit, regardless of stock price movement after that date. However, if the stock's market value were to rise above the long calls' striking price, they would increase in value three points for each point of increase in the stock. The calls can also be sold at any point prior to expiration, to create additional profit.

Table 2.2 shows a summary of the values for this strategy at various stock price levels as of expiration. No time value is considered in this

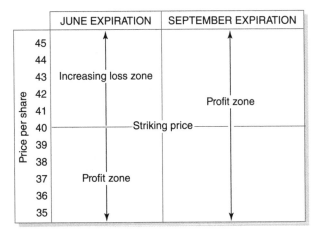

Figure 2.11 Ratio Calendar Spread Profit and Loss Zones

ratio calendar combination spread

a strategy involving both a ratio between purchases and sales and a box spread. Long and short positions are opened on options with the same underlying stock, in varying numbers of contracts and with expiration dates extending over two or more periods. This strategy is designed to produce profits in the event of either price increases or decreases in the market value of the underlying stock.

Table 2.2 Profits and Losses for Ratio Calendar Spread Example

Price	June 40	September 40	Total
$50	−$5,000	+$3,000	−$2,000
49	− 4,500	+ 2,700	− 1,800
48	− 4,000	+ 2,400	− 1,600
47	− 3,500	+ 2,100	− 1,400
46	− 3,000	+ 1,800	− 1,200
45	− 2,500	+ 1,500	− 1,000
44	− 2,000	+ 1,200	− 800
43	− 1,500	+ 900	− 600
42	− 1,000	+ 600	− 400
41	− 500	+ 300	− 200
40	+ 2,500	− 2,100	+ 400
39	+ 2,500	− 2,100	+ 400
38	+ 2,500	− 2,100	+ 400
Lower	+ 2,500	− 2,100	+ 400

summary. If the stock remains at or below the $40 per share level, the ratio calendar spread will be profitable. However, that profit will be limited as long as all positions remain open.

Expanding the Ratio

The ratio calendar spread can be expanded into an even more complex strategy through employment of the *ratio calendar combination spread.* This strategy gives another dimension to the ratio calendar spread by adding a box spread to it.

Example

Doubling Up Calls *and* Puts: As illustrated in Figure 2.12, you open the following option positions:
Buy one June 30 call at 3 (pay $300).
Sell two March 30 calls at 1.75 (receive $350).
Buy one September 25 put at 0.75 (pay $75).
Sell two June 25 puts at 0.625 (receive $125).

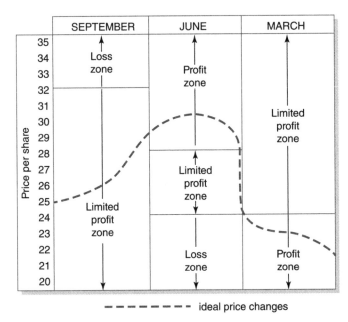

Figure 2.12 Example of Ratio Calendar Combination Spread

The net result of these transactions is a receipt of $100, before calculation of trading charges. This complex combination involves 2-to-1 ratios between short and long positions on both sides (two short option positions for each long option position). In the event of unfavorable price movements in either direction, you risk exercise on at least a segment of this overall strategy. The ideal price change pattern would enable you to close parts of the total combination at a profit, while leaving other parts open. Short positions should be closed in advance of long positions, given their least partial coverage against exercise. When prices move in one direction and then reverse and go the other way, it is called a price *whipsaw.* For the more complex options strategies, whipsaws can either create ideal profit opportunities or cause complete chaos—all depending on the timing, duration, and direction of the whipsaw.

whipsaw

a price trend in stocks when the price moves in one direction and then reverses and moves in the opposite direction.

Key Point

You will want to close short positions in advance of long positions to avoid unacceptable risk—a point worth remembering when you open the positions in the first place.

Because trading fees add up quickly, any combination using only a small number of options is a costly strategy. Considering the risk exposure, potential profits would not justify the action in many cases; the previous example is a case in point. However, for the purpose of illustration, it shows how the strategy works. In practice, such strategies would be more likely to involve much larger numbers of option contracts, and thus more money—and more risk exposure.

Exercise risk is reduced when you own shares in the underlying stock, providing full or partial coverage against short call exercise. For example, when writing two calls and buying one, the risk of a price increase is eliminated if you also own 100 shares. Those shares cover one call, and the other short call is covered by the long call.

Example

Watching the Clock: A complete ratio calendar combination spread with defined profit and loss zones is shown in Figure 2.13. In this example, you open the following positions:

Buy one July 40 call for 6 (–$600).
Sell two April 40 calls for 3 (+$600).
Buy one October 35 put for 1 (–$100).
Sell two July 35 puts for 2 (+$400).

Net proceeds in this example are $300.

This example consists of two separate ratio calendar spreads, boxed together. Profits would result if the stock's market value were to move in either direction, whereas losses are limited. Three separate expiration dates are involved. One danger in this elaborate strategy is that as earlier options expire, later open positions become exposed to uncovered option exercise, so risks are increased. This situation can be reversed—so that chances for profits are greater—by building a combination using later-expiring long positions instead of short positions. Table 2.3 provides a breakdown of profit and loss produced at various price levels based on the example.

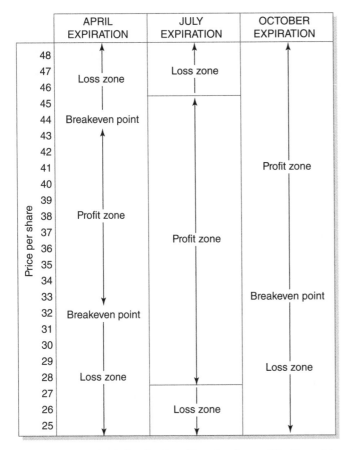

Figure 2.13 Ratio Calendar Combination Spread Profit and Loss Zones

sideways strategies

option strategies designed to produce maximum gains when the underlying stock exhibits lower than average volatility.

Strategies with a Middle Range

Another technique calls for the opening of offsetting options in middle striking price ranges, with opposing positions above *and* below. When options strategies are designed to create maximum advantages in periods of price consolidation for the stock, they are referred to as *sideways strategies*. The most popular of these is known as the *butterfly spread*. It can involve long and short positions in calls or puts. There are several possible variations of the butterfly spread. For example:

- Sell two middle-range calls and buy two calls, one with a striking price above that level and one with a striking price below that level.
- Sell two middle-range puts and buy two puts, one with a striking price above that level and one with a striking price

butterfly spread

a strategy involving open options in one striking price range, offset by open positions at higher and lower ranges at the same time.

Table 2.3 Profits and Losses for Ratio Calendar Combination Spread Example

Price	April 40 Call	July 40 Call	July 35 Put	October 35 Put	Total
$47	+$100	−$800	$ 0	+$400	−$300
46	0	− 600	0	+ 400	− 200
45	− 100	− 400	0	+ 400	− 100
44	− 200	− 200	0	+ 400	0
43	− 300	0	0	+ 400	+ 100
42	− 400	+ 200	0	+ 400	+ 200
41	− 500	+ 400	0	+ 400	+ 300
40	− 600	+ 600	0	+ 400	+ 400
39	− 600	+ 600	0	+ 400	+ 400
38	− 600	+ 600	0	+ 400	+ 400
37	− 600	+ 600	0	+ 400	+ 400
36	− 600	+ 600	0	+ 400	+ 400
35	− 600	+ 600	0	+ 400	+ 400
34	− 600	+ 600	0	+ 200	+ 200
33	− 600	+ 600	+ 100	0	+ 100
32	− 600	+ 600	+ 200	− 200	0
31	− 600	+ 600	+ 300	− 400	− 100
30	− 600	+ 600	+ 400	− 600	− 200
29	− 600	+ 600	+ 500	− 800	− 300
28	− 600	+ 600	+ 500	−1,000	− 500
27	− 600	+ 600	+ 500	−1,200	− 700
26	− 600	+ 600	+ 500	−1,400	− 900

below that level. You sell the middle options and buy the ones with strikes above and below.

- Buy two middle-range calls and sell two puts, one with a striking price above that level and one with a striking price below that level.
- Buy two middle-range puts and sell two puts, one with a striking price above that level and one with a striking price below that level. You buy the middle options and sell the ones with strikes above and below.

Example

The Butterfly in Flight: You sell two September 50 calls at 5, receiving $1,000. You also buy one September 55 call at 1 and one September 45 call at 7, paying a total of $800. Net proceeds are $200. This is a credit spread, since you receive more than you pay. You will profit if the underlying stock's price falls. And no matter how high the stock's price rises, the combined value of the long positions will always exceed the values in the two short positions.

Key Point

Exotic combinations are more often good for studying strategy than for actual use in the market. Trading costs are likely to offset potential limited profits in such strategies.

Butterfly spreads often are created when a single open position is expanded by the addition of other calls or puts, most often to protect a short position when a stock moves in a direction other than anticipated. It is difficult to create situations with risk-free combinations such as the one in the previous example.

> **Example**
>
> **Netting the Butterfly:** You sold two calls last month with a striking price of 40. The underlying stock's market value has declined to a point that the 35 calls are cheap, so you buy one to partially cover your short position. At the same time, you also buy a 45 call, which is deep out of the money. This series of trades creates a butterfly spread.

Trading costs makes butterfly spreads impractical when using a small number of options. The potential gain should be evaluated against the potential loss, trading costs, and ongoing exposure to risk.

Butterfly spreads involve either calls or puts. A bull butterfly spread will be most profitable if the underlying stock's market value rises, and the opposite is true for a bear butterfly spread.

A detailed butterfly spread, with defined profit and loss zones, is shown in Figure 2.14. In this example, the following transactions are involved:

Sell two June 40 calls at 6 (+$1,200).

Buy one June 30 call at 12 (−$1,200).

Buy one June 50 call at 3 (−$300).

The net cost is $300. This butterfly spread will either yield a limited profit or result in a limited loss. The potential yield often does not justify the strategy, since trading costs will not offset the limited

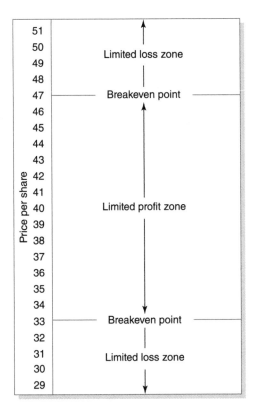

Figure 2.14 Butterfly Spread Profit and Loss Zones

potential profit. That is why the butterfly spread is often created in increments rather than all at once. Instead of executing the trades in the example, it might be more practical to simply buy one June 50 call and pay $300. In that alternative, you still have a limited potential loss ($300), but you also gain unlimited profit potential.

Table 2.4 summarizes profit and loss status at various prices of the underlying stock, using the previous example. It is based on values at expiration and assumes no remaining time value. If the stock's market value rises to $50 or more, the short position losses will be offset by an equal number of long position profits. And if the stock's market value declines, the maximum loss is $300, the net cost of opening these positions.

A variation on the butterfly spread is the *condor spread*. This is similar to the butterfly because it contains a bull and bear spread in combination; but with the condor, the striking prices of the short call and short put are not identical.

A similar variation on the use of multiple options is the *strap*. Also called a *triple option*, the strap consists of one long put and two long

condor spread

a variation of the butterfly spread using different striking prices in the short positions on either side of the middle range.

Table 2.4 Profits and Losses for Butterfly Spread Example

Price	June 30	June 40	June 50	Total
$51	+ $900	−$1,000	−$200	−$300
50	+ 800	− 800	− 300	− 300
49	+ 700	− 600	− 300	− 200
48	+ 600	− 400	− 300	− 100
47	+ 500	− 200	− 300	0
46	+ 400	0	− 300	+ 100
45	+ 300	+ 200	− 300	+ 200
44	+ 200	+ 400	− 300	+ 300
43	+ 100	+ 600	− 300	+ 400
42	0	+ 800	− 300	+ 500
41	− 100	+ 1,000	− 300	+ 600
40	− 200	+ 1,200	− 300	+ 700
39	− 300	+ 1,200	− 300	+ 600
38	− 400	+ 1,200	− 300	+ 500
37	− 500	+ 1,200	− 300	+ 400
36	− 600	+ 1,200	− 300	+ 300
35	− 700	+ 1,200	− 300	+ 200
34	− 800	+ 1,200	− 300	+ 100
33	− 900	+ 1,200	− 300	0
32	−1,000	+ 1,200	− 300	− 100
31	−1,100	+ 1,200	− 300	− 200
30	−1,200	+ 1,200	− 300	− 300
29	−1,200	+ 1,200	− 300	− 300
Lower	−1,200	+ 1,200	− 300	− 300

strap

an option strategy, also called a *triple option*, involving purchase of one put and two calls (hoping the stock's price will rise) or the purchase of one call and two puts (anticipating a stock's price decline).

triple option

alternative name for the *strap*.

calls (or one call and two puts). When the calls outnumber the puts, the position benefits if and when the underlying stock's market value rises. When the reverse is true, the position will benefit when the stock value declines. Because the in-the-money value of the heavier position will grow by two points, a favorable movement will quickly outpace the position cost. If the stock's price moves in the opposite direction, the single offsetting option will partially offset the cost (and if price movement is severe enough, it could recapture the entire cost).

In some brokerage account arrangements, you can reduce your trading cost by arranging for a *multileg options order*. This applies when several option positions are going to be opened at the same time, and the orders will be placed for a single commission rather than being charged a fee on each option position.

Any combination involving separate or offsetting options can be designed so that profits will be taken at specific points, either using stop orders or through careful tracking of the combination's status. However, in taking partial profits, you should be careful not to expose yourself to unintended risks. For example, if a short position is protected by an offsetting long position, the risk is minimal. But if the long position is closed without also closing the short position, additional risk is created.

The advantage of spreads is in their rich variety. You can create any level of risk using calls, puts, or both, and take a bullish or bearish position (or both). A related topic is that of hedges and straddles, complex strategies that are similar in some respects to spreads. However, with spreads you are focusing on different striking prices and expirations; with straddles, you set up positions based on the same striking price and expiration date. The next chapter introduces the many forms of hedges and straddles.

multileg option order

placement of an order for a single commission rather than for a commission charged for each option.

THOMSETT'S JOURNEY in ADVANCED OPTIONS

THOMSETT CONVINCES THE LAB TECHNICIAN TO LEAVE HIS HIDDEN LAB FOR THE FIRST TIME IN MONTHS.

I HAVEN'T SEEN SUNLIGHT OR THE HORIZON FOR MONTHS.

SUPER SECRET OPTIONS LAB

I FORGOT WHAT IT ALL LOOKS LIKE OUT HERE IN THE REAL WORLD.

THE NATURAL WORLD AND OPTIONS HAVE A LOT IN COMMON.

CHAPTER 3

HEDGES AND STRADDLES: MORE CREATIVITY

He that will not sail till all dangers are over must never put to sea.
— Thomas Fuller, *Gnomologia*, 1732

Whenever options are bought or sold as part of a strategy to protect another open position, the combination of positions represents a hedge.

THE TWO TYPES OF HEDGES

A *long hedge* protects against price increases. A *short hedge* protects against price decreases.

An example of a hedge, with defined profit and loss zones, is shown in Figure 3.1. In this case, you sold short 100 shares of stock at $43, and hedged that position with a May 40 call bought at 2. The cost of hedging your short position reduces potential profits by $200, but protects you against potentially greater losses without requiring that you close the position. The risk is eliminated until the call expires. At that point, there are three choices:

     1. Close the short position to eliminate risk.

2. Replace the call with another, later-expiring one.

3. Do nothing, since perception of the risk attributes might have changed.

long hedge

the purchase of options as a form of insurance to protect a portfolio position in the event of a price increase; a strategy employed by investors selling stock short and needing insurance against a rise in the market value of the stock.

Example

Trimming the Hedge: You are short on 100 shares of stock. This puts you at risk in the event the market value of that stock were to rise. You buy one call on that stock, which hedges your short stock position.

Allowing the Hedge to Grow: You own 100 shares of stock and, due to recent negative news, you are concerned that the market value could drop. You do not want to sell the shares, however. To hedge against the risk of lost market value, you have two choices: buy one put or sell one call. Both positions hedge the 100 shares. The put provides unlimited protection because it would increase in value for each in-the-money point lost in the stock's value. The call provides limited downside protection, only to the extent of the points received in premium.

short hedge

the purchase of options as a form of insurance to protect a portfolio position in the event of a price decrease; a strategy employed by investors in long positions who need insurance against a decline in the market value of the stock.

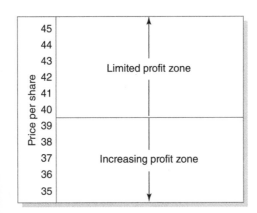

Figure 3.1 Long Hedge Profit Zones

In this example, if the underlying stock's market value increases, then profit potential is limited to the offsetting price gap between the stock's market value and the call's premium value. If the stock's market value falls, the short stock position will be profitable, with profits reduced by two points for the call premium you paid.

Table 3.1 summarizes this hedged position's overall value at various stock price levels.

Table 3.1 Profits and Losses from the Long Hedge Example

Price	Stock	Call	Total
$45	−$200	+$300	+$100
44	− 100	+ 200	+ 100
43	0	+ 100	+ 100
42	+ 100	0	+ 100
41	+ 200	− 100	+ 100
40	+ 300	− 200	+ 100
39	+ 400	− 200	+ 200
38	+ 500	− 200	+ 300
37	+ 600	− 200	+ 400
36	+ 700	− 200	+ 500
35	+ 800	− 200	+ 600

Hedging beyond Coverage

One of the disadvantages to the hedge is that potential profits may be limited. A solution is to modify the hedge to increase profit potential, while still minimizing the risk of loss.

A *reverse hedge* involves providing more protection than needed to cover another position. For example, if you are short on 100 shares of stock, you need to purchase only one call to hedge the position. In a reverse hedge strategy, you buy more than one call, providing protection for the short position *and* potential for additional profits that would outpace stock losses 2 to 1, for example; with three calls, the ratio would be 3 to 1. Three calls applied against 200 shares of stock would produce

**reverse
hedge**

an extension of
a long or short
hedge in which
more options are
opened than the
number needed
to cover the
stock position;
this increases
profit potential
in the event of
unfavorable
movement
in the market
value of the
underlying
stock.

a ratio of 3 to 2. The ratio can also be negative. For example, using two calls against 300 shares of stock provides a 2-to-3 negative reverse; you mitigate the potential loss, but you don't offset the entire potential loss.

An expanded example of a reverse hedge with defined profit and loss zones is shown in Figure 3.2. In this example, you sold short 100 shares of stock at $43 per share, and the value now has declined to $39. To protect the profit in the short position and to insure against losses in the event the price rises, you bought two May 40 calls at 2.

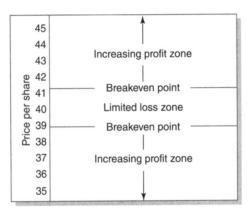

Figure 3.2 Reverse Hedge Profit and Loss Zones

This reverse hedge solves the problem of risk in the short stock position, while also providing the potential for additional gain in the calls. In order for this profit to materialize, the stock's value would have to increase enough points to offset your cost in buying the calls. This hedge creates two advantages. First, it protects the short position in the event of unwanted price increase in the stock. Second, the 2-to-1 ratio of calls to stock means that if the price were to increase in the stock, the calls would become profitable.

 Key Point

The reverse hedge protects an exposed position while adding the potential for additional profits (or losses). This makes the hedge more than a form of insurance.

Table 3.2 summarizes this position's value as of expiration at various stock prices.

Table 3.2 Profits and Losses from the Reverse Hedge Example

Price	Stock	Call	Total
$45	−$200	+$600	+$400
44	− 100	+ 400	+ 300
43	0	+ 200	+ 200
42	+ 100	0	+ 100
41	+ 200	− 200	0
40	+ 300	− 400	− 100
39	+ 400	− 400	0
38	+ 500	− 400	+ 100
37	+ 600	− 400	+ 200
36	+ 700	− 400	+ 300
35	+ 800	− 400	+ 400

The reverse hedge works to protect paper profits in long positions as well. For example, you may own 100 shares of stock that has risen in value. To protect against a possible decline in the market price, you may buy two puts, a reverse hedge that would produce 2-to-1 profits in the puts over any decline in the stock's value. You may also sell two calls for the same reason—one would be covered while the other would be uncovered. Or, looking at this another way, the hedged position would be one-half covered overall. If the stock's market value were to fall, the calls would lose value, providing downside protection to the extent of the total premium received. However, if the stock were to rise, profits in the stock would be reduced by losses in the calls. As with short positions, you can use options for partial hedging. For example, if you own 500 shares of appreciated stock, selling four calls (or buying four puts) provides you with a 4-to-5 ratio protecting against lost market value. You can also view this as having 400 shares hedged and another 100 shares without a hedge.

HEDGING OPTION POSITIONS

Hedging can protect a long or short position in an underlying stock, or it can reduce or eliminate risks in other option positions. Hedging is achieved with various forms of spreads and combinations. By varying the number of options on one side or the other, you create a *variable hedge*, which is a hedge involving both long and short positions where one side contains a greater number of options than the other.

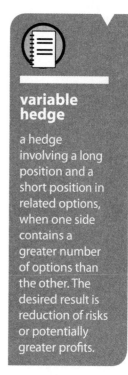

variable hedge

a hedge involving a long position and a short position in related options, when one side contains a greater number of options than the other. The desired result is reduction of risks or potentially greater profits.

> **Example**
>
> **Three to One—Nice Odds:** You buy three May 40 calls and sell one May 55 call. This variable hedge creates the potential for profits while completely eliminating the risk of selling an uncovered call. If the underlying stock's market value were to increase above the level of $55 per share, your three long positions would increase in value by three points for every point in the short position. If the stock's market value were to decrease, the short position would lose value and could be closed at a profit.

This particular situation would be difficult to create all at once with a net credit, because the lower striking price calls would probably cost more than the higher-priced short-position call. However, the variable hedge may be created in stages as a response to changing conditions. You can limit the risk exposure when short positions exceed long, by combining LEAPS and shorter-term options. A long LEAPS offset by soon-to-expire short-position calls, for example, provides a return of premium and limited time at risk.

Long and short variable hedge strategies, with defined profit and loss zones, are shown in Figure 3.3. In the long variable hedge example, you buy three June 65 calls for 1, paying $300; and you sell one June 60 call for 5. Net proceeds are $200. This long variable hedge strategy achieves maximum profits if the underlying stock's market value rises. Above the striking price of 65, long call values would increase three points for every point increase in the underlying stock. If the stock's market value decreases, all of the calls lose value and the net $200 proceeds will be all profit. The short June 60 call could also be closed at a net gain.

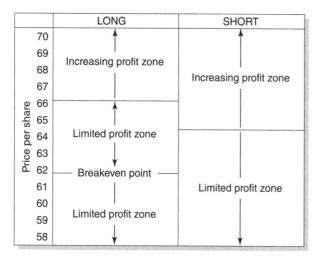

Figure 3.3 Variable Hedge Profit and Loss Zones

Table 3.3 summarizes this position's value as of expiration at various stock price levels. The problem in this strategy is that the short positions expire later than the long positions; in most circumstances, this is the most likely way to create a credit in a variable hedge. So you need to experience price movement that creates an acceptable profit before expiration of the long-position options, or be prepared to close out the short positions once the long positions expire, to avoid exposure to the risk of exercise.

Table 3.3 Profits and Losses from the Long Variable Hedge Example

Price	Stock	Call	Total
$70	+$1,200	−$500	+$700
69	+ 900	− 400	+ 500
68	+ 600	− 300	+ 300
67	+ 300	− 200	+ 100
66	0	− 100	− 100
65	− 300	0	− 300
64	− 300	+ 100	− 200
63	− 300	+ 200	− 100
62	− 300	+ 300	0
61	− 300	+ 400	+ 100
60	− 300	+ 500	+ 200
59	− 300	+ 500	+ 200
58	− 300	+ 500	+ 200

The previously discussed Figure 3.3 also shows an increasing loss zone and limited profit zone in the example of a *short* hedge. In that case, you sold five June 60 calls for 5, receiving $2,500; and you bought three June 65 calls for 1, paying $300; net proceeds were $2,200. This short variable hedge strategy is a more aggressive variation than the long example, with more proceeds up front and a corresponding higher risk level overall. When the offsetting long and short call positions are eliminated, two short calls remain uncovered. A decline in the value of the underlying stock would create a profit. However, an increase in the stock's market value creates an increasing level of loss. Beyond striking price, the loss is two points for every point of movement in the stock's price. Outcomes for this short hedge at various price levels of the stock are summarized in Table 3.4.

Table 3.4 Profits and Losses from the Short Variable Hedge Example

Price	Stock	Call	Total
$70	−$2,500	+$500	−$2,000
69	− 2,000	+ 400	− 1,600
68	− 1,500	+ 300	− 1,200
67	− 1,000	+ 200	− 800
66	− 500	0	− 500
65	0	− 300	− 300
64	+ 500	− 300	+ 200
63	+ 1,000	− 300	+ 700
62	+ 1,500	− 300	+ 1,200
61	+ 2,000	− 300	+ 1,700
60	+ 2,500	− 300	+ 2,200
59	+ 2,500	− 300	+ 2,200
58	+ 2,500	− 300	+ 2,200

ratio write

a strategy for covering one position with another for partial rather than full coverage. A portion of risk is eliminated, so ratio writes can be used to reduce overall risk levels.

Partial Coverage Strategies

One variation of variable hedging involves cutting partial losses through partial coverage. This strategy is known as a *ratio write*. When you sell one call for every 100 shares owned, you have provided 1-to-1 coverage. A ratio write exists when the relationship between long and short positions is not identical. The ratio can be greater on either the long side or the short side. See Table 3.5.

Example

Ratio Write or Wrong: You own 75 shares of stock and you sell one call. Because part of your short call is not covered, this overall position actually consists of two separate positions: 75 shares of stock are long, and one call is short. In practice, however, in the event of exercise, your 75 shares would satisfy three-quarters of the assignment. You would need to buy 25 shares at the striking price. Your short position is 75 percent covered. The ratio write is 1 to ¾.

Covered Plus Uncovered: You own 300 shares of stock and you recently sold four calls. You have two positions here: 300 shares that are associated with covered calls; and one uncovered short call. In practice, however, you have created a 4-to-3 ratio write.

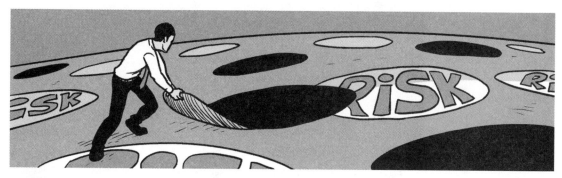

Key Point

The ratio write is appropriate when you are willing to accept some of the risk. When you think the chances of loss are minimal, the ratio write can be utilized to reduce overall costs.

Table 3.5 Ratio Writes

Calls Sold	Shares Owned	Coverage	Ratio
1	75	75%	1 to ¾
2	150	75	2 to 1½
3	200	67	3 to 2
4	300	75	4 to 3
5	300	60	5 to 3
5	400	80	5 to 4

An expanded example of the ratio write, with defined profit and loss zones, is shown in Figure 3.4.

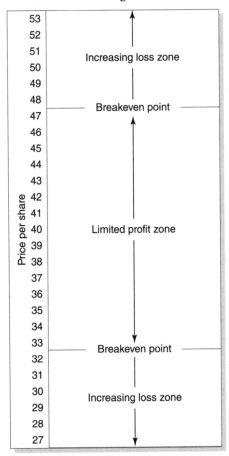

Figure 3.4 Ratio Write Profit and Loss Zones

In this example, you buy 50 shares of stock at $38 per share and you sell one September 40 call for 3. This creates a partially covered call. Half the short call risk is offset by the 50 shares. The other half of the risk is uncovered. If the value of the underlying stock rises, the risk is cut in half in the event of exercise. If the stock's market value falls, a loss in the stock will be partly offset by premium received from selling the call; there are three points of downside protection. A summary of this strategy is shown at various prices of the stock at expiration in Table 3.6.

Table 3.6 Profits and Losses from the Ratio Write Example

Price	50 Shares of Stock	September 40 Call	Total
$50	+$600	−$700	−$100
49	+ 550	− 600	− 50
48	+ 500	− 500	0

Table 3.6 (Continued)

Price	50 Shares of Stock	September 40 Call	Total
47	+ 450	− 400	+ 50
46	+ 400	− 300	+ 100
45	+ 350	− 200	+ 150
44	+ 300	− 100	+ 200
43	+ 250	0	+ 250
42	+ 200	+ 100	+ 300
41	+ 150	+ 200	+ 350
40	+ 100	+ 300	+ 400
39	+ 50	+ 300	+ 350
38	0	+ 300	+ 300
37	− 50	+ 300	+ 250
36	− 100	+ 300	+ 200
35	− 150	+ 300	+ 150
34	− 200	+ 300	+ 100
33	− 250	+ 300	+ 50
32	− 300	+ 300	0
31	− 350	+ 300	− 50
30	− 400	+ 300	− 100

STRADDLE STRATEGIES

While spreads involve buying and selling options with different terms, straddles are the simultaneous purchase and sale of options with the same striking price and expiration date.

long straddle

the purchase of an identical number of calls and puts with the same striking prices and expiration dates, designed to produce profits in the event of price movement of the underlying stock in either direction, adequate to surpass the cost of opening the position.

Middle Loss Zones

A *long straddle* involves the purchase of calls and puts at the same striking price and expiration date. Because you pay to create the long positions, the result is a middle-zone loss range above and below the striking price, and profit zones above and below that zone.

Example

Back in the Straddle Again: You open a long straddle. You buy one February 40 call for 2, and you buy one February 40 put for 1. Your total cost is $300. If the underlying stock's value remains within three points above or below the striking price, the straddle will lose money. If the stock's market value moves higher or lower by more than three points from the striking price, then the long straddle will be profitable.

Another example of a long straddle is summarized with defined profit and loss zones in Figure 3.5. In this example, you buy one July 40 call for 3 and one July 40 put for 1; total cost is $400. The long straddle strategy will be profitable if the underlying stock's market price exceeds the four-point range on either side of the striking price.

The four points required on either side of the striking price emphasize the most important fact about long straddles: The more you

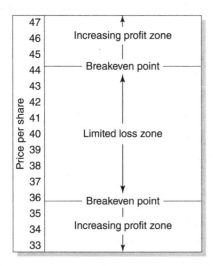

Figure 3.5 Long Straddle Profit and Loss Zones

pay in overall premium, the greater the required stock point movement away from the striking price. It does not matter which direction the price moves, as long as its total point value exceeds the amount paid to open the position. Table 3.7 summarizes the outcome of this example at various stock price levels.

You have some flexibility in the long straddle. Since both sides are long, you are free to sell off one portion at a profit while holding on to the

Table 3.7 Profits and Losses from the Long Straddle Example

Price	100 Shares of Stock	September 40 Call	Total
$47	+$400	−$100	+$300
46	+ 300	− 100	+ 200
45	+ 200	− 100	+ 100
44	+ 100	− 100	0
43	0	− 100	− 100
42	− 100	− 100	− 200
41	− 200	− 100	− 300
40	− 300	− 100	− 400
39	− 300	0	− 300
38	− 300	+ 100	− 200
37	− 300	+ 200	− 100
36	− 300	+ 300	0
35	− 300	+ 400	+ 100
34	− 300	+ 500	+ 200
33	− 300	+ 600	+ 300

other, without increasing risk. In the ideal situation, the stock will move in one direction and produce a profit on one side; and then it will move in the opposite direction, enabling you to profit on the other side as well. A long straddle may be most profitable in highly volatile stocks, but of course premium value of the options will tend to be greater as well in that situation. To show how the price swing can help to double profit potential, let's say that the stock's price moves up two points above striking price. The call can then be sold at a profit. If the stock's market value later falls three points below striking price, the put can also be sold at a profit. The strategy loses if the stock's price remains within the narrow loss range, and time value premium offsets any minor price movements. In other words, time works against you as a buyer; and when you buy both calls and puts, you have to contend with time value on both sides of the transaction.

Middle Profit Zones

In the previous example, two related long positions were opened, creating a middle loss zone on either side of the striking price. The opposite situation—a middle profit zone—is created through opening a *short straddle.* This involves selling an identical number of calls and puts on the same underlying stock, with the same striking price and expiration date. If the stock's market price moves beyond the middle profit zone in either direction, this position would result in a loss. Short straddles offer the potential for profits when stocks do not move in an overly broad trading range, and when time value premium is higher than average. Less volatile stocks also tend to contain lower time value, whereas more volatile stocks have higher time value and higher risks with short straddles. Because time value decreases as expiration approaches, the advantage in this position is the same as for sellers of calls and puts individually—time works for the short seller.

short straddle

the sale of an identical number of calls and puts with identical striking prices and expiration dates, designed to produce profits in the event of price movement of the underlying stock within a limited range.

Example

Straddling with Anticipation: You open a short straddle. You sell one March 50 call for 2 and one March 50 put for 1; total proceeds are $300. As long as the underlying stock's market value remains within three points of the striking price—on either side—the position will remain profitable. But if a change in current market value of the stock exceeds the three-point range, the short straddle will produce a loss.

The problem with the short straddle is that one side or the other is always at or in the money, so the risk of exercise is constant. The previous example does not allow for the transaction costs. In a practical application, the profit zone would be smaller for single options. The best outcome for this strategy, assuming that exercise does not take place, is that both sides will lose enough time value that they can both be closed at a profit. Considering that the profit margin will be slim and risks are considerable, you need to evaluate whether this two-sided short position would be worth the risk. As with other examples of advanced strategies, the short straddle is likely to result from opening one position and later adding the other.

Key Point

For each and every strategy with limited profit potential, always ask the critical question: Is it worth the risk?

An example of a short straddle with defined profit and loss zones is shown in Figure 3.6. In this example, you sell one July 40 call at 3, and one July 40 put at 1; total proceeds are $400. This creates a four-point profit zone on either side of the striking price.

The short straddle in this example creates a middle profit zone extending four points in both directions from the striking price. Unless the stock's market value is at the money at the point of expiration, the likelihood of exercise on one side or the other is high. Table 3.8 summarizes the outcome of this short straddle at various stock price levels.

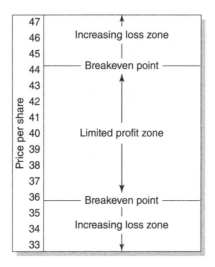

Figure 3.6 Short Straddle Profit and Loss Zones

Table 3.8 Profits and Losses from the Short Straddle Example

Price	July 40 Call	July 40 Put	Total
$47	−$400	+$100	−$300
46	− 300	+ 100	− 200
45	− 200	+ 100	− 100
44	− 100	+ 100	0
43	0	+ 100	+ 100
42	+ 100	+ 100	+ 200
41	+ 200	+ 100	+ 300
40	+ 300	+ 100	+ 400
39	+ 300	0	+ 300
38	+ 300	− 100	+ 200
37	+ 300	− 200	+ 100
36	+ 300	− 300	0
35	+ 300	− 400	− 100
34	+ 300	− 500	− 200
33	+ 300	− 600	− 300

Actual profits and losses have to be adjusted to allow for trading costs on both sides of any position. A thin margin of profit can be entirely wiped out by those fees, making more elaborate option strategies less than practical, notably when using only single options. To compare outcomes of long and short straddles, refer to Figure 3.7, which shows profit and loss zones in a side-by-side format for each strategy.

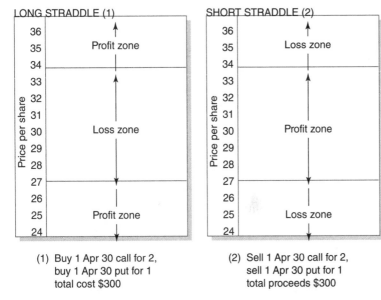

LONG STRADDLE (1)	SHORT STRADDLE (2)

Figure (left): LONG STRADDLE (1), Price per share axis 24–36
- 36, 35: Profit zone
- 34
- 33, 32, 31, 30, 29, 28: Loss zone
- 27
- 26, 25: Profit zone
- 24

Figure (right): SHORT STRADDLE (2), Price per share axis 24–36
- 36, 35: Loss zone
- 34
- 33, 32, 31, 30, 29, 28: Profit zone
- 27
- 26, 25: Loss zone
- 24

(1) Buy 1 Apr 30 call for 2,
buy 1 Apr 30 put for 1
total cost $300

(2) Sell 1 Apr 30 call for 2,
sell 1 Apr 30 put for 1
total proceeds $300

Figure 3.7 Comparison of Long and Short Straddle Strategies

THEORY AND PRACTICE OF COMBINED TECHNIQUES

Advanced option strategies expose you to the risk of loss, which could
be significant, especially when short positions are involved. If you do
decide to employ any of these strategies, remember the following seven
critical points:

1. *Brokerage fees are part of the equation.* Transaction fees reduce
   profit margins significantly, especially when you are dealing

in single-option increments. A marginal potential profit could be wiped out by fees, so approach advanced strategies from a practical point of view.

2. *Early exercise can change everything.* Buyers have the right of exercise at any time, so whenever your short positions are in the money, you could face early exercise. What seems a straightforward, easy strategy can be thrown into complete disarray by early exercise.

3. *Potential profit and risk are always related directly to one another.* Many options traders tend to pay attention only to potential profits, while overlooking potential risks. Remember that the greater the possibility of profit, the higher the potential for losses.

4. *Your degree of risk will be limited by your brokerage firm.* As long as your strategy includes short positions, your brokerage firm will restrict your exposure to risk—because if you cannot meet assignment obligations, the firm will be stuck with a loss.

5. *You need to thoroughly understand a strategy before opening positions.* Never employ any strategy before you understand how it will work out given all possible outcomes. You need to evaluate risks carefully, not only for the most likely results but for the worst-case possibilities.

6. *Using LEAPS options vastly increases the flexibility of combinations.* Combination strategies can also be designed to avoid exercise risk or naked option writing risk by employing longer-term LEAPS options. A net debit position could be transformed into a net credit position with repeated short-position offsetting sales over as long a period as three years.

7. *It doesn't always work out the way it was planned on paper.* When working out an option strategy on paper, it is easy to convince yourself that a particular strategy cannot fail, or that failure is only a remote possibility. Remember that option premium changes are not completely predictable, and neither are stock prices.

Options add a new dimension to your portfolio. You can protect existing positions, insure profits, and take advantage of momentary opportunities. However, every potential profit is associated with an offsetting risk. The market is efficient at least in that regard: Pricing of options reflects the risk level, so while a price is an opportunity, it also reflects exposure to the inherent risk in opening a position. Only through evaluation and analysis can you identify strategies that make sense for you, that protect your stock positions, and that you believe have a reasonable chance of producing profits at risk levels you are willing to undertake.

The next chapter shows how options in many configurations can be used to develop a highly leveraged program of swing trading. This may be accomplished with single contracts in either long or short positions, or with the use of spreads or straddles.

93

OPTIONS FOR SPECIALIZED TRADING: LEVERAGING THE TECHNICAL APPROACH

CHAPTER 4

No man thinks there is much ado about nothing when the ado is about himself.
—Anthony Trollope, *The Bertrams*, 1859

Most people think about options trading as an isolated and separate strategy. Options are used to speculate or to hedge existing stock positions, and, for many traders, that is the full extent and value of options. But options are so flexible and convenient that they can be used in numerous specialized situations as well.

A popular system in use today is *swing trading*. This is an excellent technical trading method for anyone who wants to become involved in short-term market plays, normally lasting between two and five days.

swing trading

a form of trading spanning 2 to 5 days in most cases, intended to take advantage of exaggerated swings in price, often in response to unexpected changes, such as earnings surprises.

setup

in swing trading, a signal indicating that a stock has reached a short-term high level (a sell setup) or a short-term low level (a buy setup). By taking action upon recognizing a setup, swing traders make small but consistent profits.

Swing traders use charting to identify a buy or sell *setup* and then time their decisions for small but consistent profits.

Options are perfect devices for swing traders, and for one simple reason. If you swing trade using stocks, your potential range of trades is severely limited and involves significant risks, at least on the short side. For example, if you want to swing trade using lots of 100 shares, a $25 stock demands a $2,500 commitment, but an option on the same stock will be available for a small fraction of that cost. An $85 stock requires $8,500 in available cash to place at risk but, again, an option on the same shares will cost far less.

Key Point

The leveraging feature of options makes swing trading practical, affordable, and less risky than using stock. This is an example of how options favor short-term traders.

With these important distinctions in mind, the swing-trading strategy is perfectly setup for options in place of stock. Remember these key points:

- *Swing traders are not interested in long-term investing.* A swing trader wants to create extremely short-term profits by moving in and out of positions in two- to five-day trading ranges. Because these traders are not interested in the long term, swing trading and options are a good match.

- *Because options cost less than stock, the range of possible swing trades is expanded with the use of options.* Imagine starting a swing-trading strategy with $10,000 available. Using stocks, you could trade four stocks in the range of $20 to $25. If you have to go short, you would be required to keep cash on hand to cover margin requirement. However, with the same $10,000, you could trade many more stocks using options, avoid the margin requirement involved with going short, and still make the same profits on each trade.

- *Swing traders want to open both buy and sell positions, meaning they may have to short stock. But with options, swing traders can buy puts instead of selling stock.* Many swing traders simply avoid opening short positions in stock because the risk is so significant. So they cut out half of their potential trades, and limit activity to only the buy side. With options, you can go long on calls and puts, meaning both sides can be involved without extra risk.

- *Swing trading is set up for very short-term positions, meaning this is a perfect strategy for in-the-money options that will expire within one month.* You are not likely to hear of very many options strategies where in-the-money options about to expire are favored above all others. But swing traders intend to be in positions for only two to five days, so soon-to-expire options are perfect for this purpose. Because time value will be at or near zero in these options, the cost of long positions will be limited to intrinsic value. Swing traders will want to use in-the-money options because they need the point-for-point price reaction, and options scheduled to expire in a month or less (but with current market value of the stock only a few points from striking price) are ideal.

- *Options present much lower risk than stock positions.* Swing traders are not going to time their decisions perfectly. No one is right 100 percent of the time. So in the use of long or short stock, the potential risks are significant. In fact, because swing traders want to move in and out of positions in only a few trading days, having capital tied up in positions beyond that time prevents swing traders from realizing their full potential and translates to many lost opportunities. In those cases where the timing is wrong, using soon-to-expire options has less risk because less cash is involved. A missed timing situation does not destroy the strategy.

SWING-TRADING BASICS

A swing trader depends on the three emotions that dominate the stock market: greed, fear, and uncertainty. These emotions cause virtually all of the short-term price aberrations that make swing trading a profitable technical strategy. Swing traders themselves, however, try to ignore their own tendency to react emotionally to price movement, and instead use logic to take advantage of market overreactions. When prices of stocks rise quickly, the market (the overall investing market, that is) tends to act out of greed, buying up shares to get in on the anticipated profits. The majority is often wrong, meaning that many people buy shares at the very top of a short-term price swing.

Key Point

Swing traders bet against majority thinking, which often leads to exceptional profits because the majority is usually wrong.

When prices of stocks fall, investors fear further declines and want to cut losses. So the tendency is to sell shares at the very bottom of the short-term price swing. And after a period of price movement, stock prices may move into a very brief period of uncertainty. At these times, the trading range narrows as traders wait out the next price movement. During uncertain times, some inexperienced investors become impatient and buy or sell impulsively.

All of these conditions present profitable opportunities, and this is where swing trading works best. Rather than timing decisions emotionally, swing traders tend to do the opposite of the majority. They attempt to time their sales for the price peaks, and time their purchases for the price bottoms. When prices settle down and the market is uncertain, swing traders wait out the period, moving their focus to other stocks and practicing patience rather than making buy or sell decisions impulsively.

Swing traders buying and selling stock have to limit their activity based on cash available (on the long side) and margin credit (on the short side). So they typically can swing trade using odd lots only and limiting their participation to only a handful of stocks. In some cases, swing traders can afford to play only one or two stocks at a time, based on their capital restrictions. This is unfortunate because it means having to miss many opportunities. Options solve this problem while reducing risks *and* setting the stage to play both sides of the price swing without ever having to go short.

Key Point

Swing trading with options presents a double advantage: You can be involved in many stocks at the same time, while costs and risks are lower than when shares of stock are used.

One argument against using options for swing trading is that they expire. But this should not be an issue, because swing trading ideally works in a very short time frame. There is no need to tie up capital in buying (or selling) 100 shares of stock, when a single option contract provides the same dollar profit when price movement takes place.

Example

A Swinging Idea: A stock on your watch list was trading in the mid-40s, and its trading range for 52 weeks had been $42 to $54 per share. Using the traditional method for measuring volatility, the stock was at 24 percent (range divided by low price). You wanted to swing trade this stock. On January 10, it was trading between $47 and $48 per share. To buy 100 shares, you would have needed more than $4,700. To go short, you would have had to assume the risk of selling short, and would have needed at least $2,400 in your account to cover the margin requirement.

Now consider using extremely short-term options. On January 10, slightly more than one week remained until expiration of the January options. There were only seven trading days remaining. This is a perfect scenario for extremely short-term in-the-money options for swing trading. Assuming a current setup signal occurred, you might anticipate a price rise (meaning you want to buy a call) or decline (meaning you want to buy a put). The January 45 call was about 2.5 points in the money, and was selling on January 10 for $2.37. This is virtually all intrinsic value. The January 47.50 put was selling that day for 0.60. So whether you believed that the price would rise or that it would fall in the next six trading days, options are clearly much cheaper than 100 shares of stock.

The example makes a strong case for swing trading. But remembering that those options are going to expire in only six trading days, buying either the call or the put must be done only if and when a strong setup signal is present.

Key Point
You can use options very close to expiration—even a matter of days—based on the swing-trading ideal of five or fewer trading days in any open position. But you also have to be willing to get in and out quickly or to accept small losses.

In most options strategies, you have to be concerned about the timing of a buy or sell decision primarily due to expiration, so the majority of strategies present a dilemma. On the long side, you want cheap options close to the money with a long time until expiration. On the short side, you seek high-time-value options with as short a time as possible until expiration. Swing trading contradicts these requirements, primarily because it is designed to work within only a few trading days.

In swing trading, you do not have strong feelings about companies one way or the other. You are trading stocks, not emotions. So when you find a setup to buy, you buy; and when you find a setup to sell, you sell. It's that simple. As a swing trader, you are exploiting the overreactions of the market at large and seeking very short-term profits based on identifiable setup signals. In a later section, Verizon Communications and Apple examples are detailed and the question of setup signals is explored in detail to show how this works.

THE SETUP SIGNAL

Swing trading depends on the setup, a buy or sell signal based on at least three days' worth of indications. Setups occur as well in combinations. In other words, a short-term trend requires at least a three-day price and pattern movement in one direction, ending with a clear reversal signal. It also requires a combination of setup indicators.

candlestick charts

technical charts for stocks summarizing a stock's daily trading range, opening and closing prices, and price direction. The candlestick chart is used in many trading systems, including swing trading.

Swing traders do well using *candlestick charts* to spot these setups. The candlestick chart is based on an ancient Japanese system originally used centuries ago to track rice prices. Today, Internet-based services offer candlestick charts on most listed stocks and save you time by computing the indicators for you. The candlestick employs a relatively simple pattern that reveals the opening and closing prices, trading range, and direction of price movement for the trading day (or other period).

While the candlestick tracks the stock's market price, the setup signals you can derive from the candlestick can be employed to time buy and sell decisions using options. As long as you use minimally in-the-money options with a short time to go until expiration (meaning there will be little or no time value remaining), the use of options will track option price movement very closely.

Key Point

The reason to use close-to-expiration options is to maximize the point-for-point price movement. If there is any time value remaining in the option, swing-trading models will not work.

Candlestick charts consist of a series of boxes (squares and rectangles) with single lines extending above and below. A white or blank box indicates that the price rose on that day, and a black box occurs when the price direction is downward. The box (the body) borders the day's opening and closing prices. The lines extending above and below the body represent the trading range for the day and are named the *upper shadow* and the *lower shadow*. For example, if a stock opened at

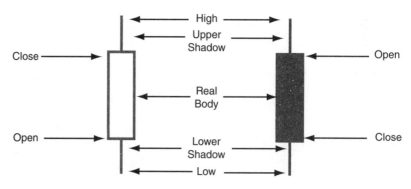

Figure 4.1 The Candlestick

upper shadow

on a candlestick formation, the line defining the highest extent of a day's trading range. The line extends above the opening or closing price for the day.

lower shadow

on a candlestick formation, the line defining the lowest extent of a day's trading range. The line extends below the opening or closing price for the day.

$23 per share and closed at $26, but had prices as high as $28 and as low as $21, the candlestick for that day would consist of a white box (because the price rose from opening to closing); the rectangle would be bordered between $23 and $26, the opening and closing prices; and the lines would extend below the box down to $21 and above the box up to $28. The attributes of candlesticks are summarized in Figure 4.1.

The buy or sell setup is found when a clearly established trend comes to an end. The setup anticipates price movement in the opposite direction and may be seen in the emergence of one or more patterns. Important patterns to know include:

- *Three or more days of clearly identified uptrend or downtrend movements.* This is the clearest of all setup signals. A minimum of three days is required. An *uptrend* occurs when you see three or more trading days consisting of a series of higher highs, offset with higher lows in price. For example, a price range over three days of $23 to $26, $24 to $28, and $26 to $29 meets these criteria. A *downtrend* also occurs over three or more days, and consists of a series of lower highs and lower lows. For example, the price pattern of $29 to $26, $28 to $24, and $25 to $23 establishes a three-day downtrend.

  The terminology is somewhat confusing, but once you see the series on a candlestick chart, the pattern becomes completely clear. The fact that uptrends consist of a series of white or clear boxes makes an uptrend jump right out and, of course, the black boxes in a downtrend are equally visible. As long as both top and bottom of each box are higher than on the previous day in an uptrend or lower in a downtrend, the pattern is clearly set. The three-day uptrend and downtrend are demonstrated in Figure 4.2.

Key Point

Short-term trends are easily identified. They open, close, and move in the same direction for three or more days.

uptrend

in swing trading, a series of three or more days consisting of higher highs and higher lows.

- *Look for the setup following the three-day pattern.* The setup will usually consist of either a *narrow-range day* (*NRD*) or a day with exceptionally high volume. The NRD is easily recognized; the rectangle and shadows are quite small.

Uptrend   Downtrend

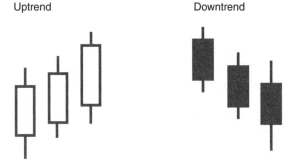

Figure 4.2 Uptrend and Downtrend Candlestick Patterns

downtrend

in swing trading, a series of three or more days consisting of lower highs and lower lows.

An NRD is considered a strong signal that the established trend may be ending. This is especially true when accompanied by a high-volume day. So when you see (1) a trend lasting three days or more, (2) an NRD, and (3) exceptionally high volume on the same day as the NRD, that combination gives you the strongest setup possible. On the upside, it is a sell signal; on the downside, it is a buy signal.

Key Point

A narrow-range day signifies price consolidation at the end of a trend. When this occurs with unusually high volume, it is the clearest possible setup, indicating time to take action.

narrow-range day (NRD)

in a candlestick chart, a trading day with an exceptionally small trading range.

TESTING THE THEORY

The two- to five-day price trends and setups can be tested by reviewing a typical candlestick chart. Figure 4.3 is a good example.

Figure 4.3 Narrow-Range Days as Reversal Signals (VZ)
Source: Courtesy of StockCharts.com.

This is a three-month candlestick chart for Verizon Communications (VZ). Two uptrends in September ended with clearly visible NRD sessions, which are pointed out. Immediately after these appeared, the trend reversed and headed downward. In both instances, the breadth of the trading range remained approximately the same even as price levels moved higher. The NRD signaled a decline in momentum among buyers, predicting the downtrend. Even though the downtrends were both short, each lasting only a few sessions, these provide a good example of how swing traders rely on two- to five-day price trends to time entry and exit.

Key Point

It is not any one signal that indicates time to take action, but a combination of an established short-term trend with a reversal signal. That is what swing traders depend on before making a move.

The chart of Apple (AAPL) provides a more complex example of reversal signals (see Figure 4.4). The first uptrend is strong, with six consecutive upward-moving sessions. This is followed by a *gap* and two black sessions, the first one an NRD. Then note the large downward gap and a second NRD, confirmation that the uptrend has ended.

Figure 4.4 Narrow-Range Days as Reversal Signals (AAPL)
Source: Courtesy of StockCharts.com.

Next are three white sessions moving sideways, the last one the setup of a bearish engulfing pattern (white followed by black body extending longer above and below). This is a very bearish signal. Following are six consecutive black sessions. Note the exceptionally long lower shadow on the NRD at the last black session, a sign that sellers tried to move price lower but failed. This is the first hint that the downtrend has ended.

The last highlighted trend is an uptrend that ends with a noticeable upside gap, three sessions, and then a downside gap. This could be interpreted as a variation of a bearish abandoned baby. The gaps on both sides of the isolated sessions are strong signals that the upside gap was a failed momentum test for buyers.

So this chart could be defined by a series of four reversal signals:

1. NRD followed by downside gap and another NRD.
2. A bearish engulfing pattern, a strong reversal signal.
3. A long lower shadow at the bottom of a downtrend, signaling declining momentum for sellers.
4. Gaps at the top of the uptrend, both before and after a series, which may be a variation of the bearish abandoned baby.

The importance of the gap as part of a reversal cannot be ignored. The gap serves as more than just spaces between trading days; it also points to the likelihood of reversal due to changes in momentum when found at the conclusion of the current trend.

Strong signals in these instances cannot be taken alone. They serve as part of a process of *confirmation* as well. For example, the bearish

gap

a trading pattern between days in which the second day's trading range opens above the highest price of the previous day or below the lowest price of the previous day.

confirmation

a signal providing support for another signal, reinforcing the belief that a trend is ending and about to reverse.

engulfing pattern confirms the change from uptrend to downtrend; and the modified bearish abandoned baby serves the same purpose, confirming what appears to be the end of the trend. The NRD is often found at these reversal moments, but NRDs also show up within trends, so confirmation of what they mean is an essential step in knowing when a reversal is actually taking place.

Regarding Figure 4.4 once again: In using options for swing trading, the signal that the downtrend had ended was clear by October 10. If you had bought a call on one of those days, especially one in the money and due to expire in the near future, you would have made a profit within five trading days. Of course, hindsight is always perfect in swing-trading situations being reviewed. Swing traders are supposed to ignore the news and just trade the price patterns and investor emotions. In this situation, the signals that the downtrend had ended by the beginning of October were quite strong, and indicators provided strong confirmation of that fact. These included the very long lower shadow on the session of the first week in October; the strong bullish engulfing pattern in the next two days; and the strong and repetitive price gaps that followed.

Key Point

The more confirmation you have that an established short-term trend is on the verge of reversing, the better. But if you wait too long—even one day—you could also miss the opportunity.

This leverage feature is compelling. A swing trader faces the constant problem of capital limitation. With a finite amount of money, you can swing trade only a limited number of stocks if you are going to be buying shares. But slightly in-the-money, soon-to-expire options are quite cheap. In the example earlier in this chapter, when a stock on your watch list was selling at about $48 per share, the closest in-the-money call was available for 2.37, or about 5 percent of the stock's price.

The next-expiring in-the-money put was at 0.60, or about 1 percent of the stock price. So your capital is easily leveraged with options in place of stock. Rather than having to buy 100 shares for almost $4,800, you could put $237 into a call and have the same potential upside profit, or invest only $60 in a put for the same downside potential (not to mention avoiding the risk of selling shares short).

A STRATEGIC VIEW OF OPTIONS FOR SWING TRADING

The success of a swing-trading program relies on following the rules: identifying the setup after an uptrend or downtrend and acting quickly to take advantage of the short-term price swing. But many stock-related considerations should be kept in mind as well, including:

- *Selection of stocks based on value.* No matter what potential profits you might earn using options for swing trading and other strategies, it remains a sensible approach to limit your trading activity to high-value stocks. Using the relatively logical and simple theory of *value investing*, you may limit your options trading to stocks that also offer long-term growth and profits for well-managed companies.
- *A stock's price volatility.* Options traders face a dilemma when considering strategies like swing trading. The strategy will not work on the exceptionally safe stocks because, by definition, they tend to trade only in a narrow price range. So the opportunities for even moderate price volatility are simply not there. At the same time, exceptionally volatile stocks are difficult to predict. Even trying to apply the principles

value investing

selection of stock in companies that are exceptionally well managed, with a long-term track record of increasing revenue and profits, and a strong competitive position—and that is currently available at a bargain price.

of swing trading to erratic stock trends is difficult and risky, so swing traders also want to avoid risky stocks. The ideal stock is one with moderate volatility—a stock that is likely to experience price swings of a few points within a few days, but not likely to go through wide swings in *either* direction due to high market interest and high market overreaction to news and rumor.

Key Point

No matter what options strategies you employ, limiting your activity to high-quality companies is simply smart investing. Those stocks will be more predictable, less volatile, and better for all types of option trading.

- *Price history (recent and potential).* The definition of various volatility levels is invariably based on past price performance. But the potential price history can be further clarified by checking the size of the stock's recent trading range. Stocks with relatively narrow trading ranges of 10 points or less are excellent candidates for swing trading in the $40 to $80 price range. These stocks display historical volatility of 12.5 percent to 25 percent. If this range has been consistent, it is reasonable to extrapolate the same volatility levels into the future. This may oversimplify the task, however. In an ever changing market, yesterday's sedate stock may be tomorrow's most volatile, and vice versa. But investors and traders have to rely on trends and trust them. Without the trend, you would have no basis for selecting one stock over another for swing-trading purposes.
- *The price-to-earnings (P/E) ratio of the stock.* The P/E ratio tells you how much the market anticipates future price appreciation. So a P/E multiple of 20 represents a price per share 20 times higher than last year's earnings per share. The P/E can be used to limit the range of stocks you consider for swing trading. An exceptionally high P/E often indicates that the market has driven the stock's price too high, that enthusiasm is higher than justified. An exceptionally low P/E ratio is a symptom of a lack of interest in the stock. The P/E ratio may foreshadow future volatility as well. High-P/E

stocks will tend to overreact to marketwide price movements and be highly volatile. Low-P/E stocks will tend to underreact, making them poor candidates for swing trading.

With this in mind, limiting a stock portfolio to those with P/E ratios between 10 and 20, for example, will help you avoid companies with overpriced stocks as well as those lacking the moderate price volatility swing traders desire. The range of 10 to 20 for P/E ratio is subjective, but if you check typical P/E ranges, you will find that this range represents the midrange of stocks. Historically, a P/E of 15 has been considered the norm for the market's P/E ratio, and the stocks in the S&P 500 have often ranged between 15 and 20; but in more volatile markets, such as the year 2002, the P/E range for the S&P 500 rose as high as 45.

Key Point

Picking a range of P/E ratios in which to consider stocks is a matter of personal preference. The multiples between 10 and 20 are reasonable, but some investors will prefer P/E ranges far higher.

Key Point

For a good overview of financial and economic indicators as part of your portfolio analysis, check www .bullandbearwise.com. Indicators such as P/E as well as broader indications classified as bullish or bearish help you to gauge the current market mood.

- *Fundamental and technical tests of the company and stock.* Any stock you pick for options trading as part of a swing-trading strategy should also pass a few basic fundamental and technical tests. You may develop your own short list of essential tests. On the fundamental side, these should include tests of working capital, the trend in debt versus equity capitalization, revenue, and net return. On the technical side, you will want to test price history and volatility, expressed in terms of the volatility percentage and breadth of the trading range for stocks at various price levels.

OPTIONS USED FOR OTHER TRADING STRATEGIES

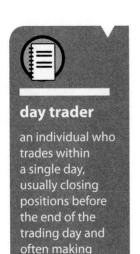

day trader

an individual who trades within a single day, usually closing positions before the end of the trading day and often making such trades on high volume.

Swing trading is only one of many possible trading strategies in which options can play a valuable role. In fact, swing trading is an extension of a better-known strategy called day trading. The *day trader* typically moves in and out of positions within a single trading day, so that the open positions do not extend from one day to the next. Day traders also tend to be high-volume traders, moving in and out of positions frequently and on the same stock, often tracking prices minute to minute. Day trading is perfectly suited to options in the same way and for the same reasons as swing trading: greater leverage and lower risk. Because day trading is extremely short-term in nature, cheap options near expiration and slightly in the money are real bargains. With little or no time value, options enable day traders to control 100 shares of stock per contract for only a fraction of the cost of trading stock. The risks are limited as well, due to lower investment requirements and the ability to use calls and puts equally in long positions.

Day traders are able to avoid a margin requirement, and this has caused problems for regulators. Under the rules, margin requirements are based on positions open at the end of each trading day. So a day trader could avoid having to meet margin requirements while still placing a large amount of capital into positions, as long as those positions were closed before the end of the day. Because this practice can lead to large losses for the trader as well as for the brokerage firm, a qualification was enacted and applied to day traders. Anyone who trades on high volume (meaning moving in and out of the same positions four or more times within five consecutive trading days) is classified as a *pattern day trader.* Traders meeting this standard are required to leave at least $25,000 in their accounts. If they do not maintain the required level, they will not be allowed to execute further trades once the pattern day trader status is triggered.

Key Point

Swing trading is the perfect solution for avoiding being classified as a pattern day trader. The typical entry and exit takes at least three days, so executing four trades within five days under these guidelines would be unlikely.

pattern day trader

any individual executing four or more transactions on the same security within five consecutive trading days; these traders are required to maintain no less than $25,000 in their brokerage accounts.

SWING- AND DAY-TRADING ADVANCED STRATEGIES

Most examples used in this book involve single option contracts, for the sake of clarity. However, swing and day trading do not necessarily have to be limited to single contracts to control 100 shares of stock. Especially when option premium levels are quite low, using multiple contracts saves on brokerage fees while increasing profit potential. In addition, using multiple contracts vastly expands your strategic potential for swing trading, including taking partial profits while keeping the remainder of a position open, and expanding swing trading into more advanced options strategies such as straddles and spreads.

For example, one popular online brokerage firm (Charles Schwab) charges $8.95 for a single online trade, plus $0.75 per contract. However, when multiple contracts are involved, the savings are substantial:

Number of Options	Transaction Fee
1	$ 9.70
2	10.45
3	11.20
4	11.95
5	12.70

At five contracts, the cost per option is only $2.54. So substantial transaction cost savings are going to be realized when trading in multiple option contracts. But there are other and more important reasons to use multiple contracts. They add flexibility to swing- and day-trading strategies. Examples of how you can vary your strategies with multiple contracts include:

- *Take partial profits.* In many cases when swing trades are executed, you face a dilemma. Do you take your profits even when setup signals are not present or do you wait? Because no system is perfect, you will at times miss profit opportunities by waiting one day too long. But with the use of multiple contracts, you can sell part of your holdings and keep the balance in the position. When profits are exceptional, this enables you to make a profit on the entire position, while keeping a portion in play and awaiting the setup signal.
- *Partial exercise.* As a holder of a long call, you have the right to exercise it or to sell it. For example, if you are swing trading on a stock you might want to also own, multiple contracts open the possibility of combining strategies. You can sell part of the overall position to gain a profit on the swing trade, and exercise the remainder. This strategy is valuable when you realize that the stock is selling at a great price. With a long call in hand, you can buy at the striking price and then hold the stock for the long term (or revert to a covered call strategy, for example).
- *Add more option contracts in times of price momentum.* From time to time, a stock's price not only moves in one direction, but gains momentum. For example, you might open a single-contract position only to later get a *second* setup signal going in the same direction. You can simply wait out the trend or buy additional option contracts based on the strong momentum of the stock's price.

Multiple contracts give you greater flexibility in a swing- or day-trading program, while also enabling you to execute trades for very little additional cost. Yet another interesting twist involves combining a swing-trading strategy with covered calls.

One of the great advantages in using options rather than stock is that you can use puts instead of the high-risk shorting of stock. But there is a mirror strategy of this, and it involves using covered calls instead of buying puts. If you do not own shares of stock and you reach a sell setup point, the obvious move is to buy puts. Then, when the stock declines, the put becomes profitable. However, if you also own stock, you can write covered calls rather than buying puts. This provides you with a double advantage.

First, the covered call is safer than the long put because time value is involved. As time value declines, your short call becomes less valuable and can be closed out (bought to a close) at a profit. Second, you have to pay money for the long put, but when you write a covered call, it produces cash that goes into your account.

Key Point

Covered calls are conservative strategies in their own right. But as part of a swing-trade strategy, covered calls make even more sense because they are tied to a sell setup. You can take profits within a few days without having to sell stock. This approach also produces cash rather than spending it.

You might consider many options-trading strategies to work as swing trades. But the strategy itself is invariably based on short-term price swings identified with specific setup signals. Swing-trading signals improve your profitability even when using options near expiration. The same advantages applied to listed stock options can be applied with equal benefit to options traded on futures contracts. The next chapter shows how this works.

THOMSETT'S JOURNEY in ADVANCED OPTIONS

DO YOU FEEL OKAY?

YES. I JUST FEEL LIKE I'M SWINGING BACK AND FORTH WITH THIS UNSETTLED STOMACH.

I TOLD YOU NOT TO ORDER THE OYSTERS.

SUPER SECRET OPTIONS LAB

I'M STILL NOT SURE HOW YOU FOUND OUT ABOUT THIS LAB.

YOU DO REALIZE, DON'T YOU, THAT EVERYONE KNOWS ABOUT THE OPTIONS MARKET, EVEN IF THEY DON'T UNDERSTAND IT?

OPTIONS ON FUTURES: LEVERAGING YOUR LEVERAGE

CHAPTER 5

Beware of all enterprises that require new clothes.
—Henry David Thoreau, *Walden*, 1854

Some traders assume that trading options on *futures contracts* is the same as trading options on stocks. This is not identical. Although the basic distinctions and definitions of options are the same in all instances, trading options on futures contracts (also broadly called commodities) involves special risks and qualifications.

In the 1980s a new investment device was introduced within the futures industry. Like stocks, futures could be traded on exchanges. The very first option with a futures contract as the underlying was introduced by the Chicago Board of Trade (CBOT) in 1982, when it introduced options on Treasury bond futures. Participation in futures options was limited for many years to insiders working as commodities brokers, with very little involvement by individual nonprofessional traders. Today, futures options are widely available,

futures contract

a contract to buy or sell a preestablished amount of a commodity (agricultural, energy, livestock, precious metals, or imports) or financial instrument at a set price and by or before a specific date (delivery date). Like options, futures are rarely exercised but are more likely to be closed prior to settlement or rolled forward.

and virtually anyone can perform minimal research to discover how to get into this market.

IMPORTANT DISTINCTIONS

There are many important differences between listed options based on an underlying stock and options on a futures contract. With a stock, the option is tied to 100 shares of stock and is a derivative of those shares. A futures option, however, is a type of derivative on a derivative. The futures contract itself exists as a contract representing an underlying commodity or financial instrument (foreign currency or interest rate, for example). So when you trade an option on a futures contract, your leverage is compounded. This can be a great advantage if the price is moving in the direction you desire, but it can also compound your losses when your timing is wrong.

Key Point

The futures option is a derivative on a derivative. This expands the potential for profits—as well as risks.

The cautionary aspects of futures options are the same as those for stock-based options. You face the same problems of time decay in long positions and the same risks of exercise in short positions. Just as many would-be stock option traders have opted instead to invest in stock-based exchange-traded funds (ETFs) or index funds, many traders interested in the futures market have channeled their capital into futures-based ETFs. For many, this makes sense. If you do not want to assume the risks of buying and holding stocks, various kinds of equity mutual funds or ETFs are appealing. And if you find the futures market too complex, then a handful of futures-based ETFs could be the perfect solution. However, some options traders will be attracted to the exponential leverage of futures on options.

Valuable Resource
For a comprehensive explanation of options on futures, download the Chicago Mercantile Exchange (CME) report, "Options on Futures" at **www.cmegroup.com/resources-for/files/G66_Options_on_Fut2001.pdf**.

Another important distinction is that the futures market is often far more volatile than the stock market, with valuation potentially moving rapidly in either direction. For example, consider the recent history of the most popularly traded commodity, oil. In 2007 and 2008, prices doubled to over $145 per barrel, and then by the end of 2008, oil fell more than $110 to under $35 per barrel. While some stocks have experienced similar upward and downward movement, it is much more common in the futures market. So if you had bought calls early in 2007 and then sold them at the top and replaced them with oil futures puts, you could have made an incredible profit. Hindsight is always perfect, however, and during the turbulent price changes of 2007–2008, uncertainty and bad timing made such perfect decisions unlikely.

Key Point
Traditional explanations of the futures market cite the equilibrium between buyers and sellers to claim that the market is more stable than the stock market. Recent history shows, however, that this assumption is not always valid. Futures can be just as volatile as stocks, and at times even more volatile.

Anyone familiar with options on underlying stock is probably quite comfortable with the knowledge that every option is based on 100 shares of stock. A complexity in the futures market is that underlying increments are different for each commodity, given its nature and method of trading. This makes the futures option industry much more complex than the stock option industry. As with any new and unfamiliar market, a lack of understanding about these basics is itself a very serious risk.

Trading increments are based on the specific future itself. Some examples:

Futures Trading Units		
Commodity		**Trading Unit**
Energy		
	Unleaded gas	Gallons
	Heating oil	Gallons
	Crude oil	Barrels
	Natural gas	MMBtus (millions of British thermal units)
Agricultural		
	Sugar	Pounds
	Corn	Pounds
	Soybean oil	Pounds
	Wheat	Bushels
	Oats	Bushels
	Soybeans	Bushels
	Soybean meal	Tons
	Lumber	b.f. (board feet)
Imports and Tropical Commodities		
	Frozen concentrated orange juice (FCOJ)	Pounds
	Coffee	Pounds
	Cotton	Pounds
	Cocoa	MTs (metric tons)
Cattle		
	Feeder cattle	Pounds
	Frozen pork bellies	Pounds
	Lean hogs	Pounds
	Live cattle	Pounds
Precious Metals		
	Aluminum	MTs
	Copper	MTs
	Lead	MTs
	Nickel	MTs
	Zinc	MTs
	Gold	t.oz. (troy ounces)
	Platinum	t.oz.
	Silver	t.oz.

In addition to the many variations in trading units for commodities, an active market in financial futures complicates the picture further. Currency rate futures are traded on a relative basis (e.g., valuation changes between the U.S. dollar and the British pound). Interest rates trade on percentage rise and fall of known rates, such as Treasury securities. A number of index futures trade based on price movement in stock market indexes, such as the Dow Jones Industrials, the S&P 500, and numerous other tracking and benchmark indexes. Another form of financial futures is futures on individual stocks, usually associated with 100 shares of the underlying. Many traders like futures because of the liberalized margin requirements. Rather than the 50 percent margin needed for stocks themselves, stock futures can be traded with 20 percent on deposit. You can also short stock with a futures contract without needing to borrow 100 shares of stock. In many ways, stock futures are very much like options. However, settlement rules are not the same, and regulatory oversight resides with the Commodity Futures Trading Commission (CFTC) rather than with the Securities and Exchange Commission (SEC).

Valuable Resource
The CFTC provides a wide range of resources for anyone wanting to know more about the futures market and options on futures. Its website is at **www.cftc.gov**.

Understanding the trading units is only part of the challenge in trading options on futures. With stocks, the increment is standardized, meaning that every listed option is related to 100 shares of the underlying stock. For futures, the incremental unit base is different in each case. So for one futures contract, the contract may be traded in a unit increment of 100, and for another it could be 5,000. Naturally, these distinctions also affect the total cost of the futures option.

Another distinction is the nature of the underlying security. While 100 shares of stock represent an equity position in the company itself, an increment of a futures contract on which options may be bought or sold does not contain any equity, only the obligatory nature of the futures contract itself. This contract is a future obligation either to accept delivery or to provide delivery of the underlying commodity. With stock, delivery means exchanging 100 shares in satisfaction of an exercised option. In the futures business, delivery rarely occurs because it means actually trading the commodity on which the futures contract and the option are based. Because this rarely occurs, exercising a futures option or allowing a short position to go into exercise is not an acceptable outcome in most situations. So while many stock options writers accept the possibility of exercise, the same is not true of futures options writers. In fact, only about 3 percent of all futures contracts result in actual delivery of the underlying commodity. So a majority of futures options traders allow expiration, sell, or roll forward their positions to avoid exercise.

Key Point

The underlying security for a stock-based option (100 shares of stock) has permanent, tangible value. But the underlying security in a futures option (a futures contract) is both intangible and finite (the futures contract has its own expiration date). This is a very important distinction between the two markets.

retender

a notice issued by a commodities broker to cancel an obligation by a short option trader to take actual physical delivery of the underlying commodity.

The actual risk of a short futures option writer having to take delivery of a massive quantity of a commodity is small. Even in the few instances when a short futures option is kept open beyond the notice date, the commodity exchange issues an intent to deliver. Even if that date passes, the commodities broker will issue what is called a *retender* notice to cancel the obligation to take delivery.

The retender involves a fee, but that is invariably preferable to having to accept delivery. Unlike stock-based options, where delivery is automatic, a futures-based option is unlikely to go through delivery. This leniency is built into the market because a majority of traders could not afford the high cost of physical delivery, so actually making such a delivery would be a disadvantage for everyone.

Options traders are constantly aware of expiration, especially as the expiration date approaches. The same is true for futures options traders. However, while stock continues to exist indefinitely, the underlying futures contract has its own expiration date. In some cases, the futures contract and related options expire on the same day. In other cases, the expiration dates for futures and futures options may be different. Expiration is also distinct for futures options in another way. If your short stock-based put option is exercised and you receive stock, you have the right to hold those shares of stock as long as you wish. However, with a futures-based put, accepting delivery is not normally a viable outcome, so an in-the-money futures short put has to be rolled forward or sold.

In one respect, the fact that exercise of a short option is unlikely (and automatic exercise does not occur), futures-based option sellers have a distinct advantage over stock-based short sellers. You can roll short positions forward indefinitely, at least in theory. However, a serious risk exists in cases where prices rise rapidly and significantly. A look back at markets in 2007–2008 for energy and agricultural commodities makes this case. Eventually, a deep in-the-money option may have to be closed, for example, when the price level no longer is available because commodity values have moved far beyond the original price ranges.

A final important distinction has to be made: anyone trading options on long stock positions earns dividends on the stocks owned when applicable, and the dividends often represent a significant portion of overall return (when included with capital gains and option premiums in covered calls and similar strategies). So for traders with a portfolio of stocks, the dividend is a major advantage to keep in mind when comparing potential profits and risks. However, futures contracts as an underlying security for options trading do not pay dividends. Although this is widely known by traders, the relative value and distinction are easily overlooked or ignored.

In situations when potential profit is similar or identical between stock and futures options trading, the dividend on long stock positions

Key Point

Don't overlook the importance of dividend income from long positions in the underlying stock as a point of comparison of profit and risk between stock-based and futures-based option trading.

may make all the difference and, when considered in the overall comparison, could make it preferable to trade the better-known stock-based option.

REGULATORY DIFFERENCES

open outcry

a method of trading futures contracts and options on futures in which buyer and seller in a commodity exchange trading pit shout bids back and forth; in comparison, options on stocks are traded using electronic bid and ask systems.

Many of the differences between stock and futures options involve not only methods of trading but also how the industries are regulated. Virtually all listed options on stocks are traded electronically, meaning execution is instantaneous or nearly instantaneous in most cases. However, although some futures exchanges use electronic trading, the prevailing method is *open outcry*, or a vocalized bidding system that has been in place for many decades.

Under this method, verbal bidding is used to trade options on futures as well as on futures contracts themselves. Buyer and seller negotiate prices by calling them out. A trader making an offer gets a completed trade if a trader on the other side and within the trading pit accepts verbally. Part of the reason for continuing to use this antiquated method involves differences in regulatory structure of the exchanges.

All trading in stocks and equity options is regulated by the SEC as well as the self-regulatory securities firm, the Financial Industry

Regulatorty Authority (FINRA). Options trading is further regulated by the Options Clearing Corporation (OCC), which facilitates the orderly market through the central exchange, the Chicago Board Options Exchange (CBOE). In addition, securities accounts and margin requirements are governed by the Federal Reserve Board (FRB) and its Regulation T, specifying how much a customer has to keep on deposit in a margin and cash account.

Valuable Resource
The National Futures Association (NFA) is the self-regulatory association for the futures industry. Its site contains a wealth of information on the industry and on options on futures: **www.nfa.futures.org**.

All trading in futures and futures options is regulated by the CFTC and the self-regulatory firm, the National Futures Association (NFA). Rules concerning how customer funds are managed and accounted for make the business of operating a commodity brokerage firm much different from that for a stock brokerage firm. The rules for maintaining cash and futures positions are far different from the requirements for the stock market and for options on stocks. The complexity of the futures market is not limited to the nature of the trading unit and settlement rules; it also includes the rules for setting up trading accounts, the costs involved, and the cash levels required.

Key Point
The differences in regulation and in regulatory bodies also distinguish levels of risk and methods of trading between stock-based and futures-based options.

For most traders focused on a portfolio of stocks and the use of options to protect positions or to enhance short-term profits, expanding into options on futures may be too exotic. The futures industry demands great expertise and often the acceptance of a different range of risks and trading costs than most stock market–based traders can absorb. As a result, many traders diversify into commodities by focusing on commodities-based ETFs and indexes; this is often the most practical alternative to directly buying or selling futures options.

For advanced traders, diversification and hedging are accomplished by combining stock-based options with futures options. For example, you may own shares in an energy company and enhance or offset those shares by trading in shares of an energy-industry ETF or in an ETF focusing on the energy sector. The same approach may be employed for numerous other market sectors or for financial instruments such as interest rates or foreign currencies. However, these methods and strategies are for the advanced trader. As with any exploration of a new method of speculating or trading, thorough knowledge of the rules for trading and of the risks involved is always a wise first step.

Expanding on the idea of seeking new markets, you may also want to explore the possibilities of trading options on the many available market indexes. This industry has exploded in popularity along with the growing volume of traditional equity options. Index-based options trading is one way to diversify while expanding potential profits and portfolio risks, but through the advantageous leveraging attributes of options. The next chapter explains how this market works.

TO BE CONTINUED...

130

TRADING INDEX OPTIONS: PLAYING THE BROADER MARKET

6

It is a very sad thing that nowadays there is so little useless information.
— Oscar Wilde, in *Saturday Review*, November 17, 1894

An *index option* is a special type of option, with the underlying not a single stock but a representation of the broader market. Popular indexes on which index options can be traded include the S&P 500, the Dow Jones Industrials, and many others.

The market for index options has been expanding rapidly in recent years, along with the popularity of more traditional options. According to the Chicago Board Options Exchange (CBOE), index option trading first exceeded one million contracts per day in 2008. By the end of 2008, volume above five million contracts per day was common. Growth in these highly specialized options has been dramatic.

Index options are traded on several U.S. exchanges, including the NYSE MKT, CBOE, and NASDAQ. Like the better-known

index option

any option traded on a market index as the underlying, rather than on an individual stock.

stock-based option, all index options are guaranteed and cleared by the Options Clearing Corporation (OCC). Indexes include not only well-known stock market indexes (S&P 500 and NASDAQ Composite, for example), but also debt securities, foreign currencies, and even economic indicators like the Consumer Price Index (CPI).

Valuable Resources
To view index options and indexes available on each exchange, check the websites for the NYSE MKT (**www.nyse.com**) (**www.amex.com/options/prodInf/ OptPiIndex.jsp**), CBOE (**www.cboe.com/products/ indexoptions.aspx**), and NASDAQ (**www.nasdaqtrader .com/Micro.aspx?id=phlxbroadbased**).

An index value is calculated in one of several ways, and the methodology for valuation of the index will affect the movement in value of any related options. In addition, while all stock-based options in the United States can be exercised or closed at any time (American style), some index options cannot and instead follow the European-style rules (meaning that options can be closed or exercised only on the day of expiration or within a short time frame immediately before expiration). Others adjust the valuation of options by contractually limiting the exercise window, which is a capped-style option. This distinction also matters to anyone considering opening trades in index options. In other words, the terms for index options are not as standardized as those for stock-based options.

ADVANTAGES TO TRADING INDEX OPTIONS

Many traders see an immediate advantage to trading an index rather than a number of individual stocks. By definition, an index tracks either a representative sample of the broader market or the whole market. It all depends on the number of issues included. For example, the Dow Jones Industrial Average (DJIA) has only 30 industrial companies but accounts for a major share of total capital in the U.S. market. The S&P 500 includes trends for 500 of the biggest companies in the United States. So depending on the index selected, the index represents an overall market trend that might not be experienced in a single stock. This means that risks are spread around; however, it also means that profit opportunities are going to be limited to overall market movement and not to the experience of any one stock.

Key Point
The great index advantage is that the index efficiently reflects price movement of a broad spectrum of issues, rather than single stocks or other securities. This is built-in diversification.

So in trading index options in place of individual stock options, you achieve effective diversification of risk. In fact, the risk of individual stock options is replaced by a marketwide risk based on the structure of the index. For many traders, this is viewed as an advantage and perhaps as the only way to truly diversify an options trading portfolio.

broad-based index

an index with a large number of components and involving many different market sectors.

If you were to attempt to approximate the movement of even a limited index such as the DJIA, you would still need to trade options in all of the 30 companies it lists. This is not practical for most traders and, in fact, would not necessarily be as effective as it is to trade in the options using the DJIA as the underlying security.

The specific price movement of an option will vary based on how the index is calculated and on how broadly the index represents the larger market. A *broad-based index* includes a larger number of components in many different market sectors. For example, the NASDAQ Composite index includes all of the stocks listed on the exchange.

In comparison, a *narrow-based index* is limited to a smaller number of issues. For example, the Dow Jones Industrial Average includes the stocks of only 30 large so-called industrial companies. Even so, the DJIA represents nearly half of the total value of all U.S. companies listed and traded on the public exchanges.

narrow-based index

an index using a small number of components rather than a larger or broader basis for its calculations.

Another very important distinction is the method used to calculate the numerical value of an index. Some indexes are *capitalization weighted* (also called *market value weighted*), including the NASDAQ Composite, S&P 500, and Wilshire 5000 indexes.

Another group of indexes are *price weighted*. To calculate their index values, these are weighted not only for changing market value per share, but also for stock splits. So the divisor is continually changing for each of the components in a price-weighted index.

A simplified method for valuing an index involves adding together the total prices of all components and dividing the result by the number of securities. This method becomes inaccurate, however, whenever there is a stock split; so, over time, the nonweighted approach will become increasingly inaccurate.

Key Point

If you trust the publisher of an index to fairly and accurately reflect the market in picking its components, the index will be easy to use as a gauge. However, some companies, publishing indexes do not reveal their criteria for removing and replacing index components.

capitalization weighted

description of the procedure used to calculate an index value, based on current market value for each of the components in the index.

Index components change periodically due to merger and acquisition activity, or because a particular company becomes less representative of the index itself, at least in the opinion of the publisher of the index. For example, Dow Jones & Company publishes numerous indexes but does not announce how it determines whether a particular company should be dropped and replaced. An index is intended to accurately report movement in the broader market, so that investors and traders will be able to track markets and make sound judgments about current market conditions; so as long as an index accurately reflects these current conditions, it continues to have validity for traders. And options that are traded on these indexes allow you to trade the overall market with a realistic expectation that the index will, in fact, move in line with market conditions.

market value weighted

alternative term for *capitalization weighted.*

EXERCISE AND EXPIRATION RULES

Unlike stock options, which contain standardized terms for all listed companies, the rules for index options will vary based on the exchange and on the publisher's requirements and rules determined when the index was created.

The trading size of an index option is not uniform, either, as it is with stock options. With stocks, each option is related specifically to 100 shares of the underlying stock. Index options are valued based on the value of the index, times a multiplier. This is usually $100, but not always; so before comparing prices of index options, check to ensure that multipliers are uniform among the various indexes being followed.

Upon exercise of an index option, the holder does not receive a proportionate number of shares in each of the companies listed in the index. Instead, cash is exchanged based on the option value at

price weighted

description of the procedure used to calculate an index value, based on current price and adjusted for all stock splits, for each of the components in the index.

cash settlement

a method for settling exercise of an index option, in which cash is paid rather than shares of stock being bought or sold.

the time of exercise. Accordingly, index options cannot be used for any strategy involving contingent purchase or sale of stock, a popular reason for employing stock-based individual options. This procedure is called *cash settlement*. One of the well-understood contractual rights of purchasers of stock options is the right to purchase 100 shares of stock (by exercising a call) or to sell 100 shares of stock (by exercising a put). That right does not exist for buyers of index options. The underlying security—the index value—is intangible, whereas the underlying value of a stock-based option—100 shares of stock—is tangible. This is what defines the difference in settlement procedures.

exercise cutoff time

the specific deadline for exercise of index options, imposed by brokerage firms on traders, varying by index and by class of option.

Exercise procedures are also different for index options. You can exercise your stock-based options at any time before expiration simply by entering an order, and this is usually executed immediately. But with an index option, you are required to notify your broker before a specified *exercise cutoff time*. This time for early exercise is not always identical to the time for exercise on expiration day. It is crucial for an index options trader to determine the rules of exercise and to ensure that the applicable cutoff times are known in advance and observed. The cutoff deadline for index options is often not the same as the time for stock-based options.

When the holder of an index option exercises, assignment is made to a writer, who is then required to pay cash for the specified exercise value of the option. The procedure is the same as that for exercise of an option with stock as the underlying; but instead of delivering shares, the writer is required to settle in cash.

Key Point

Find out how index exercise policies are set. They are not all the same, and the differences may affect whether you earn a profit or suffer a loss. Pay special attention to PM and AM settlement.

PM settlement

valuation of an index option based on the value of the index components at the close of trading on the day of exercise or expiration.

The timing of exercise will also rely on how the settlement value is calculated. Some index valuation is based on *PM settlement*, or the value of the index components at the close of a trading day. Many others are based on *AM settlement*, or valuation of the index components based on a trading day's opening prices.

If an index is traded on American-style expiration, traders can exercise at any time on or before expiration. However, many indexes are traded using European-style rules. This means that options can be exercised only during a specified and limited time period, and the period varies for each index. A capped-style rule, much like European-style, may also limit the window when exercise is allowed for index options. In any of these situations, traders are allowed to close out their positions before expiration to avoid exercise, take profits, or avoid further losses.

INDEX OPTION STRATEGIES

Many of the strategies you can apply with stock-based options also work for index options. However, because settlement occurs in cash and not in stock, some stock-based exercise strategies either will not apply or will have different outcomes.

AM settlement

valuation of an index option based on the value of the index components at the opening of trading on the day of exercise or expiration.

Following are many of the possible strategies you might consider with index options:

- *Purchase of index calls.* If you believe that the index is likely to rise in the near future, buying calls is the most basic strategy. With individual stocks, a profit in call purchasing requires that the underlying stock rise in value; with the index as the underlying, the index itself needs to move upward in value (the equivalent of a stock's price for stock options) in order to create a profit.

- *Purchase of index puts.* The opposite applies when puts are involved. If you believe that the underlying index is likely to fall in the near future, you may buy an index put in the expectation that it will therefore become profitable. Because the put is based on falling prices of the underlying, in-the-money declines in the index will be matched by increases in the index put's value.

- *Selling of index calls.* If you think the index is going to fall in value, selling calls might be preferable to buying puts. However, if the index were to rise, the risk on this short strategy is, in theory, unlimited. The possibility of a broad-based index rising in double- or triple-digit ranges is probably unlikely in the short term, but it is impossible to quantify or limit the potential risk.

- *Selling of index puts.* Selling a put will be profitable as long as the index point value remains at or above the put strike. Whereas the short call has theoretically unlimited risk, loss on the short index put is actually limited. In the very worst-case scenario, an index could go to zero, but this is quite unlikely as components involving stocks would be cushioned by the tangible book value of the companies. Futures-based or currency indexes are equally unlikely to decline to the worst-case levels, so short put traders are probably able to quantify likely losses based on historical index movements, the breadth of components, and current market conditions and sentiment.

- *Index spreading.* Another way to make use of options with indexes as the underlying is through spreading between two different indexes. Because indexes with similar underlying components (i.e., based on stock values) tend to track each other fairly consistently, the risk in spreading between indexes is limited. However, if the spread involves indexes with dissimilar components (i.e., stocks in one and commodities in another), the risk elements will be much greater, especially on the side of the spread that is shorted. (This risk can be mitigated, however, by using long calls and long puts, rather than a long side and a short side, in the spread.)

In picking an appropriate strategy, individual risk tolerance has to be a primary factor. For example, those who cannot tolerate a great deal of risk should limit their exposure to long-call and long-put positions. The use of short index options is appropriate for those willing to assume greater risks and, unlike stock-based options, short positions cannot be covered by owning the underlying directly.

Key Point

Index strategies, like single-issue option ideas, can be varied, created and combined creatively, providing maximum control over risk and portfolio management.

To cover a short position in an index option, there are some ways to approximate the protective features of a covered option. For example, you may own a long call that expires on the same date as or later than an equivalent short call. As long as the long call's strike is identical to or higher than the earlier-expiring short call position, it is completely covered. If the long position's strike is lower, it partially covers the short call, thus limiting the risk.

The same effect can be achieved with puts. A long put with an identical expiration or a later expiration than a short put covers the short position. If the long strike is identical to or lower than the short strike, the short position is covered. When the long put's strike is higher, the risk in the short position is limited to the difference between the two strikes.

A form of option covering is also accomplished when you hold long positions in the index itself, and then write calls against the same index. Each well-known market component has an equivalent index in which shares can be purchased, and many additional indexes track quite well. For example, the Value Line Index contains many of the same stocks as the S&P 500. So owning one index while writing short calls on the other index may accomplish a version of a cover for the short position. However, you should be quite familiar with these indexes and their options before embarking on an advanced spread aimed at creating a covered call situation.

STRUCTURED INDEX OPTIONS

In addition to trading options directly, you can buy or sell positions in one of many structured products offered by one of the exchanges involved with index options. The CBOE offers many structured products aimed at specific index positions or strategies.

Valuable Resource
The Chicago Board Options Exchange (CBOE) offers options on over 40 market indexes. To investigate further, check its website at **www.cboe.com** and go to the link "Index Options Overview." To see some information about options on ETFs, go to the "Products" link and then to "Options on Exchange Traded Products."

exchange-traded funds (ETFs)

types of mutual funds that trade on public exchanges like stocks and consist of portfolios of predetermined, related securities known as the basket of stocks.

Related options are also available on indexlike products, including *exchange-traded funds* (*ETFs*). An ETF is a type of mutual fund with a predetermined basket of stocks, which trades on the public exchange just like stocks (as opposed to having to buy or sell shares through the fund's management). Because the portfolio of an ETF is known in advance, investors do not have to rely on quality of management to make wise investment decisions.

The CBOE facilitates trading of options on ETFs, which are settled in cash using American-style exercise rules. In some ETFs, the CBOE also offers long-term equity anticipation security (LEAPS) options. Every ETF has a theme or characteristic. For example, ETFs specialize in specific sectors, countries, or types of securities, making it possible to participate in very narrowly focused markets and hold proportionate values of many stocks with a single position. For this reason, the ETF form of mutual fund functions very much like an index fund, but with a narrower focus.

binary option

an option based on an underlying index, which pays a fixed amount if the index is higher than a call's strike or lower than a put's strike at expiration.

Key Point

ETFs are far more flexible than old-style mutual funds. Not only can you buy and sell shares on public exchanges, but you can also trade options on many ETFs. This vastly expands your potential trading market.

The CBOE also provides interest rate options, including options on U.S. Treasury securities; on futures through its own CBOE Futures Exchange; and on specialized types of options, including *binary options*. Binary options are based on the S&P 500 index or on the CBOE Volatility Index. With different strike prices available, binaries trade much like stock-based options, but with one important difference. The buyer of a call binary option is paid $100 at close if the underlying index is higher than the call's strike. If the underlying index is lower, the call buyer gets nothing.

The CBOE also markets short-term options with life spans of a single week or quarter. These are *weeklys* and *quarterlys*. Weeklys are issued each Friday and expire the following Friday. They are good alternatives to trading traditional stock options with timing at or near important events like earnings announcements or dividend dates. The quarterlys are issued on the final business day of each calendar quarter, and they expire three months later.

Yet another innovation is the flexible exchange option, or *FLEX option*, a CBOE product whose terms can be modified. These terms include the expiration date, striking price, and exercise terms (American or European).

weeklys

specialized options issued each Friday, which expire the following Friday.

quarterlys

specialized options issued on the last day of each calendar quarter, which expire at the end of the following quarter.

FLEX option

a type of option whose terms—including expiration date, striking price, and exercise terms—can be modified during the period in which a position remains open.

In addition to providing FLEX options on several individual stocks, the CBOE also offers them on the S&P 500, S&P 100, NASDAQ 100, Russell 2000, and Dow Jones Industrial Average.

A great deal of variety and flexibility in the markets for index options and similar products expands option investing far beyond the traditional stock-based option. While the range of strategies available on traditional listed options continues to make them the most appealing to the greatest number of traders, index option trading has great potential. It broadens the possibilities for diversification of a stock portfolio and for creative advanced strategies.

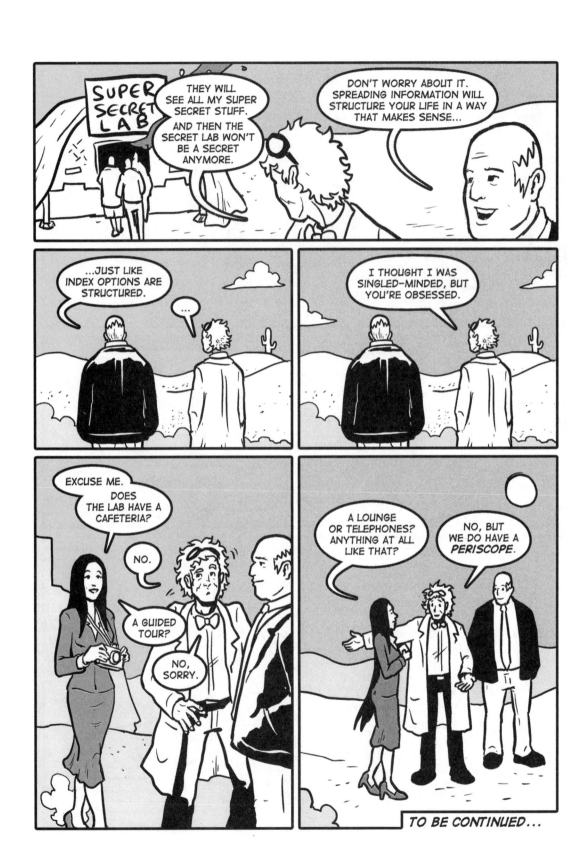

7

SYNTHETIC POSITIONS: TRACKING THE STOCK

The number of those who undergo the fatigue of judging for themselves is very small indeed.
—Richard Brinsley Sheridan, *The Critic*, 1779

Among the advanced strategies available for options trading is a group that duplicates the price movement of stock, offsets price movement to hedge risk, or works with stock to create profits without added risk. These are called *synthetic positions*, and they come in many forms.

Eight specific types of synthetic positions are explained in this chapter. These are:

1. Synthetic put, also called a protected short sale.
2. Synthetic long call, also called an insurance put or a married put.
3. Synthetic long stock.
4. Synthetic short stock.
5. Bullish split strike strategy.
6. Bearish split strike strategy.

synthetic positions

advanced options strategies that duplicate the price movement of stock, offset price movement to reduce risk, or create additional income without added risk.

7. Collars.

8. Synthetic straddles.

Key Point

Synthetics come in many shapes and sizes; what they all have in common is duplication of the price movement of a more expensive and often higher-risk position.

All examples in this chapter are based on stock and options of Altria (MO) as of November 15, 2011. On that day, the stock closed at $27.77 per share and the dividend yield was 5.91 percent, or 41 cents per share per quarter.

Striking Price	Calls			Puts		
	Dec	**Jan**	**Mar**	**Dec**	**Jan**	**Mar**
26	1.92	2.02	2.22	0.19	0.56	1.10
27	1.07	1.22	1.50	0.32	0.74	1.40
28	0.41	0.59	0.93	0.65	1.18	2.10
29	0.08	0.21	0.51	1.33	1.86	2.63

The great benefit in setting up a synthetic options strategy is that it creates a position that offsets risk, while duplicating price movement in the underlying without needing to invest in 100 shares or more. These positions create maximum leverage and cost little and, in some cases, nothing to create. The benefits of synthetic positions take three major forms:

1. *Risk reduction can be created* in the form of the limited investment required to create many synthetic positions.

Market risks may be limited while the combined options positions change in value exactly like shares, with each option representing price movement of 100 shares. The market risk of synthetics is considerably lower than the equivalent market risk of being long or short 100 shares.

2. *Leverage is maximized* when no-cost or low-cost options positions change in value exactly like the equivalent 100-share increments of the underlying.

3. *Portfolio management is created* through synthetic positions in several ways. For example, paper losses are offset with synthetic long stock positions, which rise to duplicate growth in the underlying stock. This is preferable to buying additional shares when the danger is that prices may continue to decline. By the same argument, synthetic short stock (long put, short call) contains less risk than shorting stock.

SYNTHETIC PUT (PROTECTED SHORT SALE)

A *synthetic put* (also called a *protected short sale*) is used as a strategy to reduce or eliminate risk when an investor has shorted stock. The risk in going short is that the stock price will rise; in that event, the short seller loses money in two ways. First, the loss in the shorted position increases as the stock price rises. Second, margin requirement also increases, so the investor is required to place more equity on deposit to cover the short stock loss.

synthetic put

a strategy designed to offset potential losses when stock has been shorted. For each 100 shares held short, the investor buys one call. As the stock price rises, each call offsets the loss in 100 shares of stock held short; also called a *protected short sale*.

Key Point

Anyone who has shorted stock faces high risks. The synthetic put (protected short sale) eliminates that risk with an offsetting long call.

The problem in opening a synthetic put is that it increases the amount of downward movement in the stock price required to reach or exceed a breakeven point. When an investor sells short, the required price movement only needs to equal the interest cost in the margin account for breakeven. However, the cost of the long call extends that requirement

protected short sale

a strategy in which the risk of loss in a short sale is offset by the purchase of one call per 100 shares of the underlying stock; also called a *synthetic put*.

further. In addition, the breakeven needs to be exceeded before the call expires, adding additional pressure on the short sale position.

Example

Caught by the Shorts: In November, you sell 100 shares of Altria (MO) at $27.77 per share. You expect the price to fall, after which you will take profits. The interest cost of borrowing 100 shares from your broker is minimal, but you hope to be able to close the position within one month. Your goal is to sell when the stock price has declined to $25 or below. However, you are also concerned that the price might rise, so you open a synthetic put by buying one January call with a 27 strike and pay 1.22 ($122). This means that if the stock price declines to $26.55 (original basis of $27.77 minus call price of 1.22) you are at a precost breakeven. Costs include transaction fees on stock and option and margin interest. Breakeven is going to occur somewhere near $26 per share.

The synthetic put protects against loss in the event the stock price does rise; however, it moves the breakeven further downward as well. Table 7.1 demonstrates how the synthetic put works based on the example, just on the basis of initial cost, but excluding the transaction and interest charges.

Table 7.1 Synthetic Put Example

Price	Stock Profit or Loss	Option Profit or Loss	Total Value
$23	$4.77	−$1.22	$3.55
24	3.77	−1.22	2.55
25	2.77	−1.22	1.55
26	1.77	−1.22	0.55
27	0.77	−1.22	−0.45
28	−0.23	−0.22	−0.45
29	−1.23	0.78	−0.45
30	−2.23	1.78	−0.45
31	−3.23	2.78	−0.45

The outcome of the synthetic put is clearly demonstrated. When stock is shorted, an increase in the stock value creates a frozen maximum loss at $45. This is the equivalent of value of stock at different prices, minus the cost of the call. If the stock price rises, the $45 loss is fixed because the growing value of the long call offsets the growing loss in the stock. As the stock price declines, the growing profit of the short stock is offset by the fixed cost of the long call, so that profit increases $1 per one-point drop in the stock's market value.

Key Point

Freezing losses lets traders take up positions like shorting stock without the worry that an expected price movement will lead to catastrophic losses.

SYNTHETIC LONG CALL (INSURANCE PUT OR MARRIED PUT)

A *synthetic long call* is also termed an *insurance put* or a *married put*. This is created when one put is bought for every 100 shares of long stock. It protects against a downside movement in the stock price. If the stock price does decline, growth of intrinsic value of the put offsets each point of loss in the stock.

The position is intended to offset losses in the event of a decline in the stock's price. However, if the stock price rises, additional profit is needed equal to the cost of the put to offset the cost of the synthetic long call.

Key Point

The synthetic long call protects against a price decline in the underlying stock. However, a price increase must be greater to pass breakeven, just to offset the cost of the long put.

This strategy caps the loss at anything below $27 per share, essentially locking in the $2 per share profit even if the stock price declines. This protection is good until the put's expiration in January. If the stock price rises, the actual profit will be $1 per point, adjusted by the $74

synthetic long call

the purchase of a long put to offset potential losses in 100 shares of long stock. If the stock value declines below the strike of the put, the put gains one point of intrinsic value for each point lost in the stock.

insurance put

alternate name of the *synthetic long call*.

married put

alternate name of the *synthetic long call*.

one-time cost of the put. The positions at various prices are summarized in Table 7.2.

Example

The Call Is a Put: A few months ago, you purchased 100 shares of Altria (MO) at $25 per share and in November those shares are valued at $27.77. You want to protect the profits but you do not want to sell shares. So you create a synthetic long call. You buy a January 27 put and pay 0.74 ($74). Now your net value of the stock is $27.03 (current value of $27.77 minus the cost of the put of 0.74). This leaves the value over $2 per share higher than your original purchase, while protecting against loss if the stock price falls below $27 per share.

Table 7.2 Synthetic Long Call Example

Price	Stock Profit or Loss	Option Profit or Loss	Total Value
$23	−$4.77	$3.26	−$1.51
24	−3.77	2.26	−1.51
25	−2.77	1.26	−1.51
26	−1.77	0.26	−1.51
27	−0.77	−0.74	−1.51
28	0.23	−0.74	−0.51
29	1.23	−0.74	0.49
30	2.23	−0.74	1.49
31	3.23	−0.74	2.49

As long as the stock price rises in this example, profits grow by $1 per point. However, the profit is adjusted downward by the cost of the put of $74. If the stock price declines below the strike of 27 for the long put, the maximum loss is frozen at $151.

SYNTHETIC LONG STOCK

A *synthetic long stock* position is a powerful and effective strategy. It consists of a long call and a short put opened at the same striking price and expiration. The cost of the long position is offset by income from the short position, making this a no-cost or low-cost position; and the combination of the two options acts exactly like 100 shares of stock; the overall value rises as the stock price rises, point for point; and it drops as the stock price drops, point for point.

The synthetic long stock position works best when the stock price rises. If the stock price falls, the short put goes in the money and is in danger of being exercised. When the stock price rises, the short put loses value while the long call gains.

Key Point

Synthetic long stock is a low-cost or no-cost options strategy that mirrors the price movement of 100 shares of stock—without needing to buy those 100 shares. It is the ultimate leverage.

synthetic long stock

a combination of one long call and one short put opened at the same striking price and expiration. The combined value rises and falls to the same degree as 100 shares of the underlying stock. The cost of the position is small, however, because the cost of the long call is offset by income from the short put.

The position can be left open until expiration. If the stock price has risen above the striking price, the long call can be closed at a profit or exercised; and the short put expires worthless. If the stock price has fallen below the strike, the long call will expire worthless and the short put must be closed at a loss or will be exercised. If exercised, the trader will be required to buy 100 shares of stock at the strike, which will be higher than current market value. Alternatively, the short put can be closed at a loss to avoid acquiring shares, or rolled forward to avoid or delay exercise.

Traders also have the choice of closing the short side if and when it becomes profitable, and waiting out expiration of the long put, or, if the stock price rises, being able to close the put profitably. Closing the short put is possible at a profit even if the stock price is at or in the money, due to time decay.

Example

A Mirror Image: The current value of Altria is $27.77 and you decide to open a synthetic long stock position in the stock rather than buying 100 shares. You buy one March 27 call and pay 1.50 ($150) and at the same time sell one March 27 put, receiving 1.40 ($140). Your net debit is 0.10 ($10) before transaction costs.

This example is close to a zero cost. The after-transaction cost may be more than $10 since a fee is charged for both the call and the put. The worksheet summarized in Table 7.3 is based on status prior to fees, or a $10 debit as demonstrated in the example. The table compares the outcome of the combined synthetic long stock position at expiration to changes in 100 shares of stock based on the price of $27.77 when the synthetic position was opened.

Table 7.3 Synthetic Long Stock Example

Price per Share	Long Call	Short Put	Net Options Profit or Loss	Profit on 100 Shares
$21	−$150	−$460	−$610	−$677
22	−150	−360	−510	−577
23	−150	−260	−410	−477
24	−150	−160	−310	−377
25	−150	−60	−210	−277
26	−150	40	−110	−177
27	−150	140	−10	−77
28	−50	140	90	23
29	50	140	190	123
30	150	140	290	223
31	250	140	390	323
32	350	140	490	423
33	450	140	590	523

The net difference between the synthetic position and 100 shares of stock at each price point is 0.67 ($67). This is equal to the difference between the current price of $27.77 and striking price of $27, minus the net debit in the synthetic position of 0.10 ($10).

This strategy is powerful because, for virtually no cost, it mirrors movement of 100 shares of stock. In this example, buying 100 shares would cost $2,777 whereas the synthetic long stock position costs only $10. The market risk in the position arises if and when the stock price falls. However, that market risk is identical to the market risk of owning 100 shares of stock. Given the cost difference, the synthetic long stock position is very advantageous. However, traders will not earn a dividend, which at this point was 5.91 percent or $41 per quarter.

SYNTHETIC SHORT STOCK

The opposite of synthetic long stock is *synthetic short stock*. This is an options strategy consisting of a short call and a long put opened at the same strike and expiration. If the stock price declines, the short call will expire worthless and the long put will increase in value, one point for each point of decline in the stock. If the stock price rises, the short call grows in value and presents a risk of exercise.

> **Key Point**
>
> Synthetic short stock is equally valuable when compared to synthetic long stock; the major difference is the uncovered call that is part of the strategy.

The risk of the synthetic short stock position is identical to the risk of shorting 100 shares of stock. Traders want a decline in value, and if that occurs, their short position is profitable. However, shorting stock demands margin interest payments because stock must be borrowed from the broker.

The position can be closed in parts or left until expiration. For example, if the stock price remains at or below the strike, the short call can be closed at a profit while the long put is left open in the hope of a decline in stock price prior to expiration.

Market risk is restricted to the short call. In the event of price increase in the underlying stock, the call loses one point for each point of rise in the underlying stock. This risk is eliminated by ownership of 100 shares of the underlying stock. In that case, the synthetic short stock position combines a long put with a covered call.

In this example, the synthetic short put consists of an out-of-the-money long put and an in-the-money short call, which explains why you create a net credit of 1.12 points. This is offset by the 1.77 points in the money on the short side. However, your belief that the stock price will decline is acceptable to you. Table 7.4 shows the outcome of this

synthetic short stock

a combination of one long put and one short call opened at the same striking price and expiration. The combined value rises and falls to the same degree as 100 shares of the underlying stock. The cost of the position is small, however, because the cost of the long put is offset by income from the short call.

position at various prices at expiration, compared to price movement in the stock based on the current $27.77 per share.

> **Example**
>
> **Loaded for Bear:** You believe the price of Altria (MO) will decline in the future. The current value is $27.77 per share. You open a synthetic short stock position as an alternative to shorting the stock. This consists of a long March 26 put, which you buy for 1.10 ($110), and a short March 26 call, which you sell and receive 2.22 ($222). Your net credit before transaction costs is 1.12 ($112). However, the short call is 1.77 in the money.

Table 7.4 Synthetic Short Stock Example

Price per Share	Long Put	Short Call	Net Options Profit or Loss	Profit on Short 100 Shares
$21	$390	$222	$612	$677
22	290	222	512	577
23	190	222	412	477
24	90	222	312	377
25	−10	222	212	277
26	−110	222	112	177
27	−110	122	12	77
28	−110	22	−88	−23
29	−110	−78	−188	−123
30	−110	−178	−288	−223
31	−110	−278	−388	−323
32	−110	−378	−488	−423
33	−110	−478	−588	−523

The net difference between the synthetic short put and the value of the stock is 0.65 points ($65) at each price. This is the 1.77-point difference between current value of the stock and the strike of the options, minus the net credit of 1.12 ($112) earned for opening the synthetic short position:

$27.77 – $26	= 1.77
Less: net credit	= 1.12
Difference	= 0.65

SPLIT STRIKE STRATEGY (BULLISH)

A *split strike strategy* is a variation of the synthetic stock position. This involves two striking prices instead of one. A long (or short) out-of-the-money striking price is combined with a higher, short (or long) out-of-the-money striking price.

Key Point

The desirability of the split strike is that both sides are out of the money, specifically, the short option. This makes exercise remote due to the positioning as well as time decay.

split strike strategy

a variation of the synthetic stock strategy, combining two different striking prices, both out of the money. The bullish version is a combination of a long call and a lower-strike short put; the bearish version consists of a long put and a higher-strike short call.

The bullish split strike strategy combines a long call at a higher striking price and a short put at a lower striking price. Both are out of the money. A trader opening such a position hopes for a rise in the price of the underlying stock. In that case, the long call may move in the money and can be sold at a profit or be exercised; and the short put expires worthless or can be closed at a profit.

In the bullish version, a decline in the stock's price may result in the long call expiring worthless while the short put is exercised, creating a loss because the current market value of stock is lower than the striking price.

The most desirable outcome in this bullish position is a strong rise in the stock's price. However, as long as the price remains higher than $26 per share, the short put will decline in value and can be allowed to expire worthless or be closed at a low premium. The long call striking price, in comparison, is only 0.23 points ($23) higher than current market value, so it will not take very much price movement for this call to become profitable, as shown in Table 7.5.

Example

A Split Personality: You decide to open a bullish split strike synthetic strategy on Altria instead of buying 100 shares. The current price is $27.77. You buy a March 28 call for 0.93 and sell a March 26 put for 1.10. Your net credit before fees is 0.17, or $17. If the stock price rises, your long call will appreciate. The short put is 1.77 points below the current price. If the stock price declines below the 26 strike, your position will lose money.

Table 7.5 Split Strike Strategy (Bullish)

Price per Share	Long 28 Call	Short 26 Put	Net Options Profit or Loss	Profit on 100 Shares
$21	−$93	−$390	−$483	−$677
22	−93	−290	−383	−577
23	−93	−190	−283	−477
24	−93	−90	−183	−377
25	−93	10	−83	−277
26	−93	110	17	−177
27	−93	110	17	−77
28	−93	110	17	23
29	17	110	127	123
30	117	110	227	223
31	217	110	327	323
32	317	110	427	423
33	417	110	527	523

Because the long call and short put are two striking prices apart, the differences between option outcomes and equivalent stock price movement is $2. This can be expressed in another manner:

Synthetic profit on call side	= 527
Equivalent stock profit	= 523
Net difference	= 4
Synthetic loss on put side	= 483
Equivalent stock loss	= 677
Net difference	= 194
Total, two striking prices	= 198

The six points difference on the top is also equal to the distance between the striking price of the call and the credit received for opening the option position:

Striking price of long call	= 23
Credit received	= 17
Net difference	= 6

The difference in net loss between the synthetic position and the equivalent 100-share stock position was 1.94. This is the sum of the difference between the current value of the stock and the strike of the put, plus the net credit earned by opening the synthetic position:

Current value per share	= 27.77
Less: strike of the put	= 26
Net difference	= 1.77
Plus: credit received	= 0.17
Total	= 1.94

Because of the split strikes, this position tracks upward and downward price movement differently. The tracking remains consistent, but one side reflects a spread of 0.04 and the other 1.94.

SPLIT STRIKE STRATEGY (BEARISH)

The split strike can also be bearish by reversing the call and the put. For example, instead of a long call, an out-of-the money (lower-strike) long put is used; and instead of a short put, an out-of-the-money (higher-strike) short call is used.

Key Point

A bearish split strike consists of a long put and a short call, both out of the money. The out-of-the-money call is a better choice than an in-the-money short call, but this position remains risky as long as that call is uncovered.

In this configuration, the short call is uncovered. However, if a trader also owns 100 shares of the underlying stock, the uncovered call risk is eliminated. In that case the bearish split strike synthetic stock position works as a form of no-cost or low-cost downside protective position. A trader may keep the 100 shares while offsetting losses from a price decline. In the event of a decline, the put can be exercised and stock sold at the higher strike; or the put can be sold at a profit, offsetting losses in the stock.

Example

Splitting with Pessimism: You create a bearish split strike synthetic position by opening the following positions: a long January 26 put at 0.56 and a short January 28 call at 0.59. Your net credit is 0.03, practically even before transaction costs are deducted.

Like the bullish version, this bearish split strike synthetic strategy has options two points apart. As a result, the tracking in each direction will be consistent with changes in prices of the net options the same as changes in the underlying stock. However, due to the two-point strike spread, the net spread is different for upward and for downward price movement. The comparison is made between the option price changes and an assumed change in value of 100 shares shorted. This is shown in Table 7.6.

Table 7.6 Split Strike Strategy (Bearish)

Price per Share	Long 26 Put	Short 28 Call	Net Options Profit or Loss	Profit on Short 100 Shares
$21	$444	$ 59	$503	$677
22	344	59	403	577
23	244	59	303	477
24	144	59	203	377
25	44	59	103	277
26	−56	59	3	177
27	−56	59	3	77
28	−56	59	3	−23
29	−56	−41	−97	−123
30	−56	−141	−197	−223
31	−56	−241	−297	−323
32	−56	−341	−397	−423
33	−56	−441	−497	−523

Since the two options are two striking prices apart, the differences in comparative outcomes is two dollars per share:

Synthetic profit on the put side	= 503
Equivalent short stock profit	= 677
Net difference	= 174
Synthetic loss on the call side	= 497
Equivalent short stock loss	= 523
Net difference	= 26
Total, two striking prices	= 200

The 1.74 price change on the bottom is equal to the difference between the stock price and striking price of the put, minus the net credit received:

Current value of stock	= 27.77
Less: striking price of the put	= 26
Difference	= 1.77
Minus: credit received	= 0.03
Net	= 1.74

Splitting the strikes makes the top and bottom outcomes different, and each side splits the striking price spread. However, if tracking the synthetic position in either direction, the options net out to the same level of price change as 100 shares of stock. This particular strategy presents a desirable and lower-risk alternative to shorting stock.

COLLARS

The collar (introduced in Chapter 2), also called a *protective collar*, is a synthetic position combining three separate elements: 100 shares, a covered call, and a long put.

protective collar

alternate name of the *collar*.

Key Point

A collar has three parts: 100 long shares, one long put, and one short call. The collar eliminates risk but also eliminates profit. But there are solutions to this.

The two options offset one another. The cost of buying the put is paid for or nearly all paid for by the premium received from selling the short call. This position, overall, provides downside protection for less cost than with an insurance put. In that strategy, the value of stock has to rise above the cost of the put in order to achieve a profit. The collar solves that problem. If the stock value declines, the put's value grows one point for each point the stock price falls below the strike.

The value of the collar is twofold. In addition to limiting or offsetting market risk in the event of a price decline, it also produces potential profit if the stock appreciates. This is limited because, like all covered calls, the maximum profit is going to be the difference between basis and striking price.

For this reason, the collar makes the most sense when the original basis in stock is well below current market value, and you want to protect paper profits. If you are willing to give up shares at the call's striking price while preserving the paper profits gained, the collar is a suitable strategy.

The collar usually consists of opening two out-of-the-money positions. The long put may be an increment below current value, while the short call is an increment above. This cushion provides for a small additional profit if the stock price rises above the call's strike, while also accepting a small loss (equal to the difference between the current value and the put's striking price) if the price of the stock declines.

Example

Ring around the Collar: You purchased 100 shares of Altria (MO) at $25, and today the value has risen to $27.77. You decide to protect a portion of your $2.77 per share in profit with an insurance put, but you decide to go with a collar so that the cost of the put will not take away from the profitability of the stock shares. You buy a December 27 put for 0.32 and sell a December 28 call for 0.41. Your net credit before transaction costs is 0.09 ($9).

In this example, the pretransaction effect is to create a credit close to zero. Transaction costs will offset that; however, the point here is that for almost no net cost, the paper profits are protected. If the price declines below the put strike of 27, the put can be closed and profit will offset the loss of value; it can also be exercised, in which case you sell your 100 shares at $27 per share. If the stock price rises above $28 per share, your short call will be exercised and 100 shares called away. If the price remains in between $27 and $28 until expiration, the two positions both expire. In this case, you have purchased insurance against market risk, for nearly no cost. The outcomes of the position at various prices are summarized in Table 7.7.

Table 7.7 The Collar

Price per Share	Long 27 Put	Short 28 Call	Net Options Profit or Loss	Profit on 100 Shares
$21	$568	$ 41	$609	$677
22	468	41	509	577
23	368	41	409	477
24	268	41	309	377
25	168	41	209	277
26	68	41	109	177
27	−32	41	9	77
28	−32	41	9	−23

(Continued)

Table 7.7 (Continued)

Price per Share	Long 27 Put	Short 28 Call	Net Options Profit or Loss	Profit on 100 Shares
29	−32	−59	−91	−123
30	−32	−159	−191	−223
31	−32	−259	−291	−323
32	−32	−359	−391	−423
33	−32	−459	−491	−523

The combined values of the two options track the stock price point for point. Because the strikes are one point apart, the upside tracking and downside tracking add up to that point. On the downside, the net difference between options and stock is $68 at each price level; on the upside, the net difference is $32.

Key Point

The collar works just like the synthetic stock positions, but involves options with different strikes. This changes the mirroring between options and stocks, but does not change the risk profile.

modified installment collar

a collar consisting of a long-term long put and a series of short-term short calls. The put provides downside protection through its term, and the series of short calls is planned to offset the put's cost over many months, due to rapid time decay.

The standard collar is made up of a spread above and below the stock's current price. However, this can be modified in several ways. A *modified installment collar* works like the protective collar, but combines a long-term put with a series of short-term calls. This installment method costs money to enter, since the long-term put will contain more time value than a very short-term put. Offsetting this is a series of very short-term calls, each one set up to lose time value quickly. By the time the put is close to expiration, enough calls should have been sold and then expired (or closed at a profit) to more than offset the initial cost of the long put. This allows you to enjoy downside protection for the long term while paying for the insurance put in installments of covered calls.

Another interesting variation, designed to increase net income from the collar, is the *ratio collar*. This is a collar with a long put on one side and a ratio write on the other side.

The ratio collar is considered to be a position with greater exercise risks, but it is not as risky as the uncovered call. As long as you are able to either close or cover positions in the event of an increase in the stock's price, the ratio collar may be a viable strategy; however, you do need to accept the higher risk level it involves.

Key Point

The ratio collar is interesting because of how it changes both the initial debit or credit and the potential profit or loss.

Example

Calculating the Ratio without Pi: You want to hold stock for the long term but you are concerned with the market risk, so a protective put is appealing. However, the collar is appealing as well, especially if you can produce income from the position. You buy 300 shares of Altria (MO) and pay $27.77 per share, for a total of $8,331. You buy three March 27 puts at 1.40 each and pay a total of $420. You create a 4-to-3 ratio collar by selling four March 28 calls for 0.93, and you receive $372. Your pretransaction fee debit on the option positions is $48.

In this example, the strikes of long puts and short calls spread each side of the current price of stock, so both were out of the money by less than one point. The ratio write side can be looked at in two ways. It is either a combination of three covered calls and one uncovered call or four calls that are 75 percent covered.

If the price rises above the 28 call striking price, one or more of the calls can be closed (or covered with a longer-expiration call or purchase of more shares), or that uncovered portion can be left and allowed to be exercised or even rolled forward. The outcome at various price levels is shown in Table 7.8.

Table 7.8 The Ratio Collar

Price per Share	3 Long 27 Puts	4 Short 28 Calls	Net Options Profit or Loss	Profit on 300 Shares
$21	$1,680	$372	$2,052	−$2,031
22	1,380	372	1,752	−1,731

(Continued)

Table 7.8 (Continued)

Price per Share	3 Long 27 Puts	4 Short 28 Calls	Net Options Profit or Loss	Profit on 300 Shares
23	1,080	372	1,452	−1,431
24	780	372	1,152	−1,131
25	480	372	852	− 831
26	180	372	552	− 531
27	− 120	372	252	− 231
28	− 420	372	− 48	69
29	− 420	272	− 148	369
30	− 420	− 128	− 548	669
31	− 420	− 528	− 948	969
32	− 420	− 928	−1,348	1,269
33	− 420	−1,328	−1,748	1,569

Key Point

The problem with a ratio collar is that the downside offsets stock losses, but the upside accumulates losses beyond stock profits.

variable ratio collar

a collar combining long puts with a ratio write rather than a 1-to-1 covered call; however, the short calls are split between two different striking prices. This enables the trader to produce higher current income due to the larger number of short calls, but with less risk than a single-striking-price ratio write.

The collar tracks the changes in stock quite well. On the downside, profits from the collar offset losses in the stock. Note that the net loss on the options grows as stock prices increase. As the 28 striking price is reached or surpassed by stock, disposing of one short call would solve this problem. For example, if one call is closed when the stock price reaches $28 per share, that would eliminate all of the losses (adjusted for any net loss on the call itself).

A variation of the ratio collar that reduces risk even more is the *variable ratio collar.* This is a ratio collar with one adjustment: Two separate striking prices are employed. This enables you to roll or close either striking price to avoid or defer exercise, or to close the higher-strike position if the stock price rises and approaches the at-the-money level.

By using two different strikes, the trader drastically reduces the overall position's risk. When a single strike is involved, the entire short position may end up in the money when stock prices rise; with the variable ratio write, traders have the opportunity to reduce risk exposure by closing, covering, or rolling of the excess short calls.

Example

Striking a Balance Between the Strikes: You create a variable ratio collar by purchasing 300 shares of Altria (MO) at $27.77 per share, paying $8,331. You buy three December 27 puts at 0.32, paying an additional $96. You then sell two December 27 calls at 1.07 (receiving $214) and two December 28 calls at 0.41 (receiving an additional $82). Your combined income is $296, versus the cost of puts of $96, for a net credit of $200.

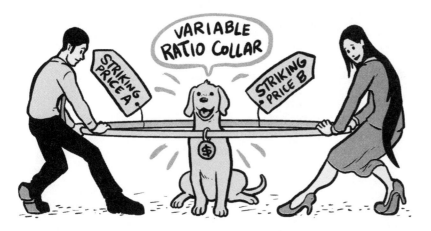

The $200 net income, equal to two points of stock price movement, offsets the in-the-money 27 call level, which is $154 (two calls, each 0.77 in the money). In fact, if these ended up exercised, you would end up with a net profit. The higher-striking-price calls can be closed or rolled to avoid exercise. The net income of $200 provides much greater flexibility in this position than in the ratio collar, for less risk. At the same time, downside protection is an important feature. The net no-cost level of three puts will offset any price decline in the 300 shares on a point-for-point basis below the 27 striking price. The outcome at different price levels is shown in Table 7.9.

Table 7.9 The Variable Ratio Collar

Price per Share	3 Long 27 Puts	2 Short 27 Calls	2 Short 28 Calls	Net Options Profit or Loss	Profit on 300 Shares
$21	$1,704	$214	$82	$2,000	−$2,031
22	1,404	214	82	1,700	−1,731
23	1,104	214	82	1,400	−1,431
24	804	214	82	1,100	−1,131

(Continued)

Table 7.9 (Continued)

Price per Share	3 Long 27 Puts	2 Short 27 Calls	2 Short 28 Calls	Net Options Profit or Loss	Profit on 300 Shares
25	504	214	82	800	−831
26	204	214	82	500	−531
27	−96	214	82	200	−231
28	−96	14	82	0	69
29	−96	−186	−118	−400	369
30	−96	−386	−318	−800	669
31	−96	−586	−518	−1,200	969
32	−96	−786	−718	−1,600	1,269
33	−96	−986	−918	−2,000	1,569

Key Point

The variable ratio collar reduces risk because the higher-strike call can be closed, covered, or rolled to avoid exercise—while it produces higher income.

Just as the ratio collar offsets stock losses on the downside, in this example, the same thing happens. The combined option positions create profits matching increasing downside losses in the stock.

On the upside, the ratio left open leads to ever-higher losses. This can be avoided easily by closing the one excess (uncovered) call by or before the stock price reaches the higher strike of 28. The position can also be rolled forward or covered with the purchase of a long call or another 100 shares of stock.

A final variation is the dividend collar (introduced in Chapter 2). In this strategy, the position is opened prior to the *record date*, and then closed entirely soon after the ex-dividend date. This creates a monthly dividend yield in place of a quarterly yield, because the strategy is repeated each month with different stocks, each with an ex-dividend date in the current month.

A dividend collar is a strategy requiring careful timing and selection. By buying shares in the ex-dividend date month and opening options expiring within one month or less from that date, the trader moves in and out of shares and earns a quarterly dividend each month.

So if a trader uses three different companies, each yielding a 4 percent dividend, the annual dividend yield will be 12 percent.

record date

the date on which the owner of stock is acknowledged as entitled to receive a dividend, even though the pay date is much later; if the stockholder of record sells shares after the ex-dividend date, the dividend is still earned.

Each company has ex-dividend dates in each of the three cycles (January, April, July, October; February, May, August, November; and March, June, September, December). Each company pays a 1 percent dividend on each of its cyclical quarterly pay dates, which occur usually within a few weeks after the ex-dividend date.

A trader buys 100 shares and at the same time opens a dividend collar. The best level of striking price is the one slightly higher than the current price. After the ex-dividend date, one of two outcomes takes place. Either the price of the stock has moved higher than the call's striking price, in which case 100 shares are called away; or the price has moved below the put's striking price, in which case the trader exercises the put and disposes of the shares. In either event, the dividend is earned every month. And by exercising out of the position through either the short call or the long put, the trader frees up capital to repeat the strategy.

Key Point

The dividend collar converts dividend income from quarterly to monthly, while completely removing market risk. It demands work and research, but can also lead to double-digit annualized returns.

The problem with the dividend collar is finding the position that works out. The proximity between current value and striking price has to be very close or the difference between long call and short put will be too great, eliminating the profit from the dividend. For this reason, it often makes the most sense to seek companies with the desirable price proximity, and open the position three to four weeks before the ex-dividend date. It may also make sense to pursue this strategy in multiples of shares and options, to achieve a better efficiency in the trading costs of both stock and options.

SYNTHETIC STRADDLES

The range of possible synthetic strategies includes the use of both spreads and straddles. A *synthetic straddle* is a position that will perform like a straightforward options-only straddle as the stock price changes.

There are several possible methods for creating a synthetic straddle. A *long call synthetic straddle* involves buying options and shorting stock. For every 100 shares shorted, the trader buys two calls. This 2-to-1

synthetic straddle

a position combining stock with options that performs like a straddle but often without the same level of risk.

long call synthetic straddle

a combination of 100 shares of short stock with two long calls at or close to the money, to create a position that acts like a call/put long straddle. If the stock price declines, the short stock position gains; if the stock price rises, the short stock position loses value but the two calls surpass the loss.

relationship between stock and long calls acts like a straddle; as the stock price declines, the short sale gains value; and if the stock price rises, the two calls offset the loss in the short stock position.

The advantage in having two long calls is that profits are possible on both sides. However, because the calls are paid for, the short seller must experience a steeper price decline in the stock to break even or achieve a profit. If the stock price rises, the two long calls appreciate at twice the rate of the loss in short stock.

Key Point

The value of doubling the number of calls is rapid price appreciation on the upside. The disadvantage is the higher long-side cost.

Example

Straddling the Short Risk: You create a long call synthetic straddle on Altria (MO). You short 100 shares at $27.77 per share. You expect the price to decline; however, in case the price rises, you also buy two January 28 calls at 0.59 each, paying $1.18 before transaction fees. Your prefee breakeven on the short stock is $26.59 per share. The trade-off is the cost of the calls versus the risk of loss if the stock price rises; the long call straddle eliminates the upside risk.

In this example, the pretransaction fee breakeven on the short stock is $26.59 per share. This is a trade-off in order to eliminate the risk that the stock price will rise. In that outcome, the market risk is eliminated and replaced by the potential to profit from the long calls. With this position open, you may earn a profit whether the stock price rises or falls. The outcome at various stock prices is summarized in Table 7.10.

Table 7.10 Long Call Synthetic Straddle

Price per Share	2 Long 28 Calls	Profit on Short 100 Shares	Net Profit or Loss
$21	−$118	$677	$559
22	−118	577	459
23	−118	477	359
24	−118	377	259
25	−118	277	159
26	−118	177	59
27	−118	77	−41
28	−118	−23	−141
29	82	−123	−41
30	282	−223	59
31	482	−323	159
32	682	−423	259
33	882	−523	359

Notice how the three-point limited loss presents a very limited risk. Above or below those price levels, the long call synthetic straddle matches price change point for point. It does not matter which direction the stock price moves; other than that middle range in which losses are very small, the position gains value. The advantage to this position is that there is a one-point gain in both directions.

The opposite strategy works in much the same way, but with the stock replaced by long stock. The *long put synthetic straddle* works when you own 100 shares and buy two puts close to or at the money.

The purpose to this strategy is to create a scenario in which you will experience a net profit in either situation: when the stock price rises or falls. This price movement must occur far enough in either direction to offset the price of the puts.

long put synthetic straddle

a combination of 100 shares of long stock with two long puts at or close to the money, to create a position that acts like a call/put long straddle. If the stock price rises, the long stock position gains; if the stock price declines, the stock position loses value but the two puts surpass the loss.

Example

Straddling the Long Risk: You create a long put synthetic straddle on Altria (MO). You buy 100 shares at $27.77 per share. You expect the price to rise; however, in case the price declines, you also buy two January 27 puts at 0.74 each, paying $1.48 before transaction fees. Your prefee breakeven on the long stock is $29.25 per share. The trade-off is the cost of the puts versus the risk of loss if the stock price falls; the long put straddle eliminates the downside risk.

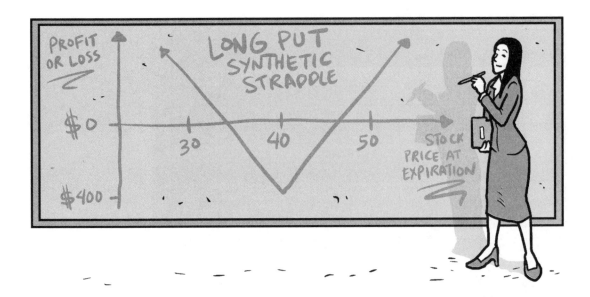

The long put synthetic straddle is elegant when you are long, just as the long call version is elegant when you are short. Profits will occur point for point whether the stock price rises or falls. However, there must be enough movement in one direction or the other to offset the cost of the puts. The outcome at different price levels is summarized in Table 7.11.

Table 7.11 Long Put Synthetic Straddle

Price per Share	2 Long 27 Puts	Profit on 100 Shares	Net Profit or Loss
$21	$1,052	−$677	$375
22	852	−577	275
23	652	−477	175
24	452	−377	75
25	252	−277	−25
26	52	−177	−125
27	−148	−77	−225
28	−148	23	−125
29	−148	123	−25
30	−148	223	75
31	−148	323	175
32	−148	423	275
33	−148	523	375

Just like the call variety against short stock, the long put synthetic straddle has a middle-range limited loss threat, but gains point for point with changes in the stock price. This growing profit applies on both sides.

The synthetic straddles overcome the chronic problem in the market of not knowing whether to go long or short on stock. Both the long call and long put strategies set up a combined position against stock (long or short) that profits with enough price movement either above or below the middle range.

Key Point

The long put or long call synthetic straddle is desirable in volatile markets, because it combines a limited midrange loss with growing profit zones both above and below.

A final strategy worth mentioning is movement of the straddles to the realm of the *ratio synthetic straddle*. For example, you may expand the long call synthetic straddle by buying three calls instead of two. This sets up a situation where you require more downward movement of stock price to exceed breakeven; but if stock prices rise, the calls accumulate at a net of two points of profit for every one-point change in the stock's price.

Synthetic positions hedge market risks and provide opportunity for profits without an accompanying greater exposure. Those synthetics that mirror price movement in stock are appealing because the same profits are possible for much less capital placed at risk.

Because synthetic positions may reduce risk so effectively, it makes sense to analyze option trading risks in greater detail. The next chapter provides an overview of the many kinds of risk you face with advanced strategies.

ratio synthetic straddle

a combination of 100 shares of stock, either long or short, with calls or puts set up in a ratio of more options than the 2-to-1 relationship of the long call or long put synthetic straddle. The ratio increases the price level required to achieve or pass breakeven; but it then enlarges the profit potential associated with price increases (for long call ratio against short stock) or price decreases (for long put ratio against long stock).

THOMSETT'S JOURNEY in ADVANCED OPTIONS

IT ALL SEEMS SO UNREAL, SO... ARTIFICIAL.

WHAT DO YOU MEAN? THE TOUR OF YOUR LAB?

YES. OPTIONS SECRETS MUST BE KEPT FROM THE GENERAL PUBLIC.

BUT WHY? I THINK IT'S BETTER IF EVERYONE KNOWS AS MUCH AS POSSIBLE.

THEN THEY CAN DECIDE WHETHER OR NOT TO USE OPTIONS BECAUSE THEY KNOW THE RISKS.

SUPER SECRET LAB

175

TO BE CONTINUED...

8 RISK: RULES OF THE GAME

All this worldly wisdom was once the unamiable heresy of some wise man.
—Henry David Thoreau, *Journal*, 1853

A tremendous opportunity awaits anyone who considers including options in a portfolio. When you review the broad range of possible uses for options, it becomes clear that they can serve the interests of a wide spectrum of investors. At the same time, you need to recognize the broad range of risks in option investing, and also to remember the complexity of income tax rules. As an options trader, your status as a stock investor could be affected by the option-related decisions that you make.

You will ultimately decide to employ options only if you conclude that they are appropriate, given your own financial and personal circumstances. If your risk tolerance and goals contradict the use of options in your portfolio, then you should avoid them altogether. Options might provide you with a convenient form of diversification, protection, or income—or all of these in various combinations. Identification of risk has to include not only knowing about *high* risk and how to avoid it, but also knowing how to contend with the risks of taking too little action. Risk comes in many forms and has to be managed constantly.

IDENTIFYING THE RANGE OF RISK

information risk

the risk that information used to make decisions could be misleading or even wrong.

In any discussion of risk, a starting point should be a discussion of *information risk*. Are you getting valid information? If you have listened to analysts in the past, or followed the crowd in deciding when to buy or sell, then you have been operating with the wrong information. But if you have picked stocks carefully and based your choices on analytical criteria (fundamental, technical, or a combination of both), then your decisions can be made based on facts rather than on the more common standards: rumors, opinions, and unsupported claims. Even the analysts' "target price" announcement is arbitrary and baseless. The popular practice of identifying earnings ranges and target price ranges has deceived many investors into making decisions for all the wrong reasons.

Key Point

Many market decisions are made based on rumors, opinions, and unsupported claims. It makes more sense to respond to facts and analysis.

Beyond the problems of information risk, you will also want to remain vigilant and watch for the whole range of risks you face whenever you are in the market. Options address the entire spectrum of risk tolerance profiles and can be used in combinations of ways to supplement income, insure other positions, leverage future long positions, or modify exposure to loss. To determine how to use options in your portfolio, first go through these three steps:

1. *Study the full range of possible option strategies.* Before opening any positions in options, prepare hypothetical variations and track the market to see how you would have done. Become familiar with valuation and changes in valuation by watching a particular series of options over time.

2. *Identify your personal risk tolerance levels.* Before picking an option strategy, determine what levels of risk you can afford to take. Set standards and then follow them. Be prepared to abandon outdated ideas and perceptions of risk, and continually refresh your outlook based on current information.

3. *Identify and understand all of the risks associated with options trading.* Consider every possible risk, including the risk that a stock's market price will not move as you expect, or that a short position could be exercised early. In option investing,

risk levels depend on the position you assume. For example, as a buyer, time is the enemy; and as a seller, time defines your profit potential.

The risk in each and every option position is that the underlying stock will do one of two things. It may move in a direction you didn't expect or want; or it may fail to move enough for a position to be profitable. A study of profit and loss zones before opening positions is a smart tactic, because it helps you to define whether a particular decision makes sense.

Margin and Collateral Risk

You may think of margin investing as buying stock on credit. That is the most familiar and common form. In the options market, margin requirements are different and margin is used in a different way. Your brokerage firm will require that short positions be protected, at least partially, through collateral. The preferred form of collateral is ownership of 100 shares of stock for each call sold; if you are short on puts, your broker will require cash or securities to be left on deposit to provide for the cost of stock in the case the short put is exercised. The combined *margin and collateral risk* is potentially substantial. Whenever you rely on borrowed funds and whenever you have to meet the collateral requirements involved, your range of investment and trading possibilities is restricted.

margin and collateral risk

the risk associated with borrowing on margin and needing to maintain collateral at the level required by law.

Whenever you open uncovered short positions in options, cash or securities will have to be placed on deposit to protect the brokerage firm's position. The level required is established by minimum legal requirements, subject to increases by the individual brokerage firm's policies. Any balance above the deposit represents risk, both for the brokerage firm and for you. If the stock moves in a direction you do not desire, the margin requirement goes up as well. In that respect, margin risk could be defined as leverage risk.

Personal Goals Risks

If you establish a goal that you will invest no more than 15 percent of your total portfolio in option speculation, it is important to stay with that goal. This requires constant review. Sudden market changes can mean sudden and unexpected losses, especially when you buy options and when you sell short. Getting away from the goals you set is all too easy.

Forgetting to adhere to the standards you set for yourself, or falling into the trap of *personal goal risks*, can be costly. Options trading is one area where this is especially difficult, but also very important. It is easy to forget goals and to end up chasing fast profits. This often ends up instead with the accumulation of fast losses.

Your goal should also include identification of the point at which you will close positions, either to take profits or to limit losses. Avoid breaking your own rules by delaying, hoping for favorable changes in the near-term future. This is tempting, but it often leads to unacceptable losses or missing a profit opportunity. Establish two price points in every option position: minimum gain and maximum loss. When either point is reached, close the position.

Key Point

Options traders, like gamblers, can succeed if they know when to fold.

personal goal risks

a range of risks associated with failing to set and follow goals and risk-related standards in how and when to trade, and related to the kinds of trades acceptable within the defined risk tolerance.

Risk of Unavailable Market

One of the least talked about risks in any investment is the potential that you will not be able to buy or sell when you want to. The discussion of options strategies is based on the basic idea that you will be able to place orders whenever you want to, without problems or delays.

The *risk of unavailable market* refers to one of two situations: Either a buyer and seller are unable to match up with one another, or the market volume is so heavy that orders cannot be placed in a timely manner. In the options market, as long as you trade in active issues, the Options

risk of unavailable market

the risk that trades may not be placed in an orderly manner, due to a lack of market on the other side or due to heavy volume leading to delays in order placement.

Clearing Corporation (OCC) ensures orderly settlement. This means the OCC acts as seller to every buyer, and as buyer to every seller. It is much more likely that heavy volume will affect trades by delaying placement of orders.

Key Point

Most traders do not need to worry about the availability of markets. The Options Clearing Corporation provides orderly settlement so that in almost every case buyers and sellers are either matched up or offset by the OCC itself.

The reality is quite different in some situations. When market volume is especially heavy, it is difficult and sometimes impossible to place orders when you want to. In an exceptionally large market correction, volume will be heavy as investors scramble to place orders to cut losses. So if you trade by telephone, your broker's lines will be overloaded and those who do get through will experience longer-than-usual delays—because so much business is taking place at the same time. If you trade online, the same problem will occur. You will not be able to get through to the online brokerage website if it is already overloaded with traders placing orders. In these extreme situations, your need to place orders will be greater than normal, as it is with all other investors. So the market may be temporarily unavailable.

Risk of Disruption in Trading

Trading could be halted in the underlying stock. For example, if rumors about a company are affecting the stock's market price, the exchange may halt trading for a day or more. When trading in stock is halted, all related option trading is halted as well. For example, a company might be rumored to be a takeover candidate. If the rumors affecting price are true, when the trading halt is lifted, the stock may open at a much higher or lower price than before. As an options investor, this exposes you to potentially significant risks, perhaps even preventing you from being able to limit your exposure to loss by offsetting the exposed side of the transaction. You will be required to wait until trading reopens, and by then it might be too late. The cost of protecting your position might be too high, or you might be subjected to automatic exercise.

The most likely reason for a disruption—halting of trading—is a short-term problem, but depending on the timing it could prevent a trader from closing a trade at the best possible moment. So *risk of disruption in trading* is not usually a serious risk, but for options trading where timing of entry and exit often is critical, this risk cannot be ignored.

risk of disruption in trading

the risk that trading is closed due to rumors or news, in anticipation of news that will affect price, or in response to unusual activity. For options traders, the timing could mean lost opportunities for entry or exit at the best possible moment.

Key Point

Losing an opportunity due to halted trading is a remote risk; but options traders need to be aware that it can affect timing and, possibly, profits. Options could be exercised during the halt.

Brokerage Risks

Another area to study and evaluate is that of *brokerage risks.* If you use a discount brokerage or online trading service, you are not exposed to this risk, because the role of the broker is limited to placement of orders as you direct. However, if you are using a broker for advice on options trading, you are exposed to the risk that a broker will use his or her discretion in placing orders, even if you have not granted permission. Never grant unlimited discretion to someone else, no matter how much trust you have. In a fast-moving market, it is difficult for a broker with many clients to pay attention to your options trades to the degree required. In fact, with online free quotations widely available, you really do not need a full-commission broker at all. In the Internet

brokerage risks

risks of discretion exercised by brokers, whether authorized or not, and errors in order placement.

environment, commission-based brokerage is becoming increasingly obsolete. As an options trader, you may want to consider using an order placement service and moving away from the practice of paying for brokerage services.

Key Point

Never give anyone unlimited discretion over your account. Also be extra cautious in placing orders, paying special attention to whether you want the order to be identified as a buy or a sell, and as an opening or a closing order.

Yet another risk, even with online brokerage accounts, is that mistakes will be made in placing orders. Fortunately, online trading is easily traced and documented. However, it is still possible for what was intended as a buy order to go in as a sell, or vice versa. Such mistakes can be disastrous for you as an options trader. If you trade by telephone or in person, the risk is increased just due to human error. If you trade online, check and double-check your order before submitting it.

Trading Cost Risk

trading cost risk

the risk of lost profits or conversion from profits to losses due to the trading fees assessed both to open and to close positions.

A calculated profit zone has to be reduced, or a loss zone increased, to allow for the cost of placing trades. Brokerage trading fees apply to both sides of every transaction. If you trade in single-option contracts, the cost is high on a per-option basis. Trading in higher increments is economical because then the cost of trading is lower on a per-option basis. So *trading cost risk* refers to the cost of opening and closing positions. Although the per-contract cost is small, it is a *round trip cost*, meaning fees are charged both for opening and for closing a position, and is applied to stock as well as to options.

Key Point

In determining a breakeven on a trade, be sure to remember the trading costs involved. For smaller trades, assume a round trip of about one-quarter point, and take this into account when calculating your profit goal.

round trip cost

name given to the double cost of transaction fees, assessed first to open and then to close positions.

This book has used examples for single contracts in most cases to make outcomes clear; in practice, such trading is not always practical because the trading fees require more profit just to break even. A thin margin of profit will evaporate quickly when trading costs are added into the mix.

When you buy and then exercise an option, or when you sell and the option is exercised by the buyer or the exchange, you not only pay the option trading fee, but you also have to pay for the cost of transacting the shares of stock, a point to remember in calculating overall return. It is possible that if you're operating on a thin profit margin, it could be taken up entirely by trading fees on both sides of the transaction, so that cost has to be calculated beforehand. In general, single-contract trades involve about one-half point for the combined cost of opening and then closing the option position; so you need to add a half-point cushion to allow for that. The calculation changes as you deal in multiple contracts, in which trading costs on a per-contract basis will be far lower.

Lost Opportunity Risks

One of the more troubling aspects of options trading involves *lost opportunity risk.* This arises in several ways, the most obvious being that

lost opportunity risk

the risk that covered call writers will lose profits from increased prices in stock because they are locked in at a fixed striking price, or that margin requirements may prevent traders from being able to take advantage of other investment opportunities.

tax consequence risk

the risk of losing tax advantages or paying additional taxes due to special options trading rules or limitations; these include ill-advised timing, loss of long-term gains rates, and limitations on loss deductions.

experienced by covered call sellers. You risk the loss of stock profits in the event of price increase and exercise. Your profit is locked in at the striking price. Covered call writers accept the certainty of a consistent, better-than-average return and, in exchange, they lose the occasional larger capital gain on their stock.

Key Point

Be aware of the lost opportunity for stock-based profits when you open a covered call. You must be willing to accept exercise in exchange for the certainty of covered call returns.

Opportunity risks arise in other ways, too. For example, if you are involved in exotic combinations including long and short positions, your margin requirements may prevent you from being able to take advantage of other investment opportunities. You will often find yourself in an environment of moderate scarcity, so you cannot seize every opportunity. Before committing yourself to an open position in options, recognize how your economic boundaries could limit your choices. You will probably lose more opportunities than you will ever be able to take.

Tax Consequence Risk

In trading options, you need to take great care to ensure that you don't incur unintended consequences. This is as true when it comes to tax liabilities as anywhere else. The potential *tax consequence risk* vulnerabilities include:

- *Poor timing of taxable outcomes.* You are going to need to perform careful tax planning to maintain control over the taxes due on your portfolio. This includes consideration of both federal and state taxes. Because so many options strategies are only marginally profitable, poor planning could result in new losses once taxes are considered in the overall outcome. For example, a small profit could result in extra tax liabilities, wiping out all of the gain. In this situation, you are exposed to risk while option positions are open, but you earn no profits.

- *Loss of favorable tax rates.* As you will see later in this chapter, some option positions automatically revert from long-term capital gains (with their lower maximum tax rate) to short-term capital gains (which are taxed at your full *ordinary income* tax rate). While *net investment income* is included on a person's tax return, it is often taxed at lower rates (long-term capital gains) or excluded from tax (qualified dividends).
- *Limitations on deductibility of losses.* Some types of advanced options trades are subject to limitations in deductibility—for example, in some cases involving two or more offsetting option positions.

There are some obvious tax advantages to some trades, especially if they are timed properly. For example, if you sell a covered call not due to expire until next year, you receive funds at the time you open the position, but taxes are not applicable until the position is closed, expires, or is exercised. But there is much more to tax planning and to tax risk. These tax risks in trading options can be quite complex, especially for anyone not completely familiar with how the tax rules work. Options taxation is exceptionally complicated, so before entering into advanced trading positions, consult with your tax adviser.

ordinary income

noninvestment income, subject to the full tax rate an individual pays and not qualified for exclusions or lower rates applicable to some forms of net investment income.

net investment income

an individual's taxable income from interest, dividends, and capital gains; distinguished from ordinary income by tax rate or potential tax exclusions.

Key Point

Tax rules for options trading are exceptionally complex. You need at a minimum a general idea of the tax consequences to specific kinds of trades.

EVALUATING YOUR RISK TOLERANCE

Everyone has a specific level of risk tolerance—the ability and willingness to accept risk. This trait is not fixed but changes over time. Your personal risk tolerance is influenced by several factors:

- *Investment capital.* How much money do you have available to invest? How much do you have committed to long-term growth, and how much can you spare for more adventurous alternatives?

- *Personal factors.* Your risk tolerance is significantly affected by your age, income, debt level, economic status, job, and job security. It changes drastically with major life events such as marriage, birth of a child, divorce, or death of a family member.

- *Your investing experience.* How experienced are you as an investor? No matter how much you study investing in theory, you do not really gain market experience until you place real money at risk.

- *Type of account.* Your risk tolerance depends on how and why you invest and the type of account involved. If you invest in your personal account, you will have greater flexibility than in a retirement account, for example.

- *Your personal goals.* Every investor's goals ultimately determine how much risk is acceptable. Remember that

definition of your personal goals should dictate how you invest.

Key Point

Risk tolerance is reflected in the way you invest. You will have a better chance of succeeding if you ensure that the risks you take are risks you can afford.

The best investment decisions invariably are made as the result of thorough evaluation of the features of an investment or strategy, the most important being risk. The evaluation process helps you to avoid mistakes and to focus attention on what will be beneficial, given your risk tolerance level. The risk evaluation worksheet for option investing in Table 8.1 will help you to classify options by degrees of risk.

Table 8.1 Risk Evaluation Worksheet

	Lowest Possible Risk
——	Covered call writing
——	Put purchase for insurance (long position)
——	Call purchase for insurance (short position)
	Medium Risk
——	Ratio writing
——	Combined strategies
	—— Long —— Short
	High Risk
——	Uncovered call writing
——	Combined strategies
	—— Long —— Short
——	Call purchases for income
——	Put purchases for income

Risk evaluation depends on your analysis of potential profits and losses under all possible outcomes. When considering an option strategy of any nature, first calculate potential profits in the event of expiration or exercise, and then set criteria for other features: maximum time value, time until expiration, the number of contracts involved in the transaction, target rate of return, and the price range at which you will close. Obviously, these criteria will be drastically different for buyers than for sellers, and for covered versus uncovered option writing. Use the option limits worksheet in Table 8.2 to set your personal limits.

Table 8.2 Option Limits

Covered Call Sale Criteria Rate of Return If Unchanged	
Dividends	$_____
Call premium	$_____
	Cost of stock $_____
	Gain ___%
Rate of Return If Exercised	
Dividends	$_____
Call premium	$_____
Stock gain	$_____
	Cost of stock $_____
	Gain ___%
Option Purchase Criteria	
Maximum time value: ___%	
Time until expiration: ___ months	
Number of options: ___ contracts	
Target rate of return: ___%	
Sell level: increase to $_____ or decrease to $_____	

THOMSETT'S JOURNEY in ADVANCED OPTIONS

I AM PROTECTING TRADERS FROM *RISK*. IF THEY DON'T KNOW ABOUT SYNTHETIC STRATEGIES, THEY ARE SAFE.

YOU REALLY DON'T HAVE TO BE SO DISTRUSTFUL OF THE AVERAGE TRADER.

IF THEY KNOW THE RISKS, THEY'RE BETTER INFORMED. KEEPING THEM GUESSING IS WHERE THE REAL RISKS COME FROM. I'M SURE YOU KNOW THAT.

BUT WE CAN'T HAVE TOO MUCH KNOWLEDGE FLOATING AROUND OUT THERE. I MEAN, IF EVERYONE KNOWS ALL THE STRATEGIES, THEN WHAT?

THEN EVERYONE CAN PICK STRATEGIES BASED ON A BETTER UNDERSTANDING OF RISK.

EXCUSE ME, BUT THIS IS A NEW IDEA TO ME. TELLING TRADERS ABOUT RISK? WHERE DOES IT *END*?

WHAT IF *EVERYBODY* KNEW HOW TO TRADE OPTIONS AND HAD ACCESS TO ALL OF MY SECRETS, LIKE SYNTHETIC STRATEGIES?

IT COULD MEAN THAT YOU HAVE TO FACE THE FACTS. YOUR SECRET LAB IS NO SECRET, AND IT'S *BETTER* FOR EVERYONE IF THEY KNOW THE RISKS.

THAT JUST MAKES EVERYONE BETTER AT TRADING AND IT REDUCES RISKS.

9

TAXES: THE WILD CARD OF OPTIONS TRADING

When there is an income tax, the just man will pay more and the unjust man less on the same amount of income.
— Plato, *The Republic*, ca. 360 BC

Taxation of options profits and losses is one of the most complex and specialized areas of the U.S. federal income tax code. This chapter summarizes the major rules and exceptions that apply to options but not to anything else.

If you are a typical trader, you have a fairly good grasp of how taxes work. However, a handful of special rules affect profitability as well as timing. Ultimately, these rules could determine whether a particular strategy makes sense.

capital gains

profits from investments, taxed the same as other income if the holding period is less than one year, and at lower rates if investments were owned for one year or more.

Key Point

More than with any other area of investing and trading, tax rules for options are specialized and in some cases could affect your basic decision to pursue a strategy.

Capital gains—taxable profits from investments—are broken down into short-term or long-term. The normal treatment of capital gains is determined by your holding period. If you own stock for 12 months or more and then sell, your profit (or loss) is treated as long-term gain (or loss); a lower tax percentage is applied than to short-term capital gains (gains on assets owned less than 12 months). This rule applies to stocks and is fairly straightforward—until you begin using options as well. Then the capital gains rules change.

Here are 11 rules for option-related capital gains taxes:

1. *Short-term capital gains.* Generally speaking, any investment you hold for less than 12 months will be taxed at the same rate as your other ordinary income (your effective tax rate). Starting in 2013, the marginal tax became 39.6 percent.

2. *Long-term capital gains.* For investments held for 12 months or more, a more favorable tax rate applies. The maximum rate of 15 percent (or 20 percent for those in the 39.6 percent bracket starting in 2013) on long-term gains applies to net capital gains (long-term capital gains less short-term capital losses).

3. *Constructive sales.* You could be taxed as though you sold an investment, even when you did not actually complete a sale. This constructive sale rule applies when offsetting

long and short positions are entered in the same security. For example, if you buy 100 shares of stock and later sell short 100 shares of the same stock, it could be treated as a constructive sale. The same rules could be applied when options are used to hedge stock positions. The determining factors include the time between the two transactions, changes in price levels, and final outcomes of both sides in the transaction. This is a complex area of tax law; if you are involved with combinations and short sales, you should consult with your tax adviser to determine whether constructive sale rules apply to your transactions.

long-term capital gains

profits on investments held for 12 months or more, which are taxed at a rate lower than other (ordinary) income.

Key Point

Many options strategies involve hedging and the use of offsetting stock and option positions. This could affect your tax liabilities due to the constructive sales rule.

4. *Wash sales.* If you sell stock and within 30 days buy it again, it is considered a wash sale. Under the wash sale rule, you cannot deduct a loss when 30 days have not passed. The same rule applies in many cases where stock is sold and, within 30 days, the same person sells an in-the-money put.
5. *Capital gains for unexercised long options.* Taxes on long options are treated in the same way as other investments. A gain is short-term if the holding period is less than 12 months, and it is long-term if the holding period is one year or more. Taxes are assessed in the year the long position is closed in either of two ways: by sale or by expiration.
6. *Treatment of exercised long options.* If you purchase a call or a put and it is exercised, the net payment is treated as part of the basis in stock. In the case of a call, the cost is added to the basis in the stock, and the holding period of the stock begins on the day following exercise. The

constructive sales

status when an investor buys and sells in separate transactions that involve substantially identical property; the holding of offsetting long and short positions may be taxed as a constructive sale even when no physical sale has occurred.

holding period of the option does not affect the capital gains holding period of the stock. In the case of a long put that is exercised, the net cost of the put reduces the gain on stock when the put is exercised and stock is sold. The sale of stock under exercise of a put will be either long-term or short-term, depending on the holding period of stock.

7. *Taxes on short calls.* Premium is not taxed at the time the short position is opened. Taxes are assessed in the year the position is closed through purchase or expiration; and all such transactions are treated as short-term regardless of how long the option position remained open. In the event a short call is exercised, the striking price plus premium received become the basis of the stock delivered through exercise.

8. *Taxes on short puts.* Premium received is not taxed at the time the short position is opened. Closing the position through purchase or expiration always creates a short-term gain or loss. If the short put is exercised by the buyer, the striking price plus trading costs become the basis of stock through exercise. The holding period of the stock begins on the day following exercise of the short put.

9. *Limitations of deductions in offsetting positions.* The federal tax rules consider a straddle to be an *offsetting position*. This means that some loss deductions may be deferred or limited, or favorable tax rates are disallowed. If risks are reduced by opening the straddle, four possible tax consequences could result. First, the holding period for the purpose of long-term capital gains could be suspended as long as the straddle remains open. Second, the wash sale rule may be applied against current losses. Third, current-year deductions could be deferred until an offsetting "successor position" (the other side of the straddle) has been closed. Fourth, current charges (transaction fees and margin interest, for example) may be deferred and added to the basis of the long-position side of the straddle.

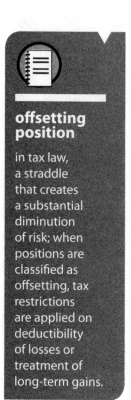

offsetting position

in tax law, a straddle that creates a substantial diminution of risk; when positions are classified as offsetting, tax restrictions are applied on deductibility of losses or treatment of long-term gains.

Key Point

Many straddles will create what the tax code calls offsetting positions. This means that some losses have to be deferred until later when the second side of the position is closed. It could also lead to an unintentional wash sale, eliminating the deduction.

qualified covered call

a covered call that meets specific definitions allowing an investor to claim long-term capital gains tax rates upon sale of stock, or to retain long-term holding period status. Qualification is determined by time to expiration and by the price difference between current market value of the stock and striking price of the call.

10. *Tax treatment of married puts.* It is possible that a married put will be treated as an adjustment in the basis of the stock, rather than taxed separately. This rule applies only when puts are acquired on the same day as stock, and when the put either expires or becomes exercised. If you sell the puts prior to expiration, the result is treated as short-term capital gain or loss.

11. *Capital gains and qualification of covered calls.* The most complicated of the special option-related tax rules involves the treatment of capital gains on stock. This occurs when you use covered calls. The federal tax laws have defined *qualified covered calls* for the purpose of defining how stock profits are treated; it is possible that a long-term capital gain could be converted to short-term if an unqualified covered call is involved. The following section provides the details and examples of how qualification is determined.

Valuable Resource
The complex tax rules of options are summarized nicely in the booklet "Taxes and Investing." You can download a PDF of this from the Options Clearing Corporation at **www.optionsclearing.com/components/docs/about/ publications/taxes_and_investing.pdf.**

QUALIFIED COVERED CALLS— SPECIAL RULES

The tax rules applied when you write in-the-money covered calls are exceptionally complicated. There are several rules to keep in mind to determine whether your in-the-money covered call is qualified or unqualified. With a qualified covered call, your stock does not risk losing its long-term capital gains status; if the covered call is unqualified, then treatment of stock profits changes as a consequence.

Example

Mind-Boggling Limitation: You wrote two covered calls last week. The first one was written with a striking price of 30; the stock's previous day's closing price was 32. The call expires in two months. The second call was written with a striking price of 45 and the stock closed the day before at the price of 52. This call expires in three weeks.

The first call is qualified in both respects. The striking price is the first available striking price below the previous day's stock closing price; and the call is scheduled to expire longer than 30 days out.

The second call is unqualified in both respects. It is not the first available striking price below the previous day's stock closing price (that would have been the striking price of 50). Also, the call is set to expire within the next 30 days.

> **Key Point**
>
> The qualified covered call rule only limits the classification of long-term gains, and only when you have not already owned the stock for the one-year term. The rule does not prevent traders from writing deep in-the-money calls.

If you write out-of-the-money covered calls, there is no effect on the status of the stock. The following explanation applies *only* when your covered calls are in the money at the time the transactions are opened.

The general rule governing in-the-money covered calls refers to time. The option must have more than 30 days until expiration. In addition, the striking price cannot be lower than the striking price immediately below the closing price of the stock on the day before you open the covered call.

The rules of qualification are more complex when the call has more than 90 days until expiration. Table 9.1 summarizes the qualification of covered calls given the stock's closing price in specific stock price ranges, and with various times until expiration.

> **Example**
>
> **A Math Challenge:** You own shares of stock in several corporations. You want to write covered calls in the money, but you want to ensure that all are qualified. One stock has current market value of $74 per share. To qualify a covered call, it must be one striking price below that level, or 70, if the call is set to expire within 31 to 90 days. If the call is set to expire beyond the 90-day point, you can write a call two striking prices below the prior day's close, which is the 65 call. If you write any in-the-money calls other than these, they will be unqualified.

Table 9.1 Qualification of Covered Calls

Previous Day's Stock Closing Price	Time until Expiration	Striking Price Limits
$25 or less	More than 30 days	One striking price below prior day's closing stock price (Exception: It is not a qualified covered call if striking price is lower than 85 percent of the stock price.)
$25.01 to $60	More than 30 days	One striking price below prior day's closing stock price
$60.01 to $150	31–90 days	One striking price below prior day's closing stock price
$60.01 to $150	More than 90 days	Two striking prices below prior day's closing stock price (but not more than 10 points in the money)
Over $150	31–90 days	One striking price below prior day's closing stock price
Over $150	More than 90 days	Two striking prices below prior day's closing stock price

antistraddle rules

tax regulations that remove or suspend the long-term favorable tax treatment of stock when the owner writes unqualified in-the-money covered calls.

What happens when you write an unqualified call? The rules governing the consequences, which are also called the *antistraddle rules*, affect long-term capital gains qualification of stock. Following is a summary of five ways the rules work:

1. *No change for at-the-money or out-of-the-money covered calls.* No effect on the tax treatment of stock will be suffered if you write calls with striking prices at or above the closing price of the stock.

2. *No change for qualified in-the-money covered calls.* As long as in-the-money calls fall within the rather limited qualification

period (see Table 9.1), no effect will be experienced on the tax treatment of the stock.

3. *Treatment of capital gains with unqualified covered call.* As a general rule, a profit on stock you own one year or more is taxed at lower long-term capital gains rates. But when you write an unqualified covered call against stock, the holding period is suspended. This means that counting up to the one-year holding period will not continue as long as the short option remains open.

> **Example**
>
> **Coming Up Short:** You have owned 100 shares of stock for 11 months. You write an unqualified covered call, and your long-term holding period is suspended. Three months later, the call is exercised and you give up your stock at a profit. Even though you owned the stock for 14 months, your gain is treated as short-term. You sold an unqualified covered call, so the period required before long-term rates apply was suspended.

4. *Treatment of covered call losses when qualified.* Any losses on qualified covered calls are treated as long-term losses when the underlying stock profits are treated as long-term capital gains.
5. *Treatment of stock holding period when covered calls are closed.* If you sell a covered call at a loss within 30 days of the end of the tax year, you have to hold on to the stock for at least 30 days in order to have the call treated as a qualified covered call.

These rules are exceptionally complicated, and the underlying reasoning for them is puzzling. It certainly requires you to use a qualified tax expert if you do engage in writing in-the-money covered calls. Additional problems may arise when you employ rolling techniques. For example, if you write a qualified covered call today, you satisfy the rules for treatment of the stock if and when the call is exercised. But what happens if the stock's price rises and you roll forward? The replacement option may end up being unqualified, based on several factors: the current price level of the stock, proximity of the stock's price to the call's striking price, and time until expiration. You could unintentionally replace a qualified covered call with an unqualified covered call.

Key Point

You may start out with a qualified covered call and end up unintentionally rolling it forward into an unqualified covered call. When you roll to the same strike after the underlying price has risen, this is a serious possibility.

If you are a typical investor, you view a roll as a single transaction: One option is replaced with another. But from the tax point of view, there are two separate transactions. When you close the original short position, you create a short-term capital gain or loss. When you open the second option, you may be either qualified or unqualified in the *new* option, because it is a separate transaction.

You may question whether it is necessary to master the special and complex tax rules governing covered call qualification. However, the problem is very narrow in focus. It is a potential problem only if you write (or roll forward to) unqualified in-the-money positions. So as long as your calls are at the money or out of the money, you are not affected.

In some situations, you may view writing in-the-money calls as advantageous. For example, you can either sell stock at a profit augmented by option profits or take advantage of stock price changes by profiting on intrinsic value price movement. If you have large unused *carryover capital losses*, you may also view the disqualification of stock status as an advantage. Because your annual losses are limited to $3,000, you can use a current-year stock profit as an offset to carryover loss. In this case, you will not be concerned with the loss of long-term favorable treatment.

carryover capital losses

sums of capital losses from prior years that exceeded annual loss limitation levels; the annual maximum capital loss deduction is $3,000, and all losses above that level have to be carried over and applied in future tax years.

Example

The Absorption Factor: You had large losses in your portfolio in the years 2011 and 2012. In the current year, you still have over $50,000 in unused carryover capital losses. It will take many years to absorb these losses at the rate of $3,000 per year. However, by selling in-the-money covered calls you create numerous short-term profits, both in calls and in stock exercised against your in-the-money short calls. You view this as one way to shelter short-term profits. The large carryover losses are applied against the current-year gains, so you have no net tax consequences this year.

qualified retirement plans

those plans qualified by the IRS to treat current income as deferred and free of tax in the year earned and, in many cases, also exempting annual contributions to the plan from current taxes.

There are two situations in which you will not be concerned about the loss of favorable long-term capital gains tax rates. First is when you have a substantial carryover loss. Because net investment income can be offset against past-year losses, current-year capital gains—even short-term gains—are fully protected from any taxes.

The second situation is when you are investing through an individual retirement account (IRA) or other retirement plan for which current income is not taxable. In these so-called *qualified retirement plans,* current income is free of tax, but in future years when withdrawals begin, all income is taxed at ordinary rates. Since you do not benefit from long-term gains rates within such plans, you are free to pursue even aggressive options strategies such as deep in-the-money covered calls.

LOOKING TO THE FUTURE

Tax problems and strategies have been made very complex by the current tax rules and, hopefully, future reforms will simplify those rules or make them easier to follow. However, taxes are only one of the many challenges you face in deciding how to plan your investment portfolio, determine which risks are acceptable, and protect capital for your future.

Options, like all investments, should always be used in the context of your individual plans. This is one of the long-term problems with taking advice from individuals whose compensation depends on generating trades: They tend to think in terms of volume rather than starting from the point of view of what works best for the client. You need to ensure that your options positions are a logical risk for your portfolio, based on your risk tolerance and personal investing goals.

Example

Defining Yourself and Your Goals: You have written down your personal investing goals, and have identified what you hope to achieve in the intermediate and long-term future. You are willing to assume risks in a low to moderate range, so all of your capital is invested in shares of blue-chip companies.

Strategy 1: Hold shares of stock as long-term investments. Aim for appreciation and continuing dividend income.

In order to increase portfolio value, you consider the following possible strategy:

Strategy 2: Increase the value of your portfolio by purchasing shares as described in strategy 1, and waiting for a moderate increase in value; then begin writing covered calls. As long as your minimum rate of return, if exercised or unchanged, will always exceed 35 percent, you will write a call and then avoid exercise through rolling techniques. If a call is exercised and stock is called away, you plan to reinvest the proceeds in additional purchases of other blue-chip company shares.

In this comparison, the rate of return from the second strategy will always be higher than the first, due to the yield from writing covered calls. A 35 percent rate of return is not unreasonable because it includes the capital gain from selling shares in the event of exercise and because calls can be closed and replaced repetitively. So an annualized double-digit rate is not only possible, but likely under this strategy. In addition to providing impressive returns, writing covered calls also provides downside protection by discounting your basis in shares of stock.

Key Point

Covered call writers will create consistent double-digit annualized returns as long as underlying prices do not decline. However, writers will lose the occasional big gain in stock due to rapid price growth.

An interesting point to remember about the covered call strategy, especially as described in strategy 2: The common argument *against* writing covered calls is that you may lose future profits in the event the stock's price rises dramatically, because your striking price locks you in. It is true that, were the stock's market value to climb dramatically, you would experience exercise and lose those profits. However, remember that well-selected stocks will also tend to be less volatile than average, so the chances of such increases—while they can happen—are lower than average. In addition, covered call writers take their double-digit returns consistently in exchange for the occasional lost paper profit. The goal of long-term growth is not inconsistent with writing covered calls, as long as you have a plan and stick to it, and as long as exercised shares are replaced with other shares of equal growth potential.

Every form of investing contains its own set of opportunities and risks. If you lose money consistently in options, you will also tend to have the following characteristics: You do not set goals, so you do not have a preestablished plan for closing positions profitably. You do not select strategies in your own best interests, describing yourself as conservative while using options in a highly speculative manner. You believe in the fundamentals but you follow only technical indicators. You have not taken the time to define your risk tolerance level, so you do not know when the risks you are taking are too high. A popular maxim in the investing community is: "If you don't know where you're going, any road will get you there."

As a successful investor, you are focused. You take the time to define your goals carefully, and you define your risk tolerance level with great care. You also define yourself in terms of what works for you and what doesn't work. This enables you to use strategies that make sense and to resist temptation when you receive advice from others. You also tend to be patient, and you are willing to wait for the right opportunities rather than taking chances when conditions are not right.

Devising a personal, individualized strategy is a rewarding experience. Seeing clearly what you need to do and then executing your strategy successfully gives you a well-deserved sense of achievement and competence, not to mention control. You will profit from devising and applying options strategies based on calculation and observation. You will also benefit from the satisfaction that comes from mastering a complex investment field and finding yourself completely in control.

TO BE CONTINUED...

10

CHOOSING STOCKS: FINDING THE RIGHT INGREDIENTS

The easiest job I have ever tackled in this world is that of making money. It is, in fact, almost as easy as losing it. Almost, but not quite.

—H. L. Mencken, in the *Baltimore Sun*,
June 12, 1922

How do you pick a stock? With about 8,000 to choose from, you need to narrow down the list. When picking stocks with call options in mind, you will need to combine fundamental and technical tests to ensure that you pick those stocks with the greatest potential for growth *and* that offer you the very best options positions.

As a starting premise, be sure to observe four basic rules for picking stocks:

1. *Always pick stocks that are strong on their own merits.* A common error is to pick stocks based only on the option premium levels offered. This is a mistake because richer

options are a symptom of higher than average stock volatility. So if you pick stocks based only on high option values, you will pick the highest-risk stocks. You will do better selecting stocks with strong fundamental and technical indicators.

2. *Combine a very short list of key indicators for stock selection.* You could spend all day applying endless tests to stock selection. But, in fact, you should be able to use six fundamental indicators and confirm these with an equally short list of technical tests.

3. *Avoid stocks of companies that have never reported a profit, or whose stock price has been falling over many years.* As obvious as this guideline might seem, it is often ignored. If a company is losing money each year or has never reported a profit, there is no rationale for expecting market value to grow. On the technical side, stock price trends tell the whole story. If a company has been experiencing a declining range of stock prices over many years, stay away. It usually means the company has lost its competitive edge and is on the way out.

4. *Look beyond option values; use past history of basic outcomes.* The basics are usually the most dependable indicators. You should check revenues, profits, capitalization, and cash flow to make sure management is operating the company wisely. The history of fundamental trends is the strongest collective indicator for picking strong companies.

In this chapter, you have a short course on the fundamental and technical indicators you need to pick strong, well-managed, and competitive companies. This is achieved with an explanation of both fundamental and technical indicators that will give you the most reliable guidance for narrowing down a list of likely stocks to buy, whether you trade options on those stocks or simply hold them for the long term. Research is the starting point.

Careful, well-researched selection is the key to consistent investing success. This is true for all forms of investing and applies to all strategies. If your stock portfolio is not performing as you expected, you might be tempted to augment lackluster profits by using options. Short-term income could close a gap to offset small losses, improve overall yields, and even recapture a paper loss. However, short-term income is not guaranteed, and poorly selected stocks cannot be converted into high performers with options. Your best chance for success in the options market comes from first selecting stocks wisely, and from establishing rules for selection and strategy that suit your individual risk tolerance. A suitable options strategy has to be a sensible match for an individual stock based on its volatility, your goal in owning it, and its original basis versus current market value.

Deciding which stocks to buy should be based on your goals and risk tolerance levels, which are part of the process of setting an investment policy for yourself. That includes defining acceptable risks and focusing on how options can and should be used in your portfolio: to speculate, enhance income, or hedge equity positions. One danger of stock market investment is the tendency of investors to follow fads. It is invariably a mistake to begin buying shares of stock *after* prices have risen significantly. This brings up a number of problems, however, all dealing with timing. How do you know when a price run-up is about to begin in a particular stock or sector, and, once invested, how do you know when to get out?

Both of these questions involve timing and risk. When you put capital at risk and when you decide whether to sell, you are making risk-oriented decisions. The difficulty in these core questions can be mitigated, and risks reduced, with the use of options. Options are not purely speculative; they can also be useful for reducing risk of loss as well as risk of lost opportunity.

For example, instead of buying shares today, you might consider buying calls. Even though they will expire, they require far less capital and risk exposure. On the other end—when you own stocks whose market value has risen significantly—you can buy puts to insure against unexpected losses, or sell covered calls to (1) discount your basis and (2) increase income without selling your shares.

Options can be coordinated with long-term goals as well. A portfolio of well-chosen stocks should be treated as a long-term investment, and, as a general rule, stocks will hold their value over the long term whether or not you write options.

Key Point

Value in your portfolio of stocks exists regardless of whether you sell options. You cannot expect to bail out poorly selected stocks by offsetting stock losses with option profits.

One of the great advantages in selling covered calls is that a minimum profit level is likely as long as you also remember that the first step always should be proper selection of the stock.

Example

A Safe Decision: You bought 100 shares of stock for $82.20 per share. At the time, you believed this would be a sound investment with excellent prospects for long-term price growth. You also considered selling a covered call and analyzed three calls, all with striking prices of 90. These expired in 4, 7, and 13 months. Premium values for these three calls were 6.10, 7.20, and 11.50. Quarterly dividends were approximately $50 at the time. (These stock, option, and dividend values are based on closing values for IBM as of December 12, 2008.) In comparing the likely outcomes for both expiration and exercise, you analyzed returns on an annualized basis.

If the call expires:			
	4-month	**7-month**	**13-month**
Call premium	$610	$720	$1,150
Dividend	50	100	200
Total profit	$660	$820	$1,350

Annualized yield if the call expires:

$$(\$660 \div \$8{,}220) \div 4 \times 12 = 24.1\%$$

$$(\$820 \div \$8{,}220) \div 7 \times 12 = 17.1\%$$

$$(\$1{,}350 \div \$8{,}220) \div 13 \times 12 = 15.2\%$$

If the call is exercised:			
	4-month	**7-month**	**13-month**
Call premium	$ 610	$ 720	$1,150
Dividend	50	100	200
Total profit on options	$ 660	$ 820	$1,350
Capital gain ($9,000 – $8,220)	780	780	780
Total profit, stock, and options	$1,440	$1,600	$2,130

Annualized yield if the call is exercised:

$$(\$1{,}440 \div \$8{,}220) \div 4 \times 12 = 52.6\%$$

$$(\$1{,}600 \div \$8{,}220) \div 7 \times 12 = 33.4\%$$

$$(\$2{,}130 \div \$8{,}220) \div 13 \times 12 = 23.9\%$$

These returns—all impressive—are typical in situations where (1) you own appreciated stock, (2) exercise would be viewed as an acceptable outcome, and (3) you are interested in improving current return on stock you own without necessarily selling.

DEVELOPING AN ACTION PLAN

Earning a consistently high yield from writing calls is not always possible, even for covered call writers. In addition to picking the right options at the right time, a covered strategy has to be structured around well-selected stocks, preferably those that have appreciated since purchase. In addition, even with the right stocks in your portfolio, you might need to wait out the market. Timing refers not only to the richness of option premiums, but also to the tendencies in the stock and in the market as a whole. You could be able to sell a call rich in time value and profit from the combination of capital gains, dividends, and call premium. But the opportunity is not always going to be available, depending on a combination of factors:

- The price of the underlying stock has to be at the right level in two respects. First, the relationship between current market value and your basis in the stock has to justify the exposure to exercise, to ensure that in the event of exercise, you will have a profit and not a loss. If this is not possible, then there is no justification in writing the call. Second, the current market value of the underlying stock also has to be correct in relation to the striking price of the call. Otherwise, the time value will not be high enough to justify the transaction.
- The volume of investor interest in the stock and related options has to be high enough to provide adequate time value to build in a profit.
- The time between the point of sale of a call and expiration should fit with your personal goals. As with all other investment decisions, no strategy is appropriate unless it represents an intelligent fit.

In evaluating various strategies you could employ as a call writer, avoid the mistake of assuming that today's market conditions are permanent. Markets change constantly, resulting in unpredictable stock price levels. The ideal call write will be undertaken when the following conditions are present:

- *The striking price of the option is higher than your original basis in the stock.* Thus, exercise would produce a profit both in the stock *and* in the option. If the striking price of the option is lower than your basis in the stock, the option premium should be higher than the difference, while also covering transaction fees in both stock and option trades.
- *The call is in or out of the money, but not deep in or out of the money.* An in-the-money call will contain a degree of intrinsic value, so stock movements will be paralleled with dollar-for-dollar price changes in option premium,

maximizing the opportunity to close the call at a profit with relatively minor stock price movement.

If the call is out of the money, all of the premium represents time value. As long as the stock's market value stays at or below the call's striking price, it will expire worthless. In the alternative, you can wait for time value to decline enough to close out the position at a profit.

- *There is enough time remaining until expiration (but not more than six months) so that most of the premium is time value.* Even with minimal or no price movement in the stock, time value evaporates by expiration. As an option writer, you are compensated by being exposed to risk for a longer period, through higher time value.

  You might not want to be locked into a striking price for too long, though, and the identification of six months as a cutoff is arbitrary. The point is that the longer the time until expiration, the higher the time value; and that time value tends to fall most rapidly during the final two to three months. As an alternative, you can employ longer-term long-term equity anticipation security (LEAPS) options, accepting the extended exposure for higher time value premium.

- *Premium is high enough to justify the risk.* You will be locked in until expiration unless you later close the short option position with an offsetting purchase. In that sense, you risk price increases in the underlying stock and corresponding lost opportunity.

Example

Ideal Circumstances: You own 100 shares of stock that you bought at $53 per share. Current market value is $57. You write a 55 call with five months to go until expiration that has a premium of 6. The circumstances are ideal. Striking price is two points higher than your basis in the stock; the call is two points in the money, so the options premium value will be responsive to price changes in the stock; two-thirds of current option premium is time value; expiration takes place in less than six months; and the premium is $600, a rich level considering your basis in the stock. It is equal to 11.3 percent of your original stock investment, an exceptional return ($600 ÷ $5,300).

In this example, you would earn a substantial return whether the option is exercised or expires worthless. If the stock's market value falls, the $600 call premium provides significant downside protection, discounting your basis to $47 per share. A worst-case analysis shows that if the stock's market value fell to $47 per share and the option then expired worthless, the net result would be breakeven.

SELECTING STOCKS FOR CALL WRITING

If you pick stocks based primarily on the potential yield to be gained from writing calls, it is a mistake—assuming you are a moderate or conservative investor. While a larger call premium discounts the stock's basis, it is not enough of a reason to buy shares. The best-yielding call premium most often is available on the highest-risk, most volatile stocks. So if you apply the sole criterion of premium yield to stock selection, you also accept far greater risks in your stock portfolio. Such a strategy could easily result in a portfolio of stocks with paper loss positions—all capital is committed in the purchase of overvalued stocks—and you would then have to wait out a reversal in market value.

Key Point

Using high-volatility stocks as a vehicle for producing current income from call writing is an appropriate strategy—as long as you accept the higher than average risks that go along with this strategy.

Example

Judging the Return: You decide to buy stock based on the relationship between current call premium and the price of the stock. You have only $4,000 to invest, so you limit your review to stocks selling at $40 per share or less. Your objective is to locate stocks on which call premium is at least 10 percent of current market value of the stock, with calls at the money or out of the money. You prepare a chart summarizing available stocks and options:

Current Value	Call Premium
$36	$3
28	3.50
25	1
39	4
27	1.75

You eliminate the first, third, and last choices because their call premiums are under 10 percent, and decide to buy the second stock on the list. It is selling at $28 per share and its call premium is 3.50, a yield of 12.5 percent. This is the highest yield available from the list. On the surface, this study and conclusion appear reasonable. The selection of the call premium discounts the stock's basis by 12.5 percent. However, there are a number of problems in this approach. Most significant is the fact that no distinction is made among the stocks other than call price and yield. The selected issue was not judged on its individual fundamental or technical merits. Also, by limiting the selection to stocks selling at $40 per share or lower, the range of potential choices is too restricted. It may be that with only $4,000 available, you would do better to select a stock on its own merits and wait until you are able to build up your portfolio.

The method in the preceding case also failed to consider time until expiration. You receive higher premiums when expiration dates are further away, in exchange for which you lock in your position for more time—meaning more change in the underlying stock's market value will be possible. Another flaw is that these calls were not judged in regard to the distance between striking price and current market value of the stock. The yield, by itself, is a misleading method for selecting options.

Key Point

Picking options based on yield alone is a popular but flawed method. It fails to recognize far more important considerations, such as the quality of the underlying stock, time until expiration, and the point distance between current market value and striking price. All of these variables affect the comparison.

Covered call writing is a conservative strategy, assuming that you first understand how to pick high-quality stocks. First and foremost should be a stock's investment value, meaning that option yield should not be the primary factor in the selection of stocks in your portfolio. On the contrary, if you are led by the attractiveness of option premium levels, you are likely to pick highly volatile stocks. If you first analyze the stock for investment value, timeliness, and safety, the option value may then be brought into the picture as an additional method for selecting among otherwise viable investment candidates.

Benefiting from Price Appreciation

You will profit from covered call writing when the underlying stock's current market value is higher than the price you paid for the stock. In that case, you protect your position against a price decline and also lock in a profit in the event of exercise.

Example

Price Appreciation: You bought 100 shares of stock last year when the value was $27 per share. Today, the stock is worth $38.

In this case, you can afford to write calls with striking prices above your original basis, even if they are in the money; or you can write out-of-the-money calls as long as time value is high enough. Remembering that your original cost was $27 per share, you have at least four choices in methods for writing covered calls:

1. *Write a call with a striking price of 25.* The premium will include 13 points of intrinsic value plus time value, which will be higher for longer-out calls. If the call is exercised, you lose two points in the stock, but gain 13 points in the call, for an overall profit of $1,100. If the stock's market value falls before exercise, or when time value disappears, you can cancel with a purchase and profit on the option trade, which frees you up to write another call. Any decline in stock market value is offset dollar for dollar by call profit in this case. The change in capital gain status and consequent tax liability on the stock should also be factored into this calculation.

2. *Write a call with a striking price of 30.* In this case, intrinsic value is 8 points, and you can apply the same strategies as in method number 1. However, because your position is not as deep in the money, chances for early exercise are reduced somewhat; in the event of exercise, you would keep the entire option premium, plus gaining $300 in profit on the stock.

3. *Write a call with a striking price of 35.* With only three points in the money, chances for early exercise are considerably lower than in the first two cases. Any decline in the stock's market value will be matched point for point by a decline in the call's intrinsic value, protecting your stock investment position. Because this call's striking price is close to current market value, there may be more time value than in the other alternatives.

4. *Write a call with a striking price of 40 or 45.* Since both of these are out of the money, the entire premium represents time value. The premium level will be lower since there is no intrinsic value; but the strategy provides you with three distinct advantages. First, it will be easier for you to cancel this position at a profit, because time value will decline even if the stock's market value rises. Second, if the option is eventually exercised, you will gain a profit in the option *and* in the stock. Third, your long-term capital gain status in the stock will not be lost, because the call is out of the money.

If you own stock with an appreciated market value, you face a dilemma that every stockholder has to resolve. If you sell and take a profit now, that is a sure thing, but you lose out in the event that further profits could also be earned by keeping those shares. You also face the risk of a decline in market value, meaning some of today's appreciated value will be lost. As a long-term investor, you may be less concerned with short-term price changes; however, anyone would like to protect paper profits.

Covered call writing is the best way to maximize your profits while providing downside protection. As long as your call is in the money, every point lost in the stock is matched by a lost point in the call; a paper loss in the stock is replaced with profits in the call position. The time value premium is potentially all profit, since it will disappear even if the stock's market value goes up, an important point that too many options traders overlook (especially buyers). When your basis is far below striking price of the call, you lock in a capital gain in the event of exercise.

Key Point

Time value declines over time, even when the stock's market value goes up. This is a problem for buyers, but a great advantage for sellers.

Example

Discounted Basis: You bought 100 shares of stock several years ago at $28 per share. Today a share is worth $45. You sell a 45 call with four months to go until expiration.

> The premium was 4, all of which is time value. This discounts your original basis down to $24. If the stock were to fall four points or less, the call premium protects the paper profit based on the current stock price. If the market value rises and the call is exercised, your shares would be called away at $45 per share, a profit of $2,100 ($1,700 on the stock plus $400 on the call).

In this example, you gain two levels of downside protection. First, the original basis is protected to the extent of the call premium; second, paper profits in the current market value also gain downside protection. When stock has appreciated beyond its original cost, it makes sense to protect current value levels, and call writing is a sensible alternative to selling shares you would not otherwise want to give up. You would probably view a decline in market value as a loss off the stock's high, even when the current stock price remains above your original cost. Call writing solves that dilemma.

AVERAGING YOUR COST

You increase your profit potential with call writing using a strategy in which you *average up*. When the price of stock has risen since your purchase date, this strategy allows you to sell in-the-money calls when the average basis in that stock is always lower than the average price you paid.

average up

a strategy
involving the
purchase of
stock when its
market value is
increasing. The
average cost of
shares bought
in this manner
is consistently
lower than
current market
value, enabling
covered call
writers to sell
calls in the
money when the
basis is below
the striking
price.

If you buy 100 shares and the market value increases, buying another 100 shares reduces your overall cost so that your basis is lower than current market value. The effect of averaging up is summarized by examples in Table 10.1.

Table 10.1 Averaging Up

Date	Shares Purchased	Price per Share	Average Price
January 10	100	$26	$26
February 10	100	28	27
March 10	100	30	28
April 10	100	30	28.50
May 10	100	31	29
June 10	100	32	29.50

How does averaging up help you as a call writer? When you write calls on several-hundred-share lots of stock, you are concerned about the possibility of falling stock prices. While price decline means you will profit from writing calls, it also means your stock loses value. Covered call writing provides downside protection, but that is limited; if price decline extends beyond the discounted basis of the stock, then you have a problem. The more shares you own of a single stock, the higher this risk. For example, if you are thinking about buying 600 shares of stock, you can take two approaches. You can either buy 600 shares at today's price or you can buy 100 shares and wait to see how market values change, buying additional lots in the future. The latter approach means you will pay higher transaction costs, but it could also protect your stock's overall market value. By averaging your investment basis, you spread your risk.

Example

A Law of Averages: You buy 100 shares on the 10th of each month, beginning in January. The price of the stock changes over six months so that by June 10, your average basis is $29.50.

This example, as illustrated in Table 10.1, allows you to reduce stock investment risk. The average price is always lower than current market value as long as the stock's price continues moving in an upward trend. Buying 600 shares at the beginning would have produced greater profits. But how do you know in advance that the stock's market value will rise?

Averaging up is a smart alternative to placing all of your capital at risk in one move. The benefits to this approach are shown in Figure 10.1.

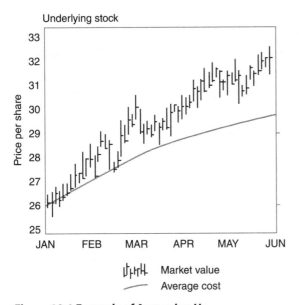

average down

a strategy involving the purchase of stock when its market value is decreasing. The average cost of shares bought in this manner is consistently higher than current market value, so a portion of the paper loss on declining stock value is absorbed, enabling covered call writers to sell calls and profit even when the stock's market value has declined.

Figure 10.1 Example of Averaging Up

By acquiring 600 shares over time, you can also write six calls. Because your average basis at the end of the period is $29.50 and current market value is $32 per share, you can sell calls with a striking price of 30 and win in two ways:

1. When the average price of the stock is lower than the striking price of the call, you will gain a profit in the event of exercise.
2. When the call is in the money, movement in the stock's price is matched by movement in the call's intrinsic value.

What happens, though, if the stock's market value falls? You also reduce your risks in writing calls if you *average down* over time. An example of this strategy is summarized in Table 10.2.

Table 10.2 Averaging Down

Date	Shares Purchased	Price per Share	Average Price
July 10	100	$32	$32
August 10	100	31	31.50
September 10	100	30	31
October 10	100	30	30.75
November 10	100	27	30
December 10	100	24	29

When a stock's market value falls, selling calls may no longer be profitable; you may need to wait for the stock's price to rebound. This does not mean that selling calls on currently owned stock is a bad idea; a decline would affect portfolio value regardless of whether you wrote calls. In fact, if you do write calls, you discount the basis of stock, mitigating the effect of a decline in market price of stock. A decline that is only temporary has to be waited out because it makes no sense to set up a losing situation. You should never sell covered calls if exercise would produce an overall loss.

Key Point

When the stock's market value declines, selling covered calls is less likely to produce profits. Never write calls when exercise will produce a net loss.

In this situation, selling calls out of the money may also fail to produce the premium level needed to justify the strategy. When stock has lost value, wait for its price to recover; meanwhile, if you continue to believe the stock is a worthwhile long-term hold, acquire more shares through averaging down.

Example

Reducing the Basis: You buy 100 shares of stock each month, beginning on July 10, when market value is $32 per share. By December, after periodic price movement, the current market value has fallen to $24 per share. Average cost per share is $29.

Your average cost is always higher than current market value in this illustration using the averaging down technique, but not as high as it would have been if you had bought 600 shares in the beginning. The dramatic difference made through averaging down is summarized in Figure 10.2.

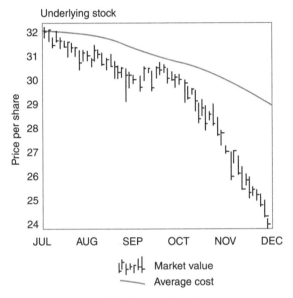

Figure 10.2 Example of Averaging Down

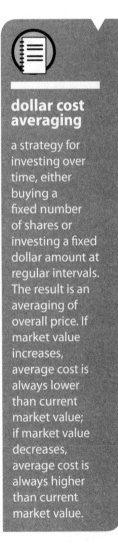

dollar cost averaging

a strategy for investing over time, either buying a fixed number of shares or investing a fixed dollar amount at regular intervals. The result is an averaging of overall price. If market value increases, average cost is always lower than current market value; if market value decreases, average cost is always higher than current market value.

When you own 600 shares, you can write up to six covered calls. In the preceding example, average basis is $29 per share. By writing calls with a striking price of 30, you gain one point of capital gain on the total of 600 shares in the event of exercise. This demonstrates how averaging down can be beneficial to call writers in the event that the stock's market value falls.

Averaging up and down are important tools that help you to mitigate the effects of quickly changing stock prices. In a fast-moving market, price changes represent a problem to the call writer, since locked-in positions cannot be sold without exposing yourself to greater risks in the short call position. Both techniques are forms of *dollar cost averaging*. Regardless of price movement, averaging protects capital. A variation of dollar cost averaging is the investment of a fixed dollar amount over time, regardless of per-share value. This is a popular method for buying mutual fund shares. However, in the stock market, direct purchase of stock makes more sense when buying in round lot increments.

By averaging out the cost of stock, you reduce exposure to loss in paper value of the entire investment. For the purpose of combining stock and option strategies, owning several hundred shares is a significant advantage over owning only 100 shares. Transaction costs involving multiple option contracts are reduced; in addition, owning more shares enables you to use many more strategies involving options. For example, if you begin by selling one call, you can avoid exercise by rolling up and increasing the number of calls sold. This provides you with more premium income as well as avoiding exercise, even when the stock's market value is rising. By increasing the number of options sold with each subsequent roll-up, you can increase profits over time. The technique is difficult, if not impossible, when you own only 100 shares of stock.

ANALYZING STOCKS

Stock selection is the starting point for covered call writing. Options are valued based on market value of the stock in comparison to striking price and expiration date of the option. So options do not contain any fundamental or technical features of their own.

Key Point

Don't look for fundamental or technical indicators in options as the starting point; instead, study the attributes of the underlying stock.

Avoid the mistake of failing to question whether the particular stock is a good match for you, given your risk tolerance level, long-term investing goals, and available capital. Options traders are especially vulnerable to the temptation to buy stocks for the wrong reason—namely, to take advantage of high-priced option opportunities.

Risks are unavoidable attributes of investing. To spot excessive risks, follow these general rules of thumb:

- *If the information provided by the company is too complicated to understand, you should not invest.* In the past, some of the explanations provided by management or disclosed in footnotes were so obscure that they could not be understood even by expert analysts. This is a danger sign.
- *If a stock continues to rise beyond reasonable expectations, it could be a sign of trouble.* It is rarely a good idea to buy shares

in a company just because the stock's price has risen to impressive levels. Are those levels justified by earnings?

- *You need to apply tests that look beyond personal recommendations, rosy estimates of future earnings, and other suspicious indicators.* Recommendations coming from analysts, stockbrokers, friends and relatives, and anyone else should be reviewed with great suspicion. You are better off investigating companies on your own, remembering that free advice may be more expensive than the kind you pay for.

- *Methods for valuing companies have to go beyond the traditional—and overly optimistic—tests so common in the market.* Question traditional assumptions and methods for picking companies. Study ratios and trends in accounts receivable, bad debt reserves, inventory levels, current and long-term liabilities, and capital assets.

- *Intelligent analysis has to be based on valuing companies rather than identifying target price and earnings levels.* You might be comfortable with short-term forecasting at the expense of longer-term analysis, which can be a problem. Analysts pick target trading ranges or prices for stocks as well as earnings per share, based on anything but fundamental information. Instead of predicting price-related value in the next three months, analysts should be studying and reporting on the value of companies over the next five to 10 years.

Standard & Poor's (S&P) has changed its method for valuing companies, and its revised definition of *core earnings* is helpful in getting around many of the creative methods used in the past to inflate earnings and mislead investors. The S&P definition of core earnings is "the after-tax earnings generated from a corporation's principal business."

core earnings

as defined by Standard & Poor's, the after-tax earnings generated from a corporation's principal business.

Key Point

Calculating core earnings does not mean that noncore line items disappear; but in calculating long-term trends, *only* core earnings should be considered. The noncore items are one-time occurrences and are not relevant to your fundamental trend.

pro forma earnings

"as a matter of form" (Latin), a company's earnings based on estimates or forecasts with hypothetical numbers in place of known or actual revenues, costs, or earnings.

Under this definition, many items are excluded from earnings, including nonrecurring gain or loss from the sale of capital assets, *pro forma earnings* such as gains on pension investments, and fees related to mergers and acquisitions. In the past, the inclusion of these items inflated reported profits, so that the market had unrealistic and inaccurate ideas of a company's operating results.

The definition includes many expenses and costs that have been excluded or capitalized in the past, such as restructuring charges, write-down of amortizable operating assets, pension costs, and purchased research-and-development costs. One of the most substantial and glaring flaws of the past has been leaving out employee stock option expense, which can be a huge number; but that flaw is gradually changing as many corporations have begun expensing stock options granted each year. As long as corporations left these and similar items out of the picture, stockholders were given a very unrealistic view of operations.

Valuable Resource

Standard & Poor's provides many useful articles and reports concerning core earnings. Check **www.standardandpoors .com** and then search "core earnings" to find a current list of articles.

The move by S&P to arrive at a standardized definition of the real earnings number is a positive trend. It enables like-kind comparisons between many different corporations, without the very real concern for inconsistent treatment and interpretation of revenues or costs and expenses. The S&P definition makes more sense than the more widely used earnings before interest, taxes, depreciation, and amortization (EBITDA). EBITDA was originally intended to serve as a measurement of cash flow or cash-based earnings for a company; however, this measurement is flawed.

Under EBITDA, no provision is included to account for purchasing of capital assets or paying down debts. Rather than a clarifying calculation, EBITDA has been used more as a way to make things appear better than they are. For example, when accounts receivable levels are rising, EBITDA does not make a distinction between cash sales and credit sales—an area where revenues have been exaggerated in some cases and where it is all too easy to alter the true numbers to inflate earnings.

Key Point

EBITDA, a well-intended calculation, has been widely misused to distort the numbers. For this reason, it should be rejected as a formula in your analytical study of a company.

As a starting point in the analysis of corporate reports, identifying core earnings helps you to analyze many different companies on a truly comparative basis. Going beyond that, you also need to quantify what analysts call the quality of earnings. While this term has many definitions, it is supposed to mean earnings that are reliable and true, as opposed to those that are overly optimistic or inflated. For example, if a company reports income based on accounts receivable that might never be collected, that does not represent good quality of earnings. The definition should include revenues that are likely to be collected and not created out of accruals, acquisitions, or accounting tricks.

In addition to the importance of selectively identifying companies based on quality of earnings, make use of specific fundamental tests. Fundamental analysis—the study of financial information, management, competitive position within a sector, and dividend history, for example—provides you with comparative analysis of value, safety, stability, and the potential for growth in the stock's long-term value. Financial and economic information, corporate management, sector and competitive position, and other indicators involving profit and loss are all part of fundamental analysis. The fundamentalist studies a corporation's balance sheet and income statement to judge a stock's long-term prospects as an investment. Other economic indicators may influence your decision about whether to invest.

The fundamentals should be reliable. If we cannot rely on what is being reported, what good is any form of analysis? Any study involving the fundamentals has to involve analysis on two levels. The traditional level includes trend analysis, for the purpose of identifying changes in financial strength and competitive position. Second is an equally important study of financial ratios, for the purpose of ensuring that a company is not artificially inflating earnings in order to deceive investors.

Valuable Resource
A more detailed analysis and comparison to GAAP standards of earnings valuation is provided by Investopedia: **www .investopedia.com/terms/e/ebitda.asp#axzz1pfPZASFG**.

The fundamental analyst believes in the numbers. However, part of a scientific analysis has to include verification of the core data as a starting point. The fundamental analyst has to be able not only to interpret the information, but also to use some basic forensic accounting skills to make sure the numbers are real. Those skills include a study of the basic ratios in a search for suspicious or questionable changes. If such changes are discovered and not adequately explained, that discovery is a warning that something could be wrong.

The technician will be less interested in the forensic aspects of current or past information. Technical analysis involves a forward-looking study relating almost exclusively to the price of the stock, market forces affecting that price, and anticipation of changes based on supply and demand, market perception, and trading ranges. The technician uses financial data only to the extent that it affects a current price trend, believing that this trend provides the key to anticipating the future price movement of the stock. Market analysts believe that price change is random, especially short-term price movement; but some technicians, notably the *chartist*, prefer to believe that patterns of price movement can be used to predict the direction of change in the stock's price.

The fundamental approach is based on the assumption that short-term price movement is entirely random and that long-term value is best identified through a thorough study of a corporation's financial status. The technical approach relies on patterns in price of the stock and other price-related indicators associated more with the market's perception of value and less with financial information. Obviously, a current report on the corporation's net income will affect the stock's market price, at least temporarily, and technicians acknowledge this. However, their primary interest is in studying pricing trends.

Both approaches have value, so it makes sense to apply fundamental and technical analysis in your analytical program. You monitor the market to make the four important decisions: buy, hold, sell, or stay away. Analysis in all of its forms is a tool for decision making, and no analysis provides insights that dictate decisions exclusively. Common sense and judgment based on experience are the extra edge that you can bring to your investment decisions. Successful investing is the result of being right more often than being wrong.

chartist

a trader who relies on analysis and interpretation of price patterns found on charts, and who also monitors volume, momentum, and reversals to time trade entry and exit.

Key Point

There are no formulas that will make you right all of the time. Investing success comes from applying good judgment, increasing your chances of being right about market decisions.

Never overlook the need to continuously track your stocks. Call writers may be inclined to ignore signals relating to the stock when, if they were not involved with writing options, they might tend to watch their portfolios more diligently. Call writers are preoccupied with other matters: movement in the stock's price (but only insofar as it affects their option positions), chances of exercise and how to avoid or defer it, opportunities to roll forward, and other matters concerning immediate strategies. As important as all of these matters are for call writers, they do not address the important questions that every stockholder needs to ask continuously: Should I keep the stock or sell it? Should I buy more shares? What changes have occurred that could also change my opinion of this stock?

The time will come when, as a call writer, you will want to close an open call position and sell the stock. For example, if you own 100 shares of stock on which you have written several calls over many months or years, when should you sell the stock and get out? For a variety of reasons, you might conclude that the stock is not going to hold its value into the future as you once believed. Even if you buy stocks for the long term, you may need to rethink your positions through constant evaluation, regardless of whether you write calls. It would be a mistake to continue holding stock because it represents a good candidate for covered call selling when in fact that stock no longer makes the grade based on the analytical tests that you use to pick stocks as a starting point.

Fundamental Tests

A number of fundamental indicators are useful in deciding when to buy or sell stock; these tests should always override the attributes in the options. Remember, options are always related to stock valuation, and trying to make a profit through options on stocks that are not worthwhile investments is a losing strategy. A worthwhile investment has to be defined as one containing fundamental strengths: revenues and earnings, dividend history, and capitalization.

One indicator that enjoys widespread popularity is the *price/earnings ratio* (P/E ratio). This is a measurement of current value that utilizes both fundamental and technical information. The technical side (price of a share of stock) is divided by the fundamental side (*earnings per share, or EPS* of common stock) to arrive at P/E.

price/ earnings ratio

an indicator combining a technical (price) and a fundamental (earnings) value, to develop a multiple. The ratio, in which price per share is divided by earnings per share, is equal to the number of years of earnings reflected in the current stock price.

Example

Calculating the P/E: A company's stock recently sold at $35 per share. Its latest annual income statement showed $220 million in profit; the company had 35 million shares outstanding. That works out to net earnings of $6.29 per share: $220 million ÷ 35 million = $6.29. The P/E ratio is:

$$\$35 \div \$6.29 = 5.6$$

A Second Calculation: A company earned $95 million and has 40 million shares outstanding, so its earnings per share is $2.38. The stock sells at $28 per share. The P/E is calculated as:

$$\$28 \div \$2.38 = 11.8$$

earnings per share (EPS)

total earnings for the year, divided by the average number of outstanding shares of common stock.

The P/E ratio is a relative indicator of what the market believes about the particular stock. It reflects the current point of view about the company's prospects for future earnings. As a general observation, a lower P/E ratio means your risks are lower. However, any ratio is useful only when it is studied in comparative form. This means not only that a company's P/E ratio may be tracked and observed over time, but also that comparisons between different companies can be instructive, especially if they are otherwise similar (in the same sector or having same product profile, for instance). In the preceding examples, the first company's 5.6 P/E would be considered a less risky investment than the second, whose P/E is 11.8. However, the P/E ratio is not always a fair indicator of a stock's risk level, nor of its potential for future profits, for at least six reasons:

1. *Financial statements may themselves be distorted.* A company's financial statement may be far more complex than it first appears, in terms of what it includes and what it leaves out. Conventional rules for reporting revenues, costs, expenses, and earnings may not convey the whole picture, and a more in-depth analysis of core earnings is an important step to take.

2. *The financial statement might be unreliable for comparative purposes.* Companies and their auditors have considerable leeway in how they report income, costs, and expenses, even within the rules. This makes valid comparison between different companies problematical.

3. *The number of shares outstanding might have changed.* Because shares outstanding is part of the P/E ratio equation, its comparative value can be affected when the number of shares changes from one year to another.

4. *The ratio becomes inaccurate as earnings reports go out of date.* If the latest earnings report of the company was issued last week, then the P/E ratio is based on recent information. However, if that report was published three months ago, then the P/E is also outdated.

5. *The P/E itself involves dissimilar forms of information.* The P/E ratio compares a stock's price—a technical value based on perceptions about current and future value—with earnings, a figure that is historical and fundamental in nature. This raises the question about whether a purely technical matter such as market price can even be compared to a purely historical and fundamental matter such as earnings, or how much weight this indicator should be given in evaluating a stock.

6. *Perceptions about P/E ratio are inconsistent.* This indicator is widely used and accepted as a means for evaluating and comparing stocks. However, not everyone agrees about how to interpret the P/E itself.

How should you use the P/E ratio? It is a valuable indicator for measuring market perception about the value of a stock, especially if you are tracking the P/E ratio for a single stock and watching how it changes over time. Comparing P/E between two different stocks may be more of a problem in terms of reliability. Companies in different industries, for example, may have widely different norms for judging profits. In one industry, a 3 percent or 4 percent return on sales might be considered average, and in another an 8 percent return is expected. So comparing P/E ratios between companies with dissimilar profit expectations is inaccurate.

The proper use of P/E can be based on comparisons between companies. Remember, the P/E represents a *multiple* that price resides above annual earnings. So when the P/E is at 10, that means current price is 10 times annual earnings per share. A P/E between 10 and 20 is usually considered reasonable by most investors' standards. But when the P/E rises to 50 or 60 (or higher), it is clear that the current price has become unrealistic.

The P/E can provide useful information as long as you also recognize its limitations. A more practical and tangible indicator is *dividend yield.* This is expressed as percentage of the share price. As the stock's market price changes, so does the yield. Compare (assuming a $3.50 per share dividend):

$$\$3.50 \div \$65 \text{ per share} = 5.4\%$$
$$\$3.50 \div \$55 \text{ per share} = 6.4\%$$
$$\$3.50 \div \$45 \text{ per share} = 6.4\%$$

A larger dividend yield could reflect a buying opportunity at the moment. That yield, added to capital gains as well as returns from selling covered calls, could add up to a very healthy overall return. Like comparisons between P/E ratios, the dividend yield is a useful indicator for narrowing the field when you are choosing stocks for investment.

A corporation's profitability is another important test. Long-term price appreciation occurs as the result of the corporation's ability to generate profits year after year. Short-term stock price changes are less significant when you are thinking about long-term growth potential of the stock, and for that, you want to compare *profit margin* from one company to another. This is the most popular system for judging a company's performance. It is computed by dividing the dollar amount of net profit by the dollar amount of gross sales. The result is expressed as a percentage.

The profit margin, as useful as it is for comparative purposes between companies and for year-to-year analysis, often is not fully understood by people invested in the market. As a consequence, many market analysts

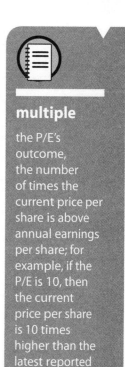

multiple

the P/E's outcome, the number of times the current price per share is above annual earnings per share; for example, if the P/E is 10, then the current price per share is 10 times higher than the latest reported earnings per share.

dividend yield

dividends paid per share of common stock, expressed as a percentage computed by dividing dividend paid per share by the current market value of the stock.

profit margin

the percentage of profit, also called net return; it is the percentage arrived at by dividing the net profit by total revenue.

total capitalization

the combination of long-term debt (debt capital) and stockholders' equity (equity capital), which in combination represent the financing of corporate operations and long-term growth.

as well as investors develop unrealistic expectations about profit margin. Two points worth remembering:

1. *An acceptable level of profit varies among industries.* One industry may experience lower or higher average profit margin than another. This makes it impractical to arrive at a singular standard for measuring profitability; the unique aspects of each sector should be used to differentiate between corporations. Comparisons should be restricted to those between corporations in the same sector.

2. *It is not realistic to expect that a particular year's profit margin should always exceed that gained in the previous year.* Once a corporation reaches what is considered an acceptable and realistic profit margin, it is unrealistic to expect it to continuously grow in terms of higher percentage returns.

Another very important fundamental indicator is the test of *total capitalization.* Corporations pay for operations through equity (stock) and debt (bonds and notes). Stockholders are compensated through dividends and capital gains, whereas bondholders are paid interest and, eventually, get their entire investment repaid. An important point for stockholders to remember is that as debt capitalization increases, a growing portion of operating profit has to be paid out in interest. That means that, in turn, there remains less profit available for dividends. The *debt ratio* tracks long-term debt as a percentage of total capitalization. (This indicator may also be referred to as the debt-equity ratio or the debt-to-equity ratio.) If the debt portion of capitalization increases steadily over time, stockholders lose out as their dividend income is eroded. A secondary consequence is the erosion of market price resulting from ever-growing reliance on debt capitalization.

These examples of fundamental indicators are important, but they do not provide the entire picture. No single indicator should ever be used as the sole means for deciding what actions to take in the market. Fundamental analysis should be comprehensive. You can employ combinations of information, including a thorough study of all of the tests that reveal trends to you. They may confirm a previous opinion, or they may change your mind. Either way, the purpose of using the fundamentals is to gather information and then to act upon that information.

You should be able to judge a company based on its fundamentals by studying 10 years' history of P/E ratio ranges, earnings per share, dividend yield, profit margin, total capitalization, and debt ratio. With these six tests, you have a good grip on the company's financial strength and profitability.

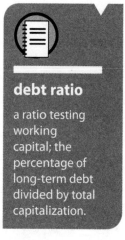

debt ratio

a ratio testing working capital; the percentage of long-term debt divided by total capitalization.

Valuable Resource
You can find 10 years' history for most listed companies by referring to the *S&P Stock Reports*. Some online brokerage services provide this valuable service free of charge. For example, Charles Schwab & Company (**www.schwab.com**) allows investors to open free accounts, and offers the *S&P Stock Reports* and other analytical reports, all free of charge.

Technical Tests

Using a combination of fundamental and technical tests helps you to review a stock from different points of view. While the fundamentals help you to gain insights into a company's overall financial and capital strength, technical indicators help you to judge market perception. The fundamentals look back at a company's history to estimate the future; technical indicators are used to forecast the future based on current market information.

Price—the primary technical indicator—is the most popular measurement used by technicians. It is an easy value to find, widely reported in the financial press and online. And while the short-term price movement of a stock is not valuable as a long-term indicator, it is of utmost importance to every options trader.

Key Point
Long-term value of stocks is inconsistent with valuation methods for options, which are by nature short-term. You need to track and monitor both.

Often overlooked in this analysis is the study of volume in a stock. You may apply volume tests to the market as a whole; they can also be applied to individual stocks. An increase in volume indicates increased market interest in the stock. High volume can have two opposite conclusions, which will be determined by the direction that the stock's price is moving on a particular day. You can track changes in volume and price in the financial press or on the Internet. Charting is widely available and free on many sites. The analysis of price and volume together improves your insight into the way that a stock acts in the market. You need to assess each stock based on historical price and volume patterns, as well as overall volatility in the stock's market price.

support level

the lowest level in a stock's current trading range, representing the lowest price at which sellers are willing to sell.

Valuable Resource
Free charts of stock price and volume are available on dozens of sites, free of charge. Check these websites for a sampling:

Investor Guide	**http://investorguide.com**
StockMaster	**www.stockmaster.com**
Financial Times	**http://ft.com**

Among the things to watch for on the technical side is a stock's *support level*, which is the lowest likely price level, given current conditions. On the other side of the chart is the *resistance level*, the highest price at which a stock is likely to trade under current conditions. The concepts of support and resistance are not only keys to the technical approach to studying stock price movement; they also are revealing because they indicate a stock's *relative volatility*. The wider the range between support and resistance, the more volatile a stock; and, of course, the narrower that trading range, the more stable the stock. So a stock with a wider-than-average trading range would contain higher relative volatility. This measurement is especially instructive when comparing stocks in the same sector or stocks with options priced at similar levels. Even when not judging relative volatility, the visualization of a stock's

resistance level

the highest level in a stock's current trading range, representing the highest price at which buyers are willing to buy.

trading pattern can help to identify a stock's overall volatility over time. The level of volatility is the best method for determining a stock's market risk.

The price range in between support and resistance price levels is called the trading range. Even when a stock's price is moving in an upward or downward direction, the trading range may remain unchanged. For example, a particular stock might consistently trade within a 15-point trading range, although the longer-term trend is upward. When price changes occur along with significant changes in the trading range, a related change in option premium is likely to occur at the same time.

The stock price is considered stable as long as it remains within the established trading range. When the price does move beyond the trading range, that is called a *breakout* pattern. The essence of charting is to try to identify in advance of the breakout when it is going to occur. The chartist believes that by studying the trading patterns, it is possible to predict price movement.

The support and resistance levels as well as breakout patterns are shown in Figure 10.3. In the illustration, an initial trading range is shown at the left, with a breakout on the upside (marked with an arrow); this establishes a new trading range that is then followed with a breakout on the downside (also indicated by an arrow).

relative volatility

the tendency for a stock to follow a specific breadth of trading between resistance and support.

breakout

movement of a stock's price above resistance or below support.

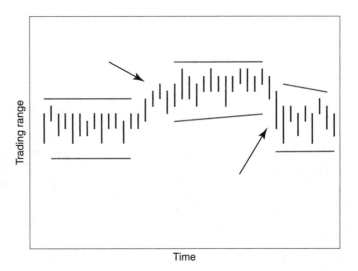

Figure 10.3 Chart Patterns

Options traders can make good use of support and resistance and other technical theories. By observing the pattern of recent trading ranges, you may better judge a stock's relative volatility. The chart reveals a pattern over time, so you can judge whether the trading range is broad or narrow; whether it is changing and, if so, to what degree; and how often previously established trading ranges have been modified by breakouts. The length of time a trading range remains unchanged is also revealing, as it helps options traders to determine a stock's tendency to react to market changes in general, or to trade with its own timing pattern.

Accompanying an in-depth review of volatility, a sound analysis of a stock may include a further study of the high and low price ranges over time. This demonstrates several things. For example, the more volatile stocks—those with broader high and low ranges—may, in fact, be volatile at the beginning of the period but not at the end, or vice versa. A simple one-year summary is not reliable in terms of today's price trend.

The stock reports in the financial press present only the 52-week high and low price ranges. Given the many possible varieties of trading patterns that can result in the same high and low summary, this information is unreliable. A more detailed study is required.

Any study in which we look at how prices have moved within a 52-week high and low range is going to be far more revealing than the more limited information about highest and lowest price levels alone. In fact, with these variations in mind, the volatility percentage is meaningless. That percentage—computed by dividing the high/low price difference by the low for the year—only provides a range distinction; it does not tell us whether a stock's trend is up, down, or flat. It also does not demonstrate price spikes.

Example

Side-by-Side Comparisons: Five different stocks have reported 52-week trading ranges as follows:

Company	Low	High	Volatility %
Company A	82	99	21%
Company B	72	94	31%
Company C	62	86	39%
Company D	35	55	57%
Company E	175	260	49%

If you were to select the least volatile stock from among this field, the choice would seem to be Company A. But is it the least volatile stock? A more detailed analysis shows that Company A's price varied during the year from low of 82 to a high of 99, but in between moved up and down quite often. In comparison, Company B, Company C, and Company E all moved steadily upward during the year; their trading ranges were consistently upward-trending, whereas Company A started and ended the year at virtually the same price. Company D did the same; it began the year at $35 per share and ended at $37, but in between surged up to $55 and back down again.

No single fundamental or technical test can be used reliably to identify good stock candidates. The high and low ranges might represent a fair starting point for stock selection, but the analysis should explore further into the timing and attributes of the stock and its trading range. You can evaluate stocks by tracking key indicators over time, looking not only for patterns but also for the emergence of *new* pricing trends.

The problem with analysis is that it takes time. And the more time you spend on analysis, the more quickly it goes out of date. Having online charting services available free of charge makes your task much easier.

Deciding Which Tests to Apply

How do you determine which of the many fundamental and technical tests are most useful for picking stocks, tracking them, and deciding when to sell? The answer depends on your own opinion. Before deciding on one form of analysis over another, be aware of these important points:

- *Many analysts love complex formulas.* A theory that is difficult to understand and that requires a lot of mathematical ability is probably useless in the real world. Avoid the complex, recognizing that useful information also tends to be straightforward and easily comprehended.
- *You can perform your own tests—you do not need to pay for analysis.* Even though some of the accounting-related ratios can be complex and difficult to follow, the actual tests leading to decisions to buy, hold, or sell will be very basic and straightforward. The process does not have to be complicated.
- *Price has nothing to do with the fundamentals.* The price of any stock reflects the market's perception about future potential value, whereas the financial condition of that company is historical. A study of fundamentals has nothing to do with today's price.
- *The net worth of a company has nothing to do with price.* Current market value is determined through auction between buyers and sellers, and not by accountants at the company's headquarters. The actual value of the stockholders' equity in a corporation is found in the *book value* of shares of stock.
- *The past is not an infallible indicator.* When you attempt to predict price movement through studying the fundamentals, you face an elusive task, since the fundamentals do not affect short-term price movement as much as other factors do, such as perception of the market as a whole. Remember the wisdom that the stock market has no past.
- *Predictions abound, but reliable predictions do not exist.* You can get lucky and make an accurate prediction once in a while. Doing so with any consistency is far more difficult.

book value

the actual value of a company, more accurately called *book value per share*; the value of a company's capital (assets less liabilities), divided by the number of outstanding shares of stock.

You can study any number of factors, either fundamental or technical, but none will enable you to accurately predict future price movement of stocks.

- *Common sense is your best tool.* You are more likely to succeed if you employ common sense, backed up with study, analysis, and comparison. Market success without hard work is no more likely in the stock market than anywhere else.
- *Stock prices, especially in the short term, are random.* Most predictive theories acknowledge that, while long-term analysis can accurately narrow down the guesswork, short-term price movement is completely random. In the stock market, where opinion and speculation are widespread, no one can control the way that stock prices change from one day to the next.

The two major theories directing opinions about stock prices are the *random walk theory* and the *Dow Theory*. The Dow Theory contends that certain signals are confirmed independently and indicate a change in market direction. The random walk hypothesis is based on the idea that market movements are not predictable based on specific tests, and that given the presumed efficiency of the auction marketplace, there is an equal chance that future prices of stocks will rise or that they will fall. The one point that both of these theories agree on is that short-term indicators are of no value in determining whether to buy or sell in the market. For the options investor, this is an interesting observation. If short-term price movement is unpredictable, that means that stock selection has to be done on a long-term basis. However, at the same time, you have an exceptional opportunity when using options. You *know* in advance how time value premium is going to change. That

random walk theory

a belief that stock prices are entirely random and cannot be predicted.

Dow Theory

a theory based on the work of Charles Dow, that stock price movement and reversal can be predicted through a series of trends and reversal confirmation.

change occurs only due to time and is not affected by changes in the stock's market price. So while you should select long-position stocks with the long term in mind regardless of which theory you accept about how price is determined, the method used for selling short calls will involve two elements not affected by stock valuation: option premium richness (meaning time value) and the amount of time remaining until expiration.

Even though you know in advance how time value is going to change over time, the degree of time value is affected by the stock's volatility. More volatile stocks (higher-risk stocks) will tend to hold higher time value. So you will have greater profit potential due to higher time value in those cases, offset by higher market risk associated with owning the stock.

efficient market hypothesis

a belief that stock prices are reasonable and efficient, and reflect all known information about the company known to the public.

Options traders should be especially aware of the principles underlying both the random walk hypothesis and the Dow Theory, since both agree on one key point: that short-term prices cannot be accurately predicted. This idea has ramifications for options traders and, if both theories agree on that point, it probably has merit.

A third idea about market pricing supports the pricing theories expressed in the random walk hypothesis and the Dow Theory. That is the *efficient market hypothesis*. An efficient market is one in which current prices reflect all information known to the public. Thus, prices are reasonable based on perceptions about markets and the companies whose stock is listed publicly. If the efficient market hypothesis is correct, then all current prices are fair and reasonable. Again, this idea has ramifications for all options traders.

Anyone who has observed how the market works understands that the efficient market is a pure theory, because prices are not always applicable. For example, Value Line divides the stocks it studies into five groups, from the highest rated for safety and timeliness down to the lowest. The first two tiers beat market averages with consistency, proving that there is value in going through the analysis of prices, price movement, and the range of fundamentals. A reasonable approach is to believe that the market is efficient, but only to a degree. Market observers know that the public tends to overreact to news in the market. Prices rise beyond a reasonable level on good news, and decline beyond a reasonable degree on bad news. So in short-term trading, prices cannot be called efficient by any means. In fact, short-term market price movement is highly chaotic and unpredictable. The often unrealistic pricing swings present momentary opportunities for you, whether operating as a speculator or as an options trader.

Like the other two theories, the efficient market hypothesis points out both danger and opportunity for options traders. Short-term price changes cannot be predicted with any reliability whatsoever, even in the efficient market; however, the characteristics of the underlying stock can be used reliably to select a profitable portfolio. It is fair to surmise that a stock with strong fundamental and technical characteristics is not only a good long-term investment, but also a viable candidate for writing covered calls. The option buyer, however, undertakes considerable risks, remembering that none of the theories place any reliability on short-term price changes. Option buyers are speculating on the short term. Their only edge is found in the ability to locate unusual price conditions in a particular stock, and to take advantage of overbought or oversold conditions by picking and timing option purchases wisely.

Key Point

All theories agree that short-term price changes provide no useful information. This presents problems for option buyers; for option sellers, the volatility of short-term prices can inflate time value, meaning greater opportunities for profits.

APPLYING ANALYSIS TO CALLS— THE "GREEKS"

Keep the major market theories in mind when you analyze stocks, and remember that exceptionally rich option premium is not a dependable standard for stock selection. Moderate volatility in a stock's price levels may work as a positive sign for options trading, as it demonstrates investor interest. A stock that has little or no volatility is, indeed, not a hot stock, and such conditions will invariably be accompanied by very low volume, a consistently low P/E ratio, and, of course, lower option premium levels. So some short-term volatility might demonstrate not only that investor interest is high, but also that option activity and pricing will be more promising as well. As a technical test of a stock's price stability, volatility should be analyzed in terms of both short-term and long-term levels. Ideally, your stocks will contain long-term stability but relatively volatile price movement in the short term.

With the distinctions in mind between different causes and patterns of volatility, the selection of stock may be based on a comparative study of the past 12 months. First, ensure that the stocks you are considering as prospects for purchase contain approximately the same causes for their volatility. Then apply volatility as a test for identifying relative degrees of safety.

Several calculations are used by options analysts to study risk and volatility in options. These are collectively referred to as the *Greeks* because they are named after letters in the Greek alphabet. These calculations are for the most part useful for comparative purposes in options analysis. It is good to know *what* they reveal, but the calculations themselves are beyond the interests of most traders. However, if you subscribe to a service that compares options for you, then it makes perfect sense to know what the Greeks reveal.

Greeks

reference to a series of tests in option pricing and volatility, designed to predict movement in the immediate future and the momentum of price changes.

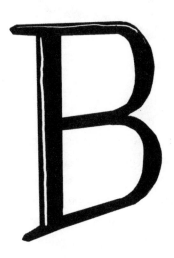

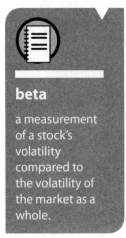

beta

a measurement of a stock's volatility compared to the volatility of the market as a whole.

Fundamental and technical tests are complemented with the use of another feature in a stock's price used to define volatility—the stock's *beta*. This is a test of relative volatility, in other words, the degree to which a stock tends to move with an entire market or index of stocks. A beta of 1 tells you that a particular stock tends to rise or fall in the same degree as the market as a whole. A beta of 0 implies that price changes of the stock tend to act independently of price changes in the broader market; and a beta of 2 indicates that a stock's price tends to overreact to market trends, often by moving to a greater degree than the market as a whole.

Because time value tends to be higher than average for high-beta stocks, premium value, like the stock's market value, is less predictable. From the call writer's point of view, exceptionally high time value that declines rapidly is a clear advantage, but it would be shortsighted to trade only in such stocks, especially if you also want stability in your stock portfolio.

delta

a comparison between price change in an option compared to price change in the underlying security.

hedge ratio

the ratio calculated by delta to determine relative price changes between the option and the underlying security.

Another interesting indicator that is helpful in selecting options is called the *delta.* When the price of the underlying stock and the premium value of the option change exactly the same number of points, the delta is 1.00. As the delta increases or decreases for an option, you are able to judge the responsiveness (volatility) of the option to the stock. This takes into consideration the distance between current market value of the stock and striking price of the call, fluctuations of time value, and changes in delta as expiration approaches. The delta provides you with the means to compare interaction between stock and option pricing for a particular stock.

The calculation of delta (the delta ratio) is a study of the relationship between the stock's price movement and value of the option. When this relationship does not move as you would expect, it indicates a change in market perception of value, probably resulting from adjustments in proximity between market price and striking price. This change is worth tracking through the delta, since it presents occasional opportunities to profit from unexpected price adjustments. The delta ratio is also called the *hedge ratio.*

Delta measures aberrations in time value. If all delta levels were the same, then overall option price movement would be formulated strictly on time and stock price changes. Because this is not the case, we also need to use some means for comparative option volatility, apart from the volatility of the underlying stock. The inclination of a typical option is to behave predictably, tending to approach a delta of 1.00 as it goes into the money and as expiration approaches. So for every point of price movement in the underlying stock, you would expect a change in option premium very close to one point when in the money. Time value tends to not be a factor when options are deep in the money. Time value is more likely to change predictably based on time until expiration. For options further away from expiration, notably those close to the striking price, delta is going to be a more important feature. In fact, the comparison of delta between options that are otherwise the same in other attributes will indicate the option-specific risks and volatility not visible in a pure study of the stock itself. Time value can and does change for longer-term options close to the money. The delta can work as a useful device for studying such options. The relative volatility of the option is the key to identifying opportunities.

Accompanying these indicators of relative volatility, you may also follow *open interest*. This is the number of open option contracts on a particular underlying stock. For example, one stock's current-month 40 calls had open interest last month of 22,000 contracts; today, only 500 contracts remain open. The number changes for several reasons. As the status of the call moves higher into the money, the number of open contracts tends to change as a result of closing sale transactions, rolling forward, or exercise. Sellers tend to buy out their positions as time value falls, and buyers tend to close out positions as intrinsic value rises. And as expiration approaches, fewer new contracts open. In addition to these factors, open interest changes when perceptions among buyers and sellers change for the stock. Unfortunately, the number of contracts does not tell you the reasons for the change, nor whether the change is being driven by buyers or by sellers.

open interest

the total of all calls and puts remaining open at the end of each trading day.

Applying the Delta

The delta of a call should be 1.00 whenever it is deep in the money. As a general rule, expect the call to parallel the price movement of the stock on a point-for-point basis, especially when closer to expiration. In some instances, a call's delta may change unexpectedly. For example, if an in-the-money call increases by three points but the stock's price rises by only two points (a delta of 1.50), the aberration represents an *increase* in time value, which rarely occurs. It may be a sign that the market perceives the option to be worth more than its previous price, relative to movement in the stock. This can be caused by any number of changes in market perception. The deeper out of the money, the lower the delta will be. Figure 10.4 summarizes movement in option premium relative to the underlying stock, with corresponding delta.

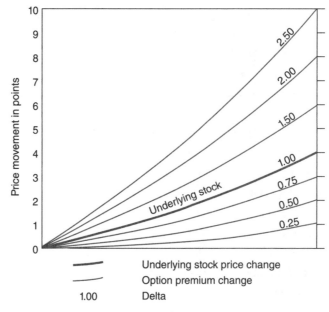

Figure 10.4 Changes in an Option's Delta

Time value is reasonably predictable in the pattern of change, given looming expiration. It does not move in a *completely* predictable manner, since perceptions about the option are changing constantly.

> **Example**
>
> **A Delta Increase:** You bought 100 shares of stock at $48 per share. During yesterday's market, the stock rose from $51 to $53, based largely on rumors of higher quarterly profits than predicted by analysts. The 60 call rose from 4 to 8, an increase of 4 points (and a delta of 2.00).

In this example, market overreaction to current news presents a call selling opportunity. Distortions in value often are momentary and require fast action. The covered call writer needs to be able to move quickly when opportunities are presented.

The same strategy can be applied when you already have an open covered call position and you are thinking of closing it. For example, suppose your call is in the money and the stock falls two points. At the same time, option premium falls by three points, for a delta of 1.50. This could be a temporary distortion, so profits can be taken immediately on the theory that the overreaction will be corrected within a short time.

The Rest of the Greeks

Beta and delta are the most popularly used and cited of the Greeks; but there are more levels of analysis as well. Another is *gamma*, which is a test of how rapidly delta moves upward or downward in relation to the price of the underlying stock.

gamma

a measurement of the speed of change in delta, relative to price movement in the underlying stock.

The gamma changes as the stock's price moves away from the option's strike price. For example, when an option moves from out of the money and goes into the money, the delta tends to increase. How quickly that occurs is where gamma comes into play. You may also consider gamma a method for measuring extrinsic value. In other words, gamma will be at its greatest level when the stock's market value is at or near the option's striking price. When options are deep in the money or deep out of the money, gamma will be close to zero.

For example, if a stock is at $39, a call with a striking price of 50 may have a delta of 0.50 and a gamma of 0.05. When the stock moves up to $40 per share, the delta is going to grow by the same degree as the gamma (0.50 plus 0.05, or 0.55). Because gamma can only be 1.00 at the most, this trend is limited and most meaningful when market value of the stock is very close to the option's striking price, which is always the most interesting price relationship where options are involved. Gamma is always expressed as a positive number, whether related to a call or a put; it is only a measurement of the delta's trend. The delta will change to the degree of the gamma. In the example of a gamma of 0.05, if the stock moves one point, delta will change by 0.05, or 5 percent of the stock change; so if the stock moves up two points, delta will increase by 0.10 (5 percent of two points), from 0.50 to 0.60. Delta moves by the percentage of the gamma.

You can use delta and gamma in combination to test the relationship between a stock and its options, and to select one company over another because of levels in these price-responsive trends. You will also observe that as expiration nears, the gamma for at-the-money options is going to increase rapidly. It is quite likely that gamma will grow at about twice the price movement of the stock, because the delta is responding to the combined forces of pending expiration and in-the-money or at-the-money price changes. In comparison, out-of-the-money options near expiration are going to have very low gamma trends; and as expiration is closer, the gamma trend confirms the ever-lower expectation that the option will move into the money.

vega
also called tau, the measurement of an option's sensitivity to volatility in the underlying security.

Another interesting Greek is the tau, better known as *vega*. This measures the relationship between an option's price and changes in the underlying stock's volatility. Whether applied to a call or a put, tau is always a positive number.

The less volatile a stock, the cheaper its options. So if and when volatility increases (especially if measured as an expansion of the stock's trading range), option values will rise as well. Defining volatility as the percentage of range off a stock's 52-week low, you can quantify vega in the same manner, on a percentage basis. This becomes very interesting because it assigns a percentage value to an option's premium, and it also places a numerical value on a stock's market risk. This is useful for comparisons between stocks and their options.

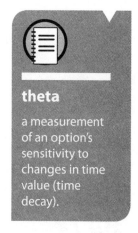

theta

a measurement of an option's sensitivity to changes in time value (time decay).

On average, stocks are expected to show around 15 percent volatility. For example, if a stock has traded between $20 and $23 per share, the three-point spread represents 15 percent volatility (3 ÷ 20 = 15 percent); as a stock's value changes, vega tracks that change.

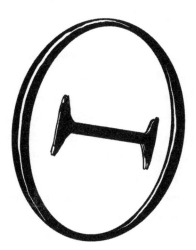

Another Greek, *theta*, reveals the strength or weakness of time value (exclusive of extrinsic value), also known as sensitivity of the price in relation to the time remaining until expiration. Many options traders consider theta the most important of the Greeks because time sensitivity defines value, notably near expiration.

Theta is valuable as a comparative study between two or more options (and their underlying stocks). Based on a stock's specific volatility, time decay may be quite rapid or fairly slow; and identifying the degree of theta characteristic of a particular stock is a valuable analytical exercise.

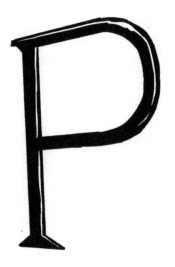

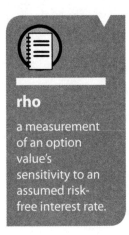

rho

a measurement
of an option
value's
sensitivity to an
assumed risk-
free interest rate.

The Greek *rho* is also a sensitivity measurement, but is far less directly involved in valuation than most other Greeks. Rho compares pricing of options to trends in interest rates, based on the theory that the higher market interest rates trend, the higher call pricing will trend. This Greek is less useful than most others, however, because it is not easy to translate long-term trends such as interest rates into action steps for fast-moving markets such as options. The general observation of rho is an oddity: As interest rates rise, call prices will follow, but put prices will tend to fall. In this regard, rho becomes an expression of market sentiment based on interest rates, with the results seen in option prices.

The Greeks are collectively an interesting series of observations concerning option trends and tendencies. All options traders are aware of changes in valuation based on the proximity issues: between striking price of options and market value of the underlying stock, and between today and expiration. The Greeks are useful for tracking the changes in all three forms of value (intrinsic, extrinsic, and time) but are also best used to make comparisons in option valuation between two different companies. Time, volatility, and chance all play roles in valuation; the Greeks are useful in observing how prices and values react to ever-changing market conditions.

ACTING ON GOOD INFORMATION

All market analysts depend on their best estimates in making decisions. You cannot time your decisions perfectly or consistently; so you have to depend on a combination of fundamental and technical indicators to provide yourself with an edge. That means that you improve your percentages, but not that you will be right every time. Base your strategy on the thorough analysis and well-thought-out selection of stocks. Pick stocks on their fundamental merits as long-term investments and not merely to provide coverage for short option positions. Also keep in mind your long-term reasons for buying the stock; keep the stock in your portfolio as long as the company's attributes remain strong. Avoid making stock-related decisions as a response to option-specific conditions. Don't take advantage of the chance to earn a short-term profit if exercise of a covered call would contradict your long-term goals.

Example

Broker or More Broke: You bought 300 shares of stock last year as a long-term investment. You have no plans to sell and, as you hoped, the market price has been inching upward consistently. Your broker is encouraging you to write calls against your shares, pointing to the potential for additional profits as well as downside protection. Your broker also observes that if exercised, you will still earn a profit. However, remembering your reasons for buying the stock, you reject the advice. Call writing is contrary to your goal in buying the stock.

Even when writing covered calls is an appropriate strategy, never overlook the need for continued monitoring of the stock. By preparing a price performance chart, you can track movement by week. A completed chart helps you to time decisions, especially for writing covered calls. If you have access to the Internet, you can also use free sites to produce price and volume charts. Three of the many sites that provide this free benefit were listed earlier in this chapter.

Track both the option and the underlying stock. If profits in one are offset by losses in the other, there is no point to a strategy except when you hedge a loss with the use of an option for insurance. By observing changes in the option and the stock, you will be able to spot opportunities and dangers as they emerge.

Example

Programmed Portfolio Losses: You bought 100 shares in each of four companies last year. Within the following months, you wrote covered calls on all four. Today, three of the four have market values below your basis, even though the overall market is higher. You add up the total of call premium, dividends, and paper capital gains and losses, and realize that if you were to close out all of your positions today, you would lose money.

This example demonstrates that stocks were poorly chosen or purchases were poorly timed. While paper losses might have been greater had you not written calls, this situation also raises questions about why a particular mix of stocks was selected. A critical review of your selection criteria might reveal that you are picking stocks based on option premium value rather than on the stocks' fundamental and technical indicators. Relatively safe stocks tend to have little options appeal, because time value is minimal in low-volatility stocks. So more volatile stocks are far more likely candidates for premium action. That does not mean they are worthwhile investments; it could mean that option profits will be offset by capital losses in your portfolio.

Perhaps the greatest risk in call writing is the tendency to buy stocks that are overly volatile because they also have higher time value premium in their options. You will do better if you look for moderate volatility as a secondary strategy. Three suggestions worth remembering:

1. *Select stocks with good growth potential* and hold them for a while without writing options. Give the stocks a chance to appreciate. This gives you much more flexibility in picking options. The combination of premium, dividends, and capital gains can be built into your strategy with ease, assuming that current market value is higher than your original cost per share.

2. *Time your decision to sell calls* on stock you already own, to maximize your potential for gains from the options.

3. *Remember the importance of patience.* You might need to wait out a market that seems to be moving too slowly. Your patience will be rewarded if you select stocks properly. Opportunity does come around eventually, but some novice call writers give in to their impatience, anxious to write calls as soon as possible. This is a mistake.

Putting Your Rules Down on Paper

Setting goals helps you to succeed in the options market. This is equally true if you buy stocks and do not write options. By defining your personal rules, you will have a better chance for success. Define several aspects of your investment plan, including:

- Long-term goals for your entire portfolio.
- Strategies you believe will help you reach those goals.
- Percentages of your portfolio that are to be placed in each type of investment.
- Definitions of risk in its many forms, and the degree of risk you are willing to assume.
- Purchase and sale levels you are willing and able to commit.
- Guidelines for review and possible modification of your goals.

Writing down your rules leads to success because it focuses your efforts. Guidelines can and should be modified as conditions change. Having self-imposed rules to follow provides you with a programmed response to evolving situations, and improves your performance and profits.

THOMSETT'S JOURNEY in ADVANCED OPTIONS

OKAY. YOU'VE CONVINCED ME. I AM CLOSING THE LAB.

WHAT WILL YOU DO NEXT?

I THINK I'LL OPEN AN ACCOUNT AND START TRADING OPTIONS.

FRAGILE

NOT SO FAST, MY NERDY FRIEND.

YOU MEAN THERE'S EVEN MORE?

PICKING $ STOCKS

YES! YOU NEED AN ACTION PLAN FOR PICKING STOCKS ON WHICH YOU WILL TRADE OPTIONS!

264

THE END!

GLOSSARY

It is better that words shall have no interpretation than an absurd one.
—*The Universal Self-Instructor*, 1883

American-style option
an option that can be exercised at any time before expiration. All equity options and some index options are American-style.

AM settlement
valuation of an index option based on the value of the index components at the opening of trading on the day of exercise or expiration.

antistraddle rules
tax regulations that remove or suspend the long-term favorable tax treatment of stock investment profits when the owner writes unqualified in-the-money covered calls.

average down
a strategy involving the purchase of stock when its market value is decreasing. The average cost of shares bought in this manner is consistently higher than current market value, so a portion of the paper loss on declining stock value is absorbed, enabling covered call writers to sell calls and profit even when the stock's market value has declined.

average up

a strategy involving the purchase of stock when its market value is increasing. The average cost of shares bought in this manner is consistently lower than current market value, enabling covered call writers to sell calls in the money when the basis is below the striking price.

bear spread

a strategy involving the purchase and sale of calls or puts that will produce maximum profits when the value of the underlying stock falls.

beta

a measurement of a stock's volatility compared to the volatility of the market as a whole.

binary option

an option based on an underlying index, which pays a fixed amount if the index is higher than a call's strike or lower than a put's strike at expiration.

book value

the actual value of a company, more accurately called *book value per share*; the value of a company's capital (assets less liabilities), divided by the number of outstanding shares of stock.

box spread

the combination of a bull spread and a bear spread, opened at the same time on the same underlying stock.

breakout

movement of a stock's price above resistance or below support.

broad-based index

an index with a large number of components and involving many different market sectors.

brokerage risks

risks of discretion exercised by brokers, whether authorized or not, and errors in order placement.

bull spread

a strategy involving the purchase and sale of calls or puts that will produce maximum profits when the value of the underlying stock rises.

butterfly spread
a strategy involving open options in one striking price range, offset by open positions at higher and lower ranges at the same time.

calendar spread
a spread involving the simultaneous purchase or sale of options on the same underlying stock, with different expirations; also called *time spread*.

calls
options providing their owners the right, but not the obligation, to purchase stock of an identified underlying security, at a fixed strike price, and on or before a fixed expiration date.

candlestick charts
technical charts for stocks summarizing a stock's daily trading range, opening and closing prices, and price direction. The candlestick chart is used in many trading systems, including swing trading.

capital gains
profits from investments, taxed the same as other income if the holding period is less than one year, and at lower rates if investments were owned for one year or more.

capitalization weighted
description of the procedure used to calculate an index value, based on current market value of each of the components in the index.

capped-style option
an option that can be exercised only during a specified period of time; if the option's value reaches the cap level prior to expiration, it is exercised automatically.

carryover capital losses
sums of capital losses from prior years that exceeded annual loss limitation levels; the annual maximum capital loss deduction is $3,000, and all losses above that level have to be carried over and applied in future tax years.

cash settlement
a method for settling exercise of an index option, in which cash is paid rather than shares of stock being bought or sold.

chartist
a trader who relies on analysis and interpretation of price patterns found on charts, and who also monitors volume, momentum, and reversals to time trade entry and exit.

collar

a spread strategy combining long stock, a covered call, and a long put, with both options out of the money. The collar limits potential gains and potential losses.

combination

any purchase or sale of options on one underlying stock, with terms that are not identical.

condor spread

a variation of the butterfly spread using different striking prices in the short positions on either side of the middle range.

confirmation

a signal providing support for another signal, reinforcing the belief that a trend is ending and about to reverse.

constructive sale

status when an investor buys and sells in separate transactions that involve substantially identical property; the holding of offsetting long and short positions may be taxed as a constructive sale even when no physical sale has occurred.

contrarian

an investor who invests opposite popular opinion in recognition of the tendency for the majority to be wrong more often than right.

core earnings

as defined by Standard & Poor's, the after-tax earnings generated from a corporation's principal business.

credit spread

any spread in which receipts from short positions are higher than premiums paid for long positions, net of transaction fees.

day trader

an individual who trades within a single day, usually closing positions before the end of the trading day and often making such trades on high volume.

debit spread

any spread in which receipts from short positions are lower than premiums paid for long positions, net of transaction fees.

debt ratio
a ratio testing working capital; the percentage of long-term debt divided by total capitalization.

delta
a comparison between price change in an option compared to price change in the underlying security.

diagonal spread
a calendar spread in which offsetting long and short positions have both different striking prices and different expiration dates.

dividend collar
a collar designed to create income from quarterly dividends, using long stock, short calls, and long puts. The strategy eliminates market risk and requires monthly entry and exit.

dividend yield
dividends paid per share of common stock, expressed as a percentage computed by dividing dividend paid per share by the current market value of the stock.

dollar cost averaging
a strategy for investing over time, either buying a fixed number of shares or investing a fixed dollar amount at regular intervals. The result is an averaging of overall price. If market value increases, average cost is always lower than current market value; if market value decreases, average cost is always higher than current market value.

Dow Theory
a theory based on the work of Charles Dow, that stock price movement and reversal can be predicted through a series of trends and reversal confirmation.

downtrend
in swing trading, a series of three or more days consisting of lower highs and lower lows.

earnings per share (EPS)
total earnings for the year, divided by the average number of outstanding shares of common stock.

efficient market hypothesis
a belief that stock prices are reasonable and efficient, and reflect all information about the company known to the public.

European-style option
an option that can be exercised only during a specified period of time immediately preceding expiration. Some index options are European-style.

exchange-traded funds (ETFs)
types of mutual funds that trade on public exchanges like stocks and consist of portfolios of predetermined, related securities known as the basket of stocks.

ex-dividend date
the date on which a stockholder is no longer stockholder of record for the purpose of earning dividends. Only those acknowledged as stockholders of record before the ex-dividend date earn the quarterly dividend.

exercise
the act of buying stock under the terms of the call option or selling stock under the terms of the put option, at the price per share specified in the option contract.

exercise cutoff time
the specific deadline for exercise of index options, imposed by brokerage firms on traders, varying by index and by class of option.

expiration
the end of an option; after expiration, every option becomes worthless. This date is the third Saturday of expiration month, and the preceding third Friday is the last trading day.

extrinsic value
the portion of an option's premium attributed to implied volatility, which combines with time value and intrinsic value to arrive at the total premium.

FLEX option
a type of option whose terms—including expiration date, striking price, and exercise terms—can be modified during the period in which a position remains open.

fundamental volatility
the tendency for a company's sales and profits to change from one period to the next, with more erratic change representing higher volatility.

futures contract

a contract to buy or sell a preestablished amount of a commodity (agricultural, energy, livestock, precious metals, or imports) or financial instrument at a set price and by or before a specific date (delivery date). Like options, futures are rarely exercised but are more likely to be closed prior to settlement or rolled forward.

GAAP

acronym for generally accepted accounting principles, the rules by which auditing firms analyze operations, and by which corporations report their financial results.

gamma

a measurement of the speed of change in delta, relative to price movement in the underlying stock.

gap

a trading pattern between days in which the second day's trading range opens above the highest price of the previous day or below the lowest price of the previous day.

Greeks

reference to a series of tests in option pricing and volatility, designed to predict movement in the immediate future and the momentum of price changes.

hedge

a strategy involving the use of one position to protect another. For example, stock is purchased in the belief it will rise in value, and a put is purchased on the same stock to protect against the risk that the stock's market value will decline.

hedge ratio

the ratio calculated by delta to determine relative price changes between the option and the underlying security.

horizontal spread

a calendar spread in which offsetting long and short positions have identical striking prices but different expiration dates.

index option

any option traded on a market index as the underlying, rather than on an individual stock.

information risk

the risk that information used to make decisions could be misleading or even wrong.

insider information

any information about a company not known to the general public, but known only to people working in the company or having nonpublic knowledge about matters that will affect a stock's price.

insurance put

alternate name of the *synthetic long call*.

intrinsic value

the portion of an option's premium equal to the points it is in the money (above a call's striking price or below a put's striking price).

iron condor

the combination of a long strangle and a short strangle on the same underlying stock. The cost is reduced due to offsetting premium payments and receipts; it is practical as long as short position exercise costs do not exceed long position profits.

long call synthetic straddle

a combination of 100 shares of short stock with two long calls at or close to the money, to create a position that acts like a call/put long straddle. If the stock price declines, the short stock position gains; if the stock price rises, the short stock position loses value but the two calls surpass the loss.

long hedge

the purchase of options as a form of insurance to protect a portfolio position in the event of a price increase; a strategy employed by investors selling stock short and needing insurance against a rise in the market value of the stock.

long put synthetic straddle

a combination of 100 shares of long stock with two long puts at or close to the money, to create a position that acts like a call/put long straddle. If the stock price rises, the long stock position gains; if the stock price declines, the stock position loses value but the two puts surpass the loss.

long straddle

the purchase of an identical number of calls and puts with the same striking prices and expiration dates, designed to produce profits in the event of price movement of the underlying stock in either direction, adequate to surpass the cost of opening the position.

long-term capital gains
profits on investments held for 12 months or more, which are taxed at a rate lower than other (ordinary) income.

lost opportunity risk
the risk that covered call writers will lose profits from increased prices in stock because they are locked in at a fixed striking price, or that margin requirements may prevent traders from being able to take advantage of other investment opportunities.

lower shadow
on a candlestick formation, the line defining the lowest extent of a day's trading range. The line extends below the opening or closing price for the day.

margin and collateral risk
the risk associated with borrowing on margin and needing to maintain collateral at the level required by law.

market value weighted
alternative term for *capitalization weighted*.

married put
alternate name of the *synthetic long call*.

modified installment collar
a collar consisting of a long-term long put and a series of short-term short calls. The put provides downside protection through its term, and the series of short calls is planned to offset the put's cost over many months, due to rapid time decay.

money spread
alternate name for the *vertical spread*.

multileg option order
placement of an order for a single commission rather than for a commission charged for each option.

multiple
The P/E's outcome, the number of times current price per share is above annual earnings per share; for example, if the P/E is 10, then current price per share is 10 times higher than the latest reported earnings per share.

mutual funds

investment programs in which money from a large pool of investors is placed under professional management. For a fee, management invests in stocks and bonds. Mutual funds may be set up to pay a sales load to salespeople, often called financial advisers; or they may be no-load, meaning investors can buy shares directly and not pay commissions.

narrow-based index

an index using a small number of components rather than a larger or broader basis for its calculations.

narrow-range day (NRD)

in a candlestick chart, a trading day with an exceptionally small trading range.

net investment income

an individual's taxable income from interest, dividends, and capital gains, distinguished from ordinary income by tax rate or potential tax exclusions.

offsetting position

in tax law, a straddle that creates a substantial diminution of risk; when positions are classified as offsetting, tax restrictions are applied on deductibility of losses or treatment of long-term gains.

open interest

the total of all calls and puts remaining open at the end of each trading day.

open outcry

a method of trading futures contracts and options on futures in which buyer and seller in a commodity exchange trading pit shout bids back and forth; in comparison, options on stocks are traded using electronic bid and ask systems.

open position

the status of a trade when a purchase (a long position) or a sale (a short position) has been made, and before cancellation, exercise, or expiration.

ordinary income

noninvestment income, subject to the full tax rate an individual pays and not qualified for exclusions or lower rates applicable to some forms of net investment income.

pattern day trader
any individual executing four or more transactions on the same security within five consecutive trading days; these traders are required to maintain no less than $25,000 in their brokerage accounts.

personal goal risks
a range of risks associated with failing to set and follow goals and risk-related standards in how and when to trade, and related to the kinds of trades acceptable within the defined risk tolerance.

PM settlement
valuation of an index option based on the value of the index components at the close of trading on the day of exercise or expiration.

premium
the price of an option, expressed in dollars and cents but without dollar signs. For example, if an option has a premium of $200, it is expressed as 2; if an option has a value of $325, it is expressed as 3.25.

price/earnings ratio
an indicator combining a technical (price) and a fundamental (earnings) value, to develop a multiple. The ratio, in which price per share is divided by earnings per share, is equal to the number of years of earnings reflected in the current stock price.

price weighted
description of the procedure used to calculate an index value, based on current price and adjusted for all stock splits, for each of the components in the index.

profit margin
the percentage of profit, also called net return; it is the percentage arrived at by dividing the net profit by total revenue.

pro forma earnings
"as a matter of form" (Latin), a company's earnings based on estimates or forecasts with hypothetical numbers in place of known or actual revenues, costs, or earnings.

protected short sale
a strategy in which the risk of loss in a short sale is offset by the purchase of one call per 100 shares of the underlying stock; also called a *synthetic put*.

protective collar
alternate name of the *collar*.

pump and dump
action by an individual holding shares of a company who spreads false rumors in order to get people to buy shares and increase the price of the stock, and then sells shares at a profit.

puts
options providing their owners the right, but not the obligation, to sell stock of an identified underlying security, at a fixed strike price, and on or before a fixed expiration date. Every put provides these rights over 100 shares.

qualified covered call
a covered call that meets specific definitions allowing an investor to claim long-term capital gains tax rates upon sale of stock, or to retain long-term holding period status. Qualification is determined by time to expiration and by the price difference between current market value of the stock and striking price of the call.

qualified retirement plans
those plans qualified by the IRS to treat current income as deferred and free of tax in the year earned and, in many cases, also exempting annual contributions to the plan from current taxes.

quarterlys
specialized options issued on the last day of each calendar quarter, which expire at the end of the following quarter.

random walk theory
a belief that stock prices are entirely random and cannot be predicted.

ratio calendar combination spread
a strategy involving both a ratio between purchases and sales and a box spread. Long and short positions are opened on options with the same underlying stock, in varying numbers of contracts and with expiration dates extending over two or more periods. This strategy is designed to produce profits in the event of either price increases or decreases in the market value of the underlying stock.

ratio calendar spread

a strategy involving a different number of options on the long side of a transaction from the number on the short side, when the expiration dates for each side are also different. This strategy creates two separate profit and loss zone ranges, one of which disappears upon the earlier expiration.

ratio collar

a collar combining long puts with a ratio write rather than a 1-to-1 covered call. This is intended to produce higher current income due to the larger number of short calls.

ratio synthetic straddle

a combination of 100 shares of stock, either long or short, with calls or puts set up in a ratio of more options than the 2-to-1 relationship of the long call or long put synthetic straddle. The ratio increases the price level required to achieve or pass breakeven; but it then increases the profit potential associated with price increases (for long call ratio against short stock) or price decreases (for long put ratio against long stock).

ratio write

a strategy for covering one position with another for partial rather than full coverage. A portion of risk is eliminated, so ratio writes can be used to reduce overall risk levels.

record date

the date on which the owner of stock is acknowledged as entitled to receive a dividend, even though the pay date is much later; if the stockholder of record sells shares after the ex-dividend date, the dividend is still earned.

relative volatility

the tendency for a stock to follow a specific breadth of trading between resistance and support.

resistance level

the highest level in a stock's current trading range, representing the highest price at which buyers are willing to buy.

retender

a notice issued by a commodities broker to cancel an obligation by a short option trader to take actual physical delivery of the underlying commodity.

reverse hedge

an extension of a long or short hedge in which more options are opened than the number needed to cover the stock position; this increases profit potential in the event of unfavorable movement in the market value of the underlying stock.

rho
a measurement of an option value's sensitivity to an assumed risk-free interest rate.

risk of disruption in trading
the risk that trading is closed due to rumors or news, in anticipation of news that will affect price, or in response to unusual activity. For options traders, the timing could mean lost opportunities for entry or exit at the best possible moment.

risk of unavailable market
the risk that trades may not be placed in an orderly manner, due to a lack of market on the other side or due to heavy volume leading to delays in order placement.

risk tolerance
the amount of risk that an investor is able and willing to take.

round trip cost
name given to the double cost of transaction fees, assessed first to open and then to close positions.

sales load
a commission charged when a financial adviser places a client's capital into a load mutual fund.

setup
in swing trading, a signal indicating that a stock has reached a short-term high level (a sell setup) or a short-term low level (a buy setup). By taking action upon recognizing a setup, swing traders make small but consistent profits.

short hedge
the purchase of options as a form of insurance to protect a portfolio position in the event of a price decrease; a strategy employed by investors in long positions who need insurance against a decline in the market value of the stock.

short straddle
the sale of an identical number of calls and puts with identical striking prices and expiration dates, designed to produce profits in the event of price movement of the underlying stock within a limited range.

short-term capital gains
profits on investments held for less than 12 months, which are taxed at the same rate as other (ordinary) income.

sideways strategies
option strategies designed to produce maximum gains when the underlying stock exhibits lower than average volatility.

split strike strategy
a variation of the synthetic stock strategy, combining two different striking prices, both out of the money. The bullish version is a combination of a long call and a lower-strike short put; the bearish version consists of a long put and a higher-strike short call.

spread
the simultaneous purchase and sale of options on the same underlying stock, with different striking prices or expiration dates, or both.

straddle
the simultaneous purchase and sale of the same number of calls and puts with identical striking prices and expiration dates.

strangle
a strategy in which an equal number of long calls and puts are bought (long strangle) or sold (short strangle). These terms include different striking prices but the same expiration date, and the strategy will be profitable only if there is a large price movement in the underlying stock.

strap
an option strategy, also called a *triple option*, involving purchase of one put and two calls (hoping the stock's price will rise) or the purchase of one call and two puts (anticipating a stock's price decline).

strikes
price points at which an option can be exercised.

striking prices
the dollar value of shares equivalent to the prices at which options are exercised.

support level
the lowest level in a stock's current trading range, representing the lowest price at which sellers are willing to sell.

swing trading
a form of trading spanning 2 to 5 days in most cases, intended to take advantage of exaggerated swings in price, often in response to unexpected changes, such as earnings surprises.

synthetic long call

the purchase of a long put to offset potential losses in 100 shares of long stock. If the stock value declines below the strike of the put, the put gains one point of intrinsic value for each point lost in the stock.

synthetic long stock

a combination of one long call and one short put opened at the same striking price and expiration. The combined value rises and falls to the same degree as 100 shares of the underlying stock. The cost of the position is small, however, because the cost of the long call is offset by income from the short put.

synthetic positions

advanced options strategies that duplicate price movement of stock, offset price movement to reduce risk, or create additional income without added risk.

synthetic put

a strategy designed to offset potential losses when stock has been shorted. For each 100 shares held short, the investor buys one call. As the stock price rises, each call offsets the loss in 100 shares of stock held short; also called a *protected short sale*.

synthetic short stock

a combination of one long put and one short call opened at the same striking price and expiration. The combined value rises and falls to the same degree as 100 shares of the underlying stock. The cost of the position is small, however, because the cost of the long put is offset by income from the short call.

synthetic straddle

a position combining stock with options that performs like a straddle but often without the same level of risk.

tax consequence risk

the risk of losing tax advantages or paying additional taxes due to special options trading rules or limitations; these include ill-advised timing, loss of long-term gains rates, and limitations on loss deductions.

theta

a measurement of an option's sensitivity to changes in time value (time decay).

time spread

alternate name for *calendar spread*.

time value
that portion of an option's premium attributed specifically to the time remaining to expiration. Time values declines as expiration approaches and the rate of decline accelerates within the final month.

total capitalization
the combination of long-term debt (debt capital) and stockholders' equity (equity capital), which in combination represent the financing of corporate operations and long-term growth.

trading cost risk
the risk of lost profits or conversion from profits to losses due to the trading fees assessed both to open and to close positions.

triple option
alternative name for the *strap*.

upper shadow
on a candlestick formation, the line defining the highest extent of a day's trading range. The line extends above the opening or closing price for the day.

uptrend
in swing trading, a series of three or more days consisting of higher highs and higher lows.

value investing
selection of stock in companies that are exceptionally well managed, with a long-term track record of increasing revenue and profits, and a strong competitive position—and that is currently available at a bargain price.

variable hedge
a hedge involving a long position and a short position in related options, when one side contains a greater number of options than the other. The desired result is reduction of risks or potentially greater profits.

variable ratio collar
a collar combining long puts with a ratio write rather than a 1-to-1 covered call; however, the short calls are split between two different striking prices. This enables the trader to produce higher current income due to the larger number of short calls, but with less risk than a single-striking-price ratio write.

vega

also called tau, the measurement of an option's sensitivity to volatility in the underlying security.

vertical spread

a spread involving different striking prices but identical expiration dates.

weeklys

specialized options issued each Friday, which expire the following Friday.

whipsaw

a price trend in stocks when the price moves in one direction and then reverses and moves in the opposite direction.

RECOMMENDED READING

Ansbacher, Max. *The New Options Market*, 4th ed. New York: John Wiley & Sons, 2000.

Fontanills, George A. *Trade Options Online*. New York: John Wiley & Sons, 1999.

Friedentag, Harvey C. *Stocks for Options Trading: Low-Risk, Low-Stress Strategies for Selling Stock Options—Profitably*. Boca Raton, FL: CRC Press, 2000.

Jabbour, George, and Philip Budwick. *The Option Trader Handbook: Strategies and Trade Adjustments*. Hoboken, NJ: John Wiley & Sons, 2004.

Kaeppel, Jay. *The Option Trader's Guide to Probability, Volatility, and Timing*. Hoboken, NJ: John Wiley & Sons, 2002.

Kolb, Robert W., and James A. Overdahl. *Financial Derivatives*, 3rd ed. Hoboken, NJ: John Wiley & Sons, 2003.

McMillan, Lawrence G. *Options as a Strategic Investment*, 3rd ed. New York: New York Institute of Finance, 1993.

McMillan, Lawrence G. *Profit with Options: Essential Methods for Investing Success*. New York: John Wiley & Sons, 2002.

Natenberg, Sheldon. *Option Volatility & Pricing: Advanced Trading Strategies and Techniques*, updated ed. New York: McGraw-Hill, 1994.

Thomsett, Michael C. *The LEAPS Strategist*. Columbia, MD: Marketplace Books, 2004.

Trester, Kenneth R. *101 Option Trading Secrets*. Stateline, NV: Institute for Options Research, 2003.

ABOUT THE AUTHOR

MICHAEL C. THOMSETT (ThomsettOptions.com) has written more than 70 books on investing, real estate, business, and management. He is the author of several Wiley books, including the eight previous editions of the bestselling *Getting Started in Options*, as well as *Getting Started in Fundamental Analysis*, *Getting Started in Stock Investing and Trading*, *Getting Started in Real Estate Investing*, and *Getting Started in Swing Trading*. He also has written numerous other stock investing and trading books, including *Winning with Stocks* (Amacom Books), *Stock Profits* (FT Press), and *Mastering Fundamental Analysis* and *Mastering Technical Analysis* (Dearborn Press). Thomsett contributes regularly to many websites, including Seeking Alpha, Global Risk Community, Yahoo! Contributor Network, and the Chicago Board Options Exchange (CBOE), and writes articles for the American Association of Individual Investors' *AAII Journal* and the National Association of Investors Corporation (NAIC). He also teaches five classes at the New York Institute of Finance (NYIF). Thomsett has been writing professionally since 1978 and full-time since 1985. He lives near Nashville, Tennessee.

INDEX

AM settlement, 137
American Institute of Certified
    Public Accountants
    (AICPA), 17
American style option, 25–26
antistraddle rule, 202
Apple, Inc., 104–105
averaging up and down,
    225–230
bear spread, 45–48
beta, 251
binary options, 141
book value, 246
box spread, 49–51
breakout pattern, 243
broad-based index, 134
brokerage risks, 183–184
bull spread, 42–44
butterfly spread, 63–69
calendar spread, 52
candlestick charts, 101–102
capital gains, 195–196
capitalization weighted index,
    134–135
capped style option, 26
carryover capital losses, 205
cash settlement, 136
chartist, 235
Chicago Board of Trade
    (CBOT), 117
Chicago Board Options
    Exchange (CBOE), 2, 125,
    131, 140
Chicago Mercantile Exchange
    (CME), 119
collars, 37–39, 162–169
combinations, 34–35
Commodity Futures Trading
    Commission (CFTC), 121

common mistake, 3–10
condor, 67–68
confirmation, 105–106
constructive sales, 196–197
Consumer Price Index (CPI), 132
contrarian investing, 10
core earnings, 231–232
cost averaging, 225–230
day trading, 110–111
debit and credit spreads, 51
debt ratio, 240
delta, 252–255
diagonal spreads, 52–57
disruption in trading risk, 183
dividend collar, 37–39, 168–169
dividend yield, 239
dollar cost averaging, 229–230
Dow Jones Industrial Average
    (DJIA), 133, 134, 142
Dow Theory, 247, 248
earnings per share (EPS),
    236–237
EBITDA, 232–233
efficient market hypothesis,
    248–249
European style option, 25–26
exchange-traded funds (ETFs),
    118, 126, 140–141
ex-dividend date, 37–38
exercise cutoff time, 136
Federal Reserve Board (FRB), 125
Financial Accounting Standards
    Board (FASB), 17
Financial Industry Regulatory
    Authority (FINRA),
    124–125
FLEX options, 141–142
fundamental analysis, 236–241
futures trading, 117–124

gamma, 255–256
generally accepted accounting
    principles (GAAP), 17, 234
Greeks, 250–258
hedge ratio, 252
hedges, 39–40, 73–77
horizontal spreads, 52–57
index options, 131–135
information risk, 178–180
insider information, 4
insurance put, 151–152
International Accounting
    Standards Board (IASB),
    17–18
iron condor, 51
JCPenney, 17
leverage, 95–97
long hedge, 73–75
long stock, synthetic, 152–155
long straddle, 84–86
long-term capital gains,
    196–197
lost opportunity risk, 185–186
margin and collateral risk, 180
market value weighted index,
    134–135
married put, 151–152, 199
modified installment collar,
    164–165
money spreads, 34–35
multileg option order, 69
multiple, 239
mutual funds, 7
narrow-based index, 134
NASDAQ, 131–132, 134, 142
National Futures Association
    (NFA), 125
offsetting positions, 198
open interest, 253

options
  advanced strategies overview, 34–41
  altering spread patterns, 57–63
  American style, 25–26
  antistraddle rule, 202
  bear spread, 45–48
beta, 251
  binary, 141
  box spread, 49–51
  bull spread, 42–44
butterfly spread, 63–69
capped style, 26
  collars, 37–39, 162–169
  combination techniques, 89–91
  condor, 41, 67–68
  debit and credit spreads, 51
delta, 252–255
  diagonal spreads, 52–57
  dividend collar, 37–39
  European style, 25–26
exercise and expiration (index), 135–137
  FLEX, 141–142
  futures, 117–124
gamma, 255–256
Greeks, 250–258
hedge ratio, 252
  hedges, 39–40, 73–83
  horizontal spreads, 52–57
  index, 131–135
leverage, 95–97
middle-range strategies, 63–69
  modified installment collar, 164–165
  open positions, 31–32, 253
protective collar, 162
qualified covered call, 199, 200–205
  quarterly, 141
ratio calendar combination spread, 64–65
ratio calendar spread, 57–58
  ratio collar, 165–166
  ratio synthetic straddle, 173
  regulatory (compared with futures), 124–126
rho, 258

risks, 177–190
  spreads, 34–36, 41–51
  stocks for call writing, 220–225
  straddle, 40, 83–89
strangle, 40–41
strap, 68
  strategies, other, 110–111, 137–139
  structured index options, 140–142
  swing trading, 107–110
  synthetic straddle, 169–173
  taxes, 195–200
theta, 257
triple option, 68
  variable ratio collar, 166–168
vega, 256–257
vertical spreads, 34–36, 41–51
  volatility of, 19–26
  weekly, 141
whipsaw, 61–62
Options Clearing Corporation (OCC), 125, 132
pattern day trader, 110–111
personal goals risks, 180–181
PM settlement, 137
portfolio action plan, 217–220
price/earnings ratio, 236, 237–239
pro forma earnings, 232
profit margin, 240
protected short sale, 149–151
protective collar, 162
pump and dump, 4
put, synthetic, 149–151
qualified covered calls, 199, 200–205
qualified retirement plans, 205–206
quarterly options, 141
random walk theory, 247, 248
ratio calendar combination spread, 64–65
ratio calendar spread, 57–58
ratio collar, 165–166
ratio synthetic straddle, 173
ratio write, 80–83
relative volatility, 243
resistance level, 242–243
reverse hedge, 75–77

rho, 258
risk tolerance, 4–5, 10–12, 188–190
risks, types of, 177–190
Russell 2000, 142
S&P 500, 132, 133–134, 142
Securities and Exchange Commission (SEC), 7, 121
set-up signals, 100–103
short hedge, 73–74
short stock, synthetic, 155–157
short straddle, 86–89
short-term capital gains, 196
split strike strategies, 157–162
stock analysis, 230–249
Stock Exchange (NYSE MKT), 131
stock selection, 213–217
straddle, 40, 83–89
strangle, 40–41
strap, 68
structured index options, 140–142
support level, 242–243
swing trading, 97–100, 103–108, 111–113
synthetic stock, 157–162
synthetic straddle, 169–173
Target, 17
tax consequence risk, 186–187
technical analysis, 241–246
theta, 257
time spread, 52
total capitalization, 240–241
trading cost risk, 184–185
triple option, 68
unavailable market risk, 181–182
value investing, 107
Value Line, 249
variable hedge, 77–80
variable ratio collar, 166–168
vega, 256–257
Verizon, 104
vertical spreads, 34–35, 41–51
volatility, 2, 13–19
Wal-Mart, 16
wash sales, 197
weekly options, 141
whipsaw, 61–62